THE ARCHITECTURE
OF THE SOUTHWEST

Indian • Spanish • American

THE

ARCHITECTURE

OF THE

SOUTHWEST

Indian · Spanish · American

BY TRENT ELWOOD SANFORD

GREENWOOD PRESS, PUBLISHERS
WESTPORT, CONNECTICUT

Copyright 1950 by W. W. Norton & Company, Inc.

Reprinted with the permission of W. W. Norton & Company, Inc.,
New York

Reprinted in 1971 by Greenwood Press, a division of Congressional
Information Service, 88 Post Road West, Westport, Connecticut 06881

Library of Congress catalog card number 76-100242

ISBN 0-8371-4012-9

Printed in the United States of America

10 9 8 7 6 5 4 3 2

TO MY WIFE

*Who reads the maps, takes the notes, packs the lunch,
repacks the luggage, sterilizes the thermos bottles, and
makes every motor court home; who remains
hushed when she wants most to speak, criticizes the
manuscript and everyone else who dares to do the same; and
who patiently awaits the outcome, realizing all the while
that the writer's greatest reward is
almost sure to be in heaven.*

CONTENTS

vii

PART FIVE: *ALTA CALIFORNIA*

PART SIX: *AMERICAN SOUTHWEST*

APPENDIX

ILLUSTRATIONS

MAPS

PLATES

THE ARCHITECTURE
OF THE SOUTHWEST

Indian • Spanish • American

PROLOGUE: Why is the Southwest?

THE BUSY El Paso agent of a Chicago manufacturing concern one day received a wire from the home office ordering him to go to Texarkana, which lies half in Texas, half in Arkansas, to call on a client who wanted to buy some of their products. The agent wired back suggesting they send someone from Chicago; it was nearer.

A large share of three fair-sized states separates Chicago and Texarkana; between the latter and El Paso lies only Texas. But the truth of the agent's statement is clear to anyone who has driven the length or the breadth of the Lone Star State. With an area of more than one quarter of a million square miles, it is larger than any country in Europe except Russia and it could swallow up all our northeastern states with ease.

But so could our second largest state, California—almost. Its Pacific coast line extends through ten degrees of latitude; San Diego is exactly west of Charleston, South Carolina, while the Golden State's northern boundary is in line with the tip of Cape Cod.

Only Montana exceeds in area the next border state in size, New Mexico. And then follows Arizona. A sizable chunk of land those four border states comprise. Nevada and Colorado follow in turn; and then only Wyoming and Oregon exceed Utah in area. Those seven states of the Southwest occupy nearly one third of the United States. Into them could be dropped all of the countries of western Europe including the Scandinavian; or, to get back home, they could house all of the twenty-seven United States east of the Mississippi including Louisiana, most of which lies to the west of that river, a fact which long caused consternation to the Spaniards in their plans for expansion.

So much for statistics. What *is* the Southwest? The old Southwest meant Kentucky and Tennessee and those states which now call themselves "deep South," just as the old Northwest meant those states which border on and extend up among the Great Lakes and are now called "Middle" West. Both terms have moved on with westward expansion.

What is now spoken of as Southwest is also South on its eastern fringes, and its western edges are definitely West. If you ask a Texan whether he considers himself a southerner he will stoutly claim a full share in the solid South, even to her political prejudices, and he will boast of the part his state played in the Civil War. But if you try to deprive him of the right to call himself a part of the great Southwest, he will tell you glowingly of the part his grandpappy played in making Texas a republic, independent of Mexico; and he may tell you that the western tip of Texas is farther west than most of Colorado.

A Californian will proudly tell you of his great Western state which looks out over more than a thousand miles of rugged and beautiful Pacific coast line to the Orient, but if you dare to divorce him from the Southwest he will recite a long list of Spanish place names which were brought in from New Spain with the great and good lame friar Junípero Serra; and he will probably tell you too about the swallows coming back to Capistrano.

But the qualifications of New Mexico and Arizona to be called Southwest are unquestioned. To many people they *are* the Southwest. They are Southwest and nothing else—neither South nor West. In the very early days New Mexico territory included not only most of Arizona but parts of Colorado and Utah. Nevada dips into the area. Coronado even marched as far as Wichita, Kansas.

For our part, then, let us include them all—what is sometimes called the Greater Southwest—and add to them the Mexican states of Chihuahua and Sonora and the territory of Baja California; in short, that part of the land which was first explored and then settled by the Spaniards as they pushed northward from New Spain. No slight is intended to Florida, but that surely is *not* Southwest. However, for her part in early Spanish exploration, which left its mark and its influence, even Florida cannot be omitted entirely from this book.

So much then for what, or who, is the Southwest. *Why* is the Southwest? What is there about that part of the country which makes it distinctive? What does it have that the rest of the country does not have? A native or a convert or one who has been cured by its sunshine will tell you that a large share of that distinction is climate. A nature lover or an artist or anyone who has been overawed (and that means everyone who has been there) by its beauty will tell you that it is scenery: snow-covered mountains contrasted with arid desert, huge painted rocks and forests of tall pines and scrubby mountain cedar and piñon, river valleys that are golden with cotton-woods in the autumn and mountainsides that are golden with aspens, rivers that are rushing torrents of mud in the rain and wide strips of hot sand in the sun, deep and colorful canyons, limitless caves and great natural bridges, flat desert seas with unexpected mesas that are really mesas and mirages that are not, daytime skies that are painted brilliantly blue and white and sunset skies that are kaleidoscopic.

But there is much more to it than that. Other places have at least some of the climate and some of the scenery. But no other part of the country has the same human background. Despite the near perfection of the climate and despite the overwhelming beauty of the scenery, it is not the work of nature that gives the Southwest its greatest distinction; it is the influence of man. Its greatest distinction lies then in how it is peopled, how it has been peopled for centuries, and in the marks left by that human occupation. Those marks are to be found high up in caves on the sides of steep cliffs, on the flat sandy bottoms of seemingly inaccessible canyons, on the tops of well-nigh unscalable mesas, on broad desert wastes, beside rushing rivers, in scattered and lonely mission outposts, and now in modern cities that are among the most beautiful in the land.

In that part of the country are blended three cultures: Indian, Spanish, and Anglo-American. All three have left their imprints— in language and in customs, in work and in play, in religious beliefs and their expression in folklore and in art, and especially and most visibly in architecture. It is the only part of the United States where the life and the work, the arts and the crafts, and particularly the architecture—because it is the *only* part that had a permanent, indigenous architecture—of the Indians have left any permanent impression. It is the only part of the country, with the exception of certain remnants in Florida and occasional faint wafts in the French atmospheric breezes of New Orleans, where the effect of Spanish occupation is felt. And in that part of the country the best work of the Americans of today is not without the influence of one or the other, or both, of the two earlier cultures.

Yet in one respect—in the names of places—the Spanish influence has reached farther afield, as if to lure the traveler on in the direction whence those names came. There is a charm in those names which spread even beyond the Southwest, to many of which we have become so accustomed that we take them for granted without inquiring into their origin or derivation but without which our geography and our travel would be so much more prosaic.

On a recent trip, beginning in what I think of as the Middle West but which to a southwesterner is East, and without any intent to pick places for their names but rather for the quality of their motor courts, my overnight stops were at Sandoval, El Dorado, Nacogdoches, San Antonio, Del Rio, Sierra Blanca, El Paso, and Las Cruces. On the way to Los Angeles, Wickenburg broke the spell, but from there on for several weeks I stopped overnight in but few places that did not have Spanish names. San Diego, San Juan Capistrano, Laguna, Santa Barbara, San Luís Obispo, Paso Robles, Monterey, Santa Cruz, San Francisco are names which recall not only the early power and energy of Spain but the fervent zeal of the Franciscan friars and the love of beauty which always attended it.

The names of Spanish saints fill New Mexico too, and sprinkled among them, even though sometimes corrupted by the Spaniards, is the magic of names going much farther back. Unlike Indian names in other parts of the country which have been applied and left to the not-too-tender mercy of foreigners, these names still live. Nowhere else in the country could there be Zuñi, Ácoma, Jemez, Nambé, Zía, Tesuque, Cochití, Picurís, Taos.

That is the *why* of the Southwest.

It is the land where the Indians built the only permanent homes—and still do; where the Spaniards first planted the Cross, and fought to keep it there; and where the Americans of today, although they have added much of their own, cannot even if they wanted to (and they don't) get entirely away from the influences of both. It is a land where the red people still pray to their gods for rain and the whites speak both Spanish and English. It is a land where the selfless energies of the friars left an indelible impression and where American economic strides of the past hundred years have been amazing but still have not erased the earlier cultures. It is Indian America. It is Spanish America. And it is Anglo-America, with all that is implied by that unsatisfactory, limited term.

All were builders of the Southwest. To tell of what and how they built is the underlying purpose herein. But that means little without telling who these men were, where they came from and what they brought with them, what inspired them and what kept them there—in a word, *why* they built. Nor can that be done without at least a brief picture, first, of what they found in that rare land. So let us go back to the beginning and see.

PART ONE: *ANCIENT SOUTHWEST*

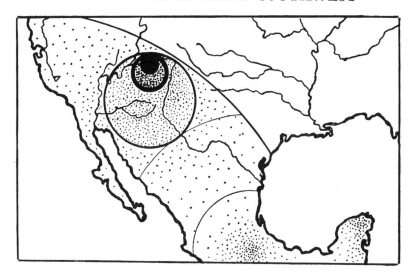

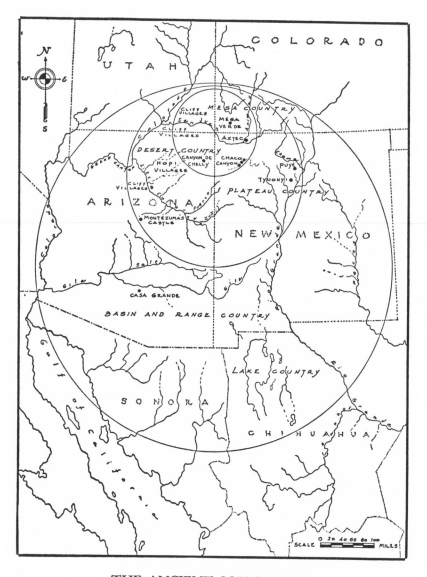

THE ANCIENT SOUTHWEST

1

The Country

THE MOST noticeable change that is sensed on driving west, whether from the eastern part of the United States, or from just the Mississippi Valley, is one of scale. It is a change that is felt as much as seen. The farther one has come the more is this true. In the northeastern corner of the country, where the states are the smallest and the cities and villages closest together, one drives, between white fences or stone walls, among low-lying hills and intimate fields and orchards. On leaving them behind and reaching the Middle West, or the "old" Southwest, distances between towns become greater, cornfields and pastures larger, the countryside flatter.

But it is on leaving the states that lie on the western banks of the Mississippi that the difference becomes most apparent. It is keenly felt on the western plains of Oklahoma, where the wind howls, the dust blows, and it is necessary for hours at a time to maintain a firm grip on the wheel of the car, until, in the Panhandle of Texas, where there is more land and sky than anywhere else in the country, intimacy has given way completely to vastness. Land and sky are everything—except one's self, and duststorms, cloudbursts, and northers and, latterly, cattle, wheat, barbed wire, and windmills. On driving across that country one can readily understand why Coronado, in search of a phantom Gran Quivira and finding only grass covering the whole round disk of the earth and sky forming a dome to complete the view, marched around in circles and then, with the sun as a guide, squared himself with the world and did not stay.

There is a gradual, steady rise too, but distances are so great that it is imperceptible. Only the altimeter registers it. Gently-rolling cottonfields give way to level grazing ranges—the high plains which mark the beginning of the West where the buffalo used to roam and where the grass that once fattened them now feeds great herds of cattle and sheep. Land, sky, and grass. Vastness. Whether one has come over the curving highways and hills of Missouri and across the length of Oklahoma, or whether it has been by way of the tortuous trails of Arkansas, the pine woods of eastern Texas, and on through Dallas and Fort Worth, the feeling is the same.

On approaching from farther south, the change is more abrupt. San Antonio lies at the upper edge of the Coastal Plain, and after leaving Del Rio and the Rio Grande the irrigated fields are suddenly left behind, the traveler climbs up onto a plateau, and there is no doubt that he is on a high shelf—barren, desolate, and interrupted only by the deep cut of Pecos River Canyon. Mesquite and sage and an occasional fox are his only companions. On approaching El Paso isolated ranges of mountains interrupt the scene, and on reaching the Rio Grande higher up on its course, cottonfields and ranches again appear.

On the more northerly route New Mexico comes into the Panhandle to meet Texas, for beyond Amarillo buttes—which in the Southwest are called mesas—suddenly appear to the right and left, scattered but rising abruptly from the plain; and as if to return the compliment Texas extends into New Mexico, where through the eastern part of that state stretch miles of ranch country, high but flat—and vast.

Beyond Tucumcari buttes appear in all directions, scattered at first and then continuous, to become truly mesas; then, as the arrow on the altimeter climbs to six thousand feet, mountains are seen close around, dotted green with scrubby mountain cedar, like the mesas scattered at first, then appearing as low, green forests. Another long and barren plateau leads to the cardboard cutout mountains in the distance that hide the valley of the upper Rio Grande. The road winds over these mountains as they gradually achieve a very real third dimension, and emerges at the upper edge of a gradual slope that leads gently down the length of Albuquerque's Central Avenue to the river which determined that city's site.

Many people think of the Rio Grande only as the boundary line between Mexico and Texas, but the upper part of that river, flowing from north to south to cut the state of New Mexico into two parts, plays an all-important role in the life of that section of the country, as it has for hundreds of years.

Tributaries of the Mississippi rise in this country: notably the Canadian River, which flows through the Panhandle of Texas to join the Arkansas on its way east, and the Red River, which forms the border between Texas and Oklahoma. The Pecos drains the eastern part of New Mexico and joins the Rio Grande halfway down the Texas-Mexico boundary. But much more important in history is that long river which the Spaniards first called Rio Bravo del Norte, the swift river of the North, and which is sometimes not a river at all but a wide strip of white sand baking in the sun.

Rising in the mountains of Colorado, the Rio Grande enters New Mexico in a broad valley which soon becomes a narrow gorge, and then, alternately wandering through green valleys and cutting its way through canyons, it continues on down to El Paso to become an international boundary but still maintains its temperamental variations. Roughly parallel ranges of mountains border its banks, with many rugged fingers pointing down the high plateau into the trough some five to fifty miles wide through which the river makes its way. On the east, continuing down from the Rockies of Colorado, is the Sangre de Cristo Range, which boasts the highest peaks in the state, reaching an elevation of more than thirteen thousand feet; and farther down are several isolated ranges, including the Sandías just to the east of Albuquerque, and the Manzano Range to the south. On the west the San Juan Mountains cross the southwestern corner of the state of Colorado and extend into New Mexico until they are interrupted by the canyon of the Rio Chama, which flows into the Rio Grande near Española. To the south of the Chama are other isolated ranges, including the Jemez Mountains west of Santa Fe which reach as high as eleven thousand feet, and the Black Range much farther south where the Gila River has its source.

All through this country detached ranges of mountains suddenly appear out of the plateau, and mesas with precipitous sides raise their streaked banks like great layer cakes. On the mountaintops, where the rain gods sit in council, pine trees and spruces give way to aspens and, farther down, piñon and dwarf cedars only partly cover the rolling hills while in the river valleys the cottonwoods, golden in the autumn, contrast with scarlet peppers hung out on racks to dry. For the most part it is at least a semiarid country, but it is a region of sudden and fierce downpours. Without warning black clouds begin to form out of nothing and quickly fill the sky, to swallow up the mountains. The rain gods flash their signals and shout their commands, and the deluge strikes. The sandy river bottoms become rushing torrents of mud, the roller-coaster ribbon of pavement between Albuquerque and Santa Fe becomes awash, and the cautious driver gropes his way with headlights on, wary of plunging too rapidly into the depressions. Almost as quickly the blue sky peers through the darkness, the sun smiles benignly on the cottonwoods, and the golden aspens on the mountainsides ripple in contentment as if they had never been aware of the presence of the rain gods venting their furious wrath.

At what appears on the map to be only a stone's throw away from where the Rio Grande rises, the San Juan River has its source. But extending between these headwaters is the Continental Divide, the great ridgepole of America, zigzagging through the western part of New Mexico and continuing on to form the boundary line between the Mexican states of Chihuahua and Sonora. Rivers to the east of that sometimes imperceptible line empty into the Gulf of Mexico or the Atlantic Ocean; rivers to the west empty into the Gulf of California or the Pacific. Thus the two great rivers of the Southwest, the Rio Grande and the Colorado—in its largest tributary the San Juan—rise almost together to flow into their respective gulfs. Mark them well; over their sandy bottoms flows, as it has for centuries, the lifeblood of the Southwest. Water has always been more important to that country than all the gold which the Spaniards so eagerly sought—and all other minerals combined.

The San Juan is not only the largest tributary of the Colorado; it is the largest river in New Mexico. Flowing through only a hundred miles of the northwest corner of that state, and not as well known and possibly not as romantic as the Rio Grande, it discharges more than twice as much water. Nor is it by any means without its romance. It is the San Juan that gave birth to the greatest of all pre-Columbian residential architecture.

The Gila River and its principal tributary, the Salt, both flow west across southern Arizona to join the Colorado less than a hundred miles from its silt-strangled mouth at the head of the Gulf of California. Halfway between the Gila to the south and the San Juan to the north, picking up the Zuñi and the Puerco on its way, and on through the Petrified Forest flows the Little Colorado, continuing through a canyon of its own to meet the main river about where the Grand Canyon begins.

Between the Little Colorado and the San Juan and extending on beyond to include parts of four states is the Colorado Plateau. It is raw, jagged country, much of it inaccessible and noted today more for its works of nature than for its utility to man. Its vast desert expanse includes great natural bridges of rock, stone monuments rise sheer out of the sandy waste, the famous Painted Desert lies within the area, and canyons cut great gashes across its surface. Greatest of these is the Grand Canyon of the Colorado River, generally conceded to be America's most magnificent spectacle.

The muddy waters of the Colorado flow on through other great canyons, to be impounded now by Boulder Dam, again properly called Hoover Dam (it is not in Boulder Canyon at all, but in Black Canyon), to create the largest artificial lake in the world. To the north, in Nevada and western Utah, is the Great Interior Basin, but little less arid than the desert to the south and covered with fingerlike ranges extending north and south. Its streams have no outlet but flow into salt-encrusted lakes or disappear into the porous soil. Southward, forming the border first between Nevada and Arizona and then between California and the youngest state, the Colorado flows on through some eighty miles of the Mexican desert to separate the mainland of Sonora from the peninsula of Baja California, and then pours the ruddy waters which gave it its name into the blue Gulf of California.

Forming a fringe along the south and extending all the way from Texas to California is what is known as the Basin and Range Province. Its eastern part, which includes the lower Rio Grande above the juncture of the Pecos, stretches north along that river valley like a finger pointing to Santa Fe. On the south it extends into the state of Chihuahua to join the great tableland of northern Mexico. Its western part, stretching across southern Arizona and into California, is a northern extension of the Sonoran Desert. Its surface is characterized by desert plains broken by short mountain ranges generally running from northwest to southeast. The broad plains maintain only vegetation characteristic of the desert, and the mountains, devoid of trees or grass, are bare and rugged.

Once known as the Great American Desert, it is a country which is nevertheless responsive to irrigation, a science which has been employed since prehistoric times, especially along the Gila and Salt Rivers. It is significant that in the whole area of the Colorado River drainage there are almost no cities of any size. Phoenix is the one exception, and irrigation is the answer. The acres of citrus trees, date palms, and vegetable gardens surrounding that city do not look like the Sahara. The Great American Desert has shrunk.

Even more amazing is what has happened to the desert to the west of the Colorado River. Much of it which was once a burning waste is now included among the most productive gardens in the land, and the more equable grassy valleys toward the coast have through irrigation made that country a paradise for fruit. Those phenomena and the salubrious sunshine have combined to make Los Angeles by far the largest city west of the Mississippi.

To the north and east, however, the desert still rules. Beyond the San Bernardino Mountains and stretching across southern Nevada into Utah the sandy, wind-blown expanse of the Mojave reaches its climax in Death Valley, almost three hundred feet below the level of the sea, and, as if to emphasize that fact, the highest mountains in the United States rise boldly from its depths.

The Sierra Nevada extends to the north to hem in the dry wilderness of the Great Basin on the east and to water the long valley on the west. Numerous streams flow down from the snow-covered peaks to empty into the twin rivers, the San Joaquin flowing north and the Sacramento flowing south. These rivers join to empty ultimately into San Francisco Bay and do for the Great Valley of California what the lower Rio Grande now does for Texas. Serving as a massive, sheltering wall for the valley, the Sierra Nevada deals in superlatives. Not only does it include the highest peaks but it nourishes the most magnificent forests in the country and surrounds some of the most beautiful valleys and lakes.

Along the west extend the complex Coast Ranges, broken in two by those rivers which combine to make a superb harbor for San Francisco. Toward the south these ranges dip into the interior to protect the coastal plain from the desert and provide that mild Mediterranean climate that has made southern California so famous. Farther north the broken chains of those ranges strike the sea obliquely, many of their rocky peaks rising almost sheer out of the Pacific to provide a strikingly beautiful and rugged coast, from whose heights the rare Indian can look out over thousands of miles of blue ocean

toward that continent whence his ancestors came by circuitous route
thousands of years ago.

2

The People

A T SOME period in the remote past, perhaps twenty thousand years ago, man began to migrate from the tablelands of
Asia and, filtering out over the barren icy wastes, spread on down
through the woods and the prairies, over the mountains and the
deserts, and through the bottleneck of the Isthmus of Panama all the
way to the tip of South America.

These people all belonged to a race which we call by the misnomer
"Indians" because the first Europeans to encounter them thought
they had landed in the East Indies. The period during which these
migrations took place probably occupied a long time, and there are
physical variations in the types whose remains have been unearthed,
but we shall not here concern ourselves with that; suffice it to say
that they all belonged to the Mongoloid division of the human
race.

These Indians spread out over almost all of that part of the Western Hemisphere occupied by what is now the United States. Europeans landing on various parts of both coasts invariably encountered
them. Their living habits varied considerably according to the part
of the country in which they found themselves and were governed
principally by the very necessary search for food, which was probably responsible for bringing them over here in the first place. Those
who occupied the southwestern part of this country, with which
we are concerned, varied considerably among themselves and, again,
it was the nature of the country and the food it supplied that determined their habits and the kind of culture they developed.

The earliest date so far established by the study of tree rings is A.D. 217, but archaeological investigation aided by geology has unearthed evidences of cultures going back more than ten thousand years. Whatever may be the significance, most of these discoveries have been made in the Southwest, though there has been enough brought to light in other parts of the country to make it certain that the Indians were already widespread as long ago as that.

No evidence of shelters, either permanent or temporary, has been found in any of these ancient sites, but the presence of charcoal, bones of extinct animals, and simple hearths indicates that fire was used for heating and cooking, and the discovery of stones for grinding wild edible foods testifies that these early occupants of the country prepared for consumption seeds, berries, and nuts as well as depending upon wild animals for food. All evidences so far uncovered indicate that this method of life was pursued until about the beginning of the Christian Era, before agriculture, pottery, and, in some favorable localities, architecture began to develop.

By the time this began to occur all of the states of the Southwest were doubtless well populated. But the occupants developed along radically different lines and living habits varied considerably from one locality to another. Those who have been encountered in historic times have been named, tagged, and fairly thoroughly studied as to background, habits, and language. We are not concerned here, however, with a detailed enumeration of Indian tribes by name nor to any great extent with the various language groups to which they belonged, but with the different culture groups and their effect on the part of the country they occupied. No one knows just *why* certain groups of Indians found their way into Colorado, Arizona, and New Mexico while others remained on the California coast and still others penetrated to the Great Plains area and beyond. But environment had a definite effect on the culture they developed, which in turn accounts for what they left behind them in the way of buildings or lack of them. Why, for example, are there no evidences of permanent buildings along the California coast and on the Great Plains east of the Rocky Mountains whereas there are many on the plateaus and in the mountains and valleys of the region between?

California would seem perhaps the most likely place in the country to attract a large population. And indeed it was. But the Indians of California never developed the degree of culture acquired by the

Indians of the drier country in New Mexico and Arizona—based on agriculture and therefore conducive to the development of the arts —for the simple reason that they did not have to. California was the ideal place to engage in the three early ways of life: hunting, fishing, and gathering. Wild nuts and fruits were plentiful, the mountains provided game, and the ocean and the rivers provided shellfish. It was not necessary to pursue game great distances as the Plains Indians had to do; so the California Indians remained sedentary.

They did migrate seasonally, from seashore to mountain slopes, but within a narrow range of climatic conditions. This limited migration precluded the possibility of permanently occupied homes and the mild climate made them unnecessary for shelter or warmth. There was an abundance of grasses which provided material for their basketmaking, the one art in which they excelled, and groves of oaks supplied them with food. Acorns formed a principal staple article of diet. They were gathered in baskets, stored in bins, and ultimately ground into a yellow meal from which, after leaching to remove the tannic acid, bread was made. The California Indians, then, did store food but, except in basketry, they did not develop far in the arts or crafts. Life was simple; they wore little clothing and their shelters were the simplest kind of huts, round, oval, or dome shaped of thatch or sod.

Life was really *too* easy; the people were soft; they could not resist the influences which destroyed their simple culture; they could not adapt themselves to the European ideas of life, thrust upon them by the well-meaning Franciscan friars who were forced to give up their work before it was completed (if it ever could have been at all); they were helpless when deserted and left to their own devices; and they could not even survive.

The Indians of the Great Plains led a very different life. The vast grassy highlands bred the buffalo, which roamed in great herds and provided the Indian inhabitants of the region with all three of the necessities of life, food, clothing, and shelter. The earliest occupants of that country were nomads, or at least seminomads; the development of agriculture in the cultivation of corn, beans, and squash made the later tribes more or less sedentary; but the still-later introduction of the horse caused many of them to revert to the nomadic life in pursuit of the buffalo. Even with agriculture, however, farming was secondary; the Indians were primarily hunters. Tents of buffalo skin (tepees) are commonly associated with the region. They were supported by light poles, and in the somewhat more permanent villages were semisubterranean. The more sedentary Indians built lodges of earth, partly underground, either circular or rectangular, and covered with a domical or cone-shaped roof of brush. They banded in comparatively small groups and therefore never developed much in the way of social organization, as was true also of the California Indians. Although their distant neighbors to the east built huge earthen mounds, building on the part of the Plains Indians was confined to their simple and more or less temporary shelters. Such a culture could not withstand the impact of civilization. When the buffalo became extinct it was doomed.

Between the land of the California Indians on and near the Pacific Coast and that of the Indians of the Great Plains were numerous groups who lived in the country of mountains, plateaus, and desert. They had apparently reached that region from various directions, at various times, and spoke a number of widely differing languages. Many of them were nomads and lived a life not greatly different from that of the Plains Indians.

Many familiar tribal names are applied to them, to differentiate one group from another, but one of the best known, coming down to play a part in modern history, is that of the Apache, of which there are several divisions. All of them were nomadic and in historic times took readily, even greedily, to the horse. They were a warlike, troublesome group and we shall, because of their depredations, come across them again both in Spanish times and in the nineteenth century. They lived—or rather camped—as they still do today on reservations, in temporary shelters called wikiups. These shelters are elliptical in form—in summer merely rude brush shelters, in winter made of a rough framework of poles thrust into the ground and covered with earth or coarse canvas.

The well-known Navaho Indians, linguistic cousins of the Apache, are famous now for their wool blankets and their silver jewelry. Living on a large reservation occupying a substantial section of northeastern Arizona and part of northwestern New Mexico, they are much the most numerous of all Indian tribes and, evidently thriving on their pastoral life on the rugged and picturesque grazing ranges, are rapidly increasing in numbers.

They were not always the peaceful people that they are today. At the time the Spaniards came into the country they were a raiding, warlike tribe whose incursions into the territory of the village Indians was as great a menace as their plundering of the Spanish

1. CLIFF CANYON, Mesa Verde, Colorado

2. (*Top*) CLIFF PALACE, Mesa Verde.   (*Bottom*) CLOSE-UP OF KIVAS, Cliff Palace

3. (*Top*) ROUND TOWER, Cliff Palace. (*Bottom*) SQUARE TOWER HOUSE, Mesa Verde

4. (*Top*) SPRUCE TREE HOUSE, Mesa Verde. (*Bottom*) RUINS OF DWELLINGS, Spruce Tree House

© *Frashers Photos. Pomona, Calif.*

5. MONTEZUMA'S CASTLE, Arizona

6. (*Top*) PUEBLO BONITO, Chaco Cànyon, New Mexico. (*Bottom*)
RUINS OF TYUONYI, Frijoles Canyon, New Mexico

7. (*Top*) CLAN KIVA, Aztec Ruins, New Mexico. (*Bottom*) INTERIOR OF GREAT KIVA, Aztec Ruins

8. (*Top*) A MODERN KIVA, Taos Pueblo, New Mexico. (*Bottom*) A MODERN KIVA, San Ildefonso Pueblo, New Mexico

settlements was later. It is only in comparatively modern times that they have acquired and developed the arts for which they are now so well known; but their chief source of income is from their sheep, goats, and horses. In the care of their flocks they are content to lead a seminomadic and pastoral life, the housing for which is provided by simple shelters called hogans. They are not grouped in villages but are widely scattered, singly or in groups of two or three. In the summer they live in crude shelters of brush; but the winter house, simple as it is, is substantially built of logs, laid up like a log cabin and sometimes including some stone, and covered with mud or sod. To the Navaho, however, it is "built of poles of white shell, turquoise, obsidian, jet, and red sandstone," and at the entrance is "a fourfold curtain of dawn, skyblue, evening twilight, and darkness." These hogans are to be seen scattered along the highways and are as distinctive a part of the Navaho landscape as the Navaho horsemen and their flocks and the women in their wide, flounced skirts, purple or green velvet blouses, and always a wealth of silver and turquoise jewelry, their reserve capital, carried with them.

In contrast to these formerly wandering, warlike, more or less limited-culture groups of hunters and despoilers was a very different type who had developed agriculture to a high plane and lived in permanent villages of mature and unique architecture. Alone among the Indians of the United States they can be said to have developed a civilization comparable to those of the Mayas and the Aztecs in Mexico. Because of their accomplishments, they and their work merit more-detailed discussion later.

Thus, in summarizing, the Indians who occupied the Southwest may be divided into two broad classifications, not according to tribe or language but according to method of life. There were many tribes who wandered over the plains and the mountains or down to the seashore in search of food, who lived on seeds and wild berries and nuts, on what they hunted and fished, and who lived in brush shelters or tents of skins or in huts of mud. Some of them, especially those who spent the greater part of their time in search of game, were nomads and others, who found food more readily available, were at least semisedentary; still others whose predatory habits gained for them the classification "Apache," which means enemy, supplemented the chase and their limited agriculture with plunder.

There were, on the other hand, sedentary tribes who raised corn and beans in sufficient quantities to maintain a stored food supply, who thereby gained sufficient leisure to develop the arts and crafts, and who lived in permanent homes built of stone and adobe. These latter people are generally spoken of as Pueblo Indians. It must be borne in mind that Pueblo is not the name of a tribe. It is a Spanish word meaning village or town, or any inhabited place, and was first applied by the Spaniards to those tribes who built and lived in villages in contrast to the types of nomadic hunters and warriors they had generally encountered up to that time as they had pushed northward from the Valley of Mexico. The most advanced and complete of these villages, which had been built centuries before the Spaniards arrived—all of them already long deserted—lie in an area the approximate center of which is what is now sometimes called the "Four Corners."

3

Early Builders in the Four Corners

THE POINT where the four states of Utah, Colorado, New Mexico, and Arizona meet is unique: it is the only one in the United States where such a meeting occurs. It is unique in another way: it is almost the geographical center of settlement and occupation by those American tribes who built apartment-house villages long before the time of Columbus.

Their descendants continued to build apartment-house villages up to the time of the arrival of the Spaniards, and even almost to this day, through an area extending well down into New Mexico. They and their villages play an important part both in recorded history and in their influence on the architecture of the Southwest; and will therefore be discussed later. For the time being we are concerned with what has been discovered of the ancestors.

The San Juan River, after rising in the mountains of Colorado, makes a dip into the state of New Mexico for a distance of about one hundred miles and then crosses in a northwesterly direction almost the exact point of the Four Corners, from where it flows on in a generally westerly direction through Utah for a distance of about two hundred miles to meet the Colorado River a similar distance northeast of the Grand Canyon. It flows through a fertile valley in New Mexico, which irrigation has made amazingly productive, but from there on its course is a wild region of desert, canyons, and natural stone monuments all the way from the Four Corners to the greatest canyon of them all.

The land to the north and east is crossed diagonally from northwest to southeast by the San Juan Mountains, and between these mountains and the river of the same name is a series of mesas, or tablelands, thrust up out of a broad valley. Their flat tops are covered with stunted piñon and juniper and are cut into fragments by canyons a thousand feet deep or more.

Throughout this region there have been discovered many evidences of occupation by men who at an early date lived a sedentary life based on agriculture, who had developed arts and crafts to a high degree, and who lived in securely built, permanent dwelling groups of stone and adobe. Some of these dwellings are built in caverns high up in the sides of cliffs while others are built on mesa tops or in valleys. Probably because of the association with primitive rock shelters or caves, it was once thought that the "cliff dwellings" were much older than the multiple-roomed, so-called "pueblos" built on mesas, in valleys, or on a plain. Actually they are all pueblos, or villages, the difference being one of location only; and it is now known that the two kinds are contemporaneous and that they were built by Indians of the same culture.

Before engaging in brief descriptions of some of the better-known sites, a brief chronological outline of the development of the "pueblo" seems called for. But, first, how do we know what that chronology is? It was thought for a long time that it never would be known. Since the Indians left no written records, and those who occupied the early villages had abandoned them long before the coming of the Spaniards, any accurate dating seemed an impossibility. Until very recently the nearest approach to placing the occupants of those villages on a calendar was a comparison of pottery types which they left behind. Then, a little less than thirty years ago, a method was devised whereby most of the important ruins have since been quite accurately dated.

It all came about because of sunspots and the work of an astronomer at the University of Arizona. Dr. A. E. Douglass, director of the Steward Observatory there, was busily engaged in studying cross sections of trees to determine whether the variations in annual rings, caused by varying wet and dry years, bore any relationship to that recurring solar phenomenon. If it could be shown that the record of such years recurred in any significant relationship to sunspots, a great step would be made in long-range weather forecasting. But that is another story. It was found that all trees in a given region, under similar circumstances, carried the same pattern of annual rings. From this a master chart was devised giving the age record of the oldest living trees and telling accurately, from the width of the annual rings, which had been the lean years and which the fat ones. The next step was to employ trees which had been cut by the Spaniards for use as beams three hundred years ago and extend the time count farther back into history.

It was then that archaeology came into the picture. Desiring still older specimens, Dr. Douglass requested beam sections from archaeological sites under excavation and was able to match patterns from one site with those of another and thus determine, to the unbounded delight of archaeologists, that the latest beam in the ceiling of the Aztec ruin in northern New Mexico, for example, was cut exactly nine years before the latest beam from Pueblo Bonito in Chaco Canyon not far away. It had been known from their material culture that they were roughly contemporaneous, but now their time relationship could be told accurately. There remained only to bridge the gap between those beams and the modern ones. Dr. Douglass put aside his astronomy temporarily and engaged enthusiastically in this new and thrilling archaeological search.

After several years of intensive investigations a piece of a charred beam from an Arizona site, carefully wrapped with twine to preserve it for analysis, yielded the secret, showing rings belonging both to the latest years of the ancient specimens and to the earliest years of the historical specimens. Thus the gap was bridged; the pine trees of the Southwest, with the help of Dr. Douglass, had silently kept the records of the Indians and archaeological surmise in that part of the country became architectural history.

In all of the pre-Columbian United States, it was only in the dry country of the Southwest that agriculture was developed to a degree which enabled the Indians to engage extensively in permanent home building and thus earn for themselves the title of Pueblo Indians. Paradoxical as it may seem, it was there only, where water was so scarce and so valuable that it had to be carefully hoarded, that the Indians became *primarily* farmers and remained only secondarily hunters. But that country had its advantages for agriculture. In that sunbaked land the minerals of the soil are close to the surface, and the same soil could be used over and over again for planting crops once an adequate supply of water was assured. Unlike the forests of the East or the jungles of Yucatán, the land did not have to be cleared and then the cornfields periodically moved because of the rapid exhaustion of the soil. Thus there developed the cultures which made ancient history in the United States mainly the story of the Pueblo Indians and ancient architecture their works. The architecture did not take the form of monumental ceremonial structures as was the case with the Mayas and the Toltecs; but in all of North America it was in the Southwest only that it took the form of permanent house building for residential purposes.

The cliff dwellings and the multiple-roomed pueblos did not spring up full blown, however. As with all building peoples, the evolution was gradual. Those Anasazi people—the word comes from the Navaho and means "old peoples"—who grew up in the Four Corners at first lived in simple shelters, either in caves or in the open. Even as early as the first quarter of the Christian Era they were farmers as well as hunters and gatherers of wild seeds, maize and pumpkins being their principal products. For their hunting they had no bows and arrows but used a spearthrower, and for their farming a simple digging stick sufficed. Their shelters were "pit houses," consisting of rectangular or oval excavations from two to six feet deep with saucer-shaped floors. Each had a single room containing a fire pit and a storage bin. Upright poles supported a flat roof of saplings, twigs, and mud.

At a somewhat later date, when the bow and arrow had replaced the spearthrower, when beans had been added to their diet, and when pottery had replaced baskets, the pit houses were made two rooms wide and were used both for living and for ceremonial purposes. The houses were walled with slabs of stone and were built in groups of ten or twenty to form the earliest kind of permanent village in the Southwest.

About the year 1000 these pit villages were spread over a much greater area than formerly, and the houses were made larger and more elaborate. They were built in units, in single or double rows of rooms above the surface of the ground, and the pit house became a *kiva*, a separate chamber used primarily for ceremonial purposes and secondarily as a lounging place for males. Kiva is a Hopi word meaning "old house," and to this day the circular or square semisubterranean chamber is a distinctive feature of all Indian pueblos.

Then came that period known as Pueblo III and variously spoken of as the "Great Period," the "Classic Period," and the "Golden Age." It lasted from about the year 1050 to 1300 and, though it covered a smaller area and the sites were fewer, the villages were far larger. About half of them were composed of cliff houses while the others were built on mesa tops or in river valleys. In general plan the villages were similar, with a mass of contiguous rooms numbering anywhere from twenty to a thousand. They varied from one to four stories in height, were often terraced with setbacks, and were built in a variety of shapes, commonly rectangular, oval, or D shaped. Where they were built in caverns on the faces of cliffs, the living rooms were set back a short distance facing the cave openings while the kivas were located along the front of the cave. The setbacks on the dwellings provided a series of ledges against which ladders could be placed, and in time of attack these ladders could be drawn up for safety, access to the first story being through a trap door in the roof.

This was the period of the cliff dwellings of Mesa Verde and of the great community houses in Chaco Canyon. Far to the south it was also the period of the greatest monuments of the Mayas, and across a continent plus an ocean to the east it was the period of the great Gothic cathedrals. Some three hundred years were to elapse before Columbus was born.

The first seeds of corn, which formed the principal crop of these Indian builders, were probably introduced from the south where on the plateaus of Mexico and Central America its wild ancestor is native. At first the grain was stored in caves, which later gave way to granaries, probably the first stone buildings erected by the Indians. Later these grew into dwellings and then, because of depredations of warlike nomads, into forts as well. The evolution had begun. The leisure permitted by an adequate stored-food supply brought pottery, cotton garments, and increasingly elaborate communal dwellings. It also brought religion and ritual—dances to the gods to bring rain—and a ceremonial center to be used as a sanctuary. The kiva was the structural germ of every community and played an all-important part in the ceremonial life. The kivas varied greatly in size, usually ranging from ten to forty feet in diameter, although in rare instances they have been found to have been as great as sixty feet in diameter. It was the nucleus of every settlement and was the first structure to be located, the living rooms being built around it. In the words of an Indian priest: "Before a man can build a dwelling, he must select a place and make it sacred, and then about that consecrated spot he can erect a dwelling where his family can live peacefully." The great number of kivas found in all ancient Indian sites and their presence in all of the pueblos of today testify to their importance.

All the way to where the San Juan River meets the Colorado, and even beyond, and as far north from there as a hundred and fifty miles, remains of cliff houses and of pueblos built in the bottom lands have been found. All of them had long been deserted when the Spaniards came to this country. They are widely scattered, the outlying villages probably representing an overflow from the concentrated center of occupation. In the Grand Gulch fork of the San Juan and farther north in White Canyon in the region of Utah's stupendous "natural bridges," and in the gorges near by, are hundreds of cliff dwellings. In some places the village is made up of a group of houses on the edge of a precipice with small cliff dwellings built into caves in the rocks below. Towers, both round and square, perched on high points in front of the villages indicate a thorough system of defense. Montezuma Canyon, in the southeastern corner of Utah, and the territory just over the Colorado line are particularly rich in the ruins of villages.

Directly to the south, some distance across the Arizona line, in the heart of the Navaho Indian Reservation is the stupendous Canyon de Chelly with its tributary canyons Del Muerto and Monument. Tucked away in the crevices in the towering red sandstone walls and protected by the overhanging ledges are hundreds of substantially built masonry houses. Most spectacular of all the ruins there is that of the "White House" perched in a cave high up on the canyon wall. The evidence of tree-ring dates shows it to have been occupied between 1050 and 1300 during the Great Period. It was abandoned about the close of that period, probably upon the arrival of the Navaho who, under different conditions, still tend their sheep in the canyon bottom.

Farther to the north and west, across the Navaho Reservation and in a relatively inaccessible location, are two of the largest cliff villages in Arizona: the Betatakin Ruin and Keet Seel. The former cave pueblo contained a hundred and fifty ground-floor rooms and the latter more than two hundred and fifty. In the region around Flagstaff there are many ruins, both of cliff dwellings and surface pueblos. There are several groups to the north in Wapatki National Monument and near-by Walnut Canyon boasts a village of about three hundred cliff dwellings built under the canyon walls in scattered units of six to eight rooms each.

One of the most striking of all cliff dwellings is that known, unfortunately, as "Montezuma's Castle," some sixty miles south of Flagstaff. A large sinkhole in the vicinity, equally confusingly named "Montezuma's Well," once furnished water for those who dwelt in that region. Almost five hundred feet in diameter and said to be "bottomless," its circling cliff rises eighty feet from the black water. Wedged in between the strata of the rock walls of the Well are a number of small cliff houses. Several miles away, in a huge natural cavity in the face of a cliff a hundred and fifty feet high and some eighty feet up from the foot, is built the stately pile of Montezuma's Castle. It is about fifty feet high, built of pink stone in five diminishing stories in the form of a crescent. The first floor is composed of a horizontal row of eight rooms. The fifth floor, set far back from the lower face, contains but two rooms, with a spacious terrace formed by the roof of the fourth story. The only means of access is by ladders from the horizontal ledges below. Up such ladders the builders must have climbed, carrying on their backs load after load of stone and mortar and sycamore beams with which to build their castle home.

But it was in southwestern Colorado on the high forest-covered shelf known as the Mesa Verde that the life and the work of the cliff dwellers reached their zenith.

The road into Mesa Verde National Park begins to climb almost immediately. One can see its sinuous path doubling on itself high up ahead. In the autumn, as one winds through its high valleys, the variegated reds of the scrub oaks make a beautiful picture; but parts of the road cut out of the edge of the precipice—especially the "Knife Edge" where one can look straight down almost half a mile to the valley below, if one dares to look—make the traveler feel that he is indeed approaching the top of the world. But after driving the additional sixteen miles to the park headquarters, and in spite of the dizzy views from there down into the deep canyons, he is actually at a lower elevation than when, with a sigh of relief, he has gained the summit above the Knife Edge.

That corner of Colorado on which lies the Green Tableland slopes to the south, the mesa sloping with it, so that in spite of a gradual downgrade from the precipitous entrance at the north one is still high up above the canyons into which the many ridges extend to the south like giant fingers on an outstretched hand. Along the walls of these canyons is a multitude of fortresslike cliff villages, and on the mesa top are many pit houses built by the earlier Indians before protection from marauding tribes became necessary. The whole gamut, in fact, of ancient Indian architecture is exhibited at the Mesa Verde, for the inhabitants of the vicinity graduated from pit houses to surface pueblos before the pressure of enemies prompted them to build the cliff villages for which the park is so justly famous.

Greatest of these is Cliff Palace, which was first discovered by white people in 1888 when two cattlemen in search of some of their wandering charges suddenly confronted it across a canyon, completely filling a cavern three hundred feet long and a hundred feet high, just under the mesa rim. It stood much as it must have appeared when completed six hundred years earlier, the group having been built between 1073 and 1273 and probably abandoned shortly thereafter.

Largest of all the cliff villages, it is also the most interesting architecturally. Because the floor of the cave slopes outward, terraces had to be built up, with the result that there are eight different floor levels from the lowest part to the highest rooms. More than two hundred living rooms probably sheltered as many as four hundred people. There are twenty-three kivas, which were made by building up their circular walls as the terracing progressed and by filling in around them, very little excavation being required. Many small storerooms were needed to supply food for the large population and these were partitioned into bins by means of thin slabs of stone. There are square towers four stories high and of especial interest is a slightly tapering conical tower near the center, with each stone rounded to produce the proper curvature.

The quantity of masonry wall in the group is amazing and the quality of the workmanship is almost as much so, much of it remaining in excellent condition. The mesa top was the quarry and from it sandstone blocks were lowered over the walls to the floor of the cave a hundred and fifty feet down and more than two hundred feet above the bed of the canyon.

Even more spectacular is Balcony House, hanging like a swallow's nest seven hundred feet above the canyon floor. For the purpose of defense against enemies it was ideally situated, being virtually an impregnable fortress. Its only approach for the Indians was along a narrow ledge and through a tunnel passable only on hands and knees. An unusual architectural feature, which gives the group its name, is the spot where floor beams have been projected beyond a supporting wall to form a balcony and provide communication between upper rooms. The twenty rooms and two kivas, built between 1190 and 1272, are among the best preserved in the park, several ceilings being still intact. A spring of clear, cold water still flowing at the rear of the cave would, with storage bins filled, have made it possible for the occupants to withstand a long siege.

Square Tower House, built between 1204 and 1246, occupies a shallow cave and contains sixty rooms and eight kivas. The square stone tower for which it is named is thirty-five feet high and is built against the cliff as one wall, and the three masonry walls still bear the original red-and-white clay plaster. The largest of the kivas, seventeen feet in diameter, still has half of its original roof in place.

Spruce Tree House, near the end of a narrow canyon close to the park headquarters, is two hundred and sixteen feet long and eighty-nine feet wide, one of the largest in the park, once sheltering some two hundred people in a hundred and fourteen rooms. There are eight kivas ranging from twelve to fifteen feet in diameter. Many of the walls were carried to the top of the cave, which served as a roof for the upper rooms. Constructed between 1230 and 1274, the masonry walls were laid up with great care and are in an excellent state of preservation, some of the red plaster covering being still intact.

The Fire Temple, consisting of two massive stone buildings flanking a court fifty feet wide, entirely fills a shallow cave and is believed to have been used for ceremonial purposes only. On the plastered walls of the rooms are symbols, in red, of wild animals. A short distance to the east is the New Fire House, built in two narrow slits of caves one above the other. The lower cave contains several kivas; the upper was probably used for storage only. Oak Tree House, a little farther along, is believed to be one of the oldest cliff dwellings, dating between 1112 and 1184; but the first date established for any of the dwellings goes back almost another hundred years to 1019.

On the mesa top above these groups is a curious structure known as the Sun Temple. It is in the shape of a letter "D," with two concentric walls surrounding an open courtyard which contains two kivas, the spaces between walls being partitioned into small rectangular chambers. The absence of roof beams makes it impossible to date the building, but it is believed that it was one of the later structures and there are indications that it never was completed. Perhaps its construction was interrupted by the great drought of 1276–1299 which drove the cliff dwellers of Mesa Verde from their fortress homes beneath the overhanging rocks of the Green Tableland's many precipitous canyons.

If Mesa Verde represents the culmination of the cliff dwellers' architecture, Chaco Canyon in northwestern New Mexico certainly is the acme of the surface pueblo builders' prowess.

The approach is very different. Highway 44 leads over an arid plain interrupted by sudden colorful buttes to where, at a filling station, a narrow road branches off, winding south through the dust for twenty-five miles. At that distance the rough and rocky surface of the dry canyon banks becomes the road, and with one final leap one's car lands quite safely in the canyon bottom.

After recovering from the shock of the landing, the traveler's first reaction is one of amazement that such a barren, sandy country could ever have supported a large population. Later, on seeing the tremendous pile of Pueblo Bonito and adjacent ruins almost equally impressive, he wonders from where the roof beams could have come. There is no sign of a tree for many miles. That once densely peopled sandy canyon bottom has in fact been described by the archaeologists who dug into the maze to expose its secrets as "one hundred miles from anywhere"—one hundred miles south of Mesa Verde, one hundred miles north of Zuñi, one hundred miles east of the Hopi mesas, and one hundred miles from Gallup, the nearest base of supplies.

Present-day Navahos claim that within the memory of their old people there was a living stream in the Chaco, that there were cultivated fields from one wall of the canyon to the other, and that pine trees grew in the vicinity. There are also evidences of ancient irrigation systems. There is little doubt that the sandy strip of land ten miles long and a mile wide has been drying up through the last several hundred years.

But a thousand years ago it was a thriving, productive valley which may well have supported a population of ten thousand. Ruins of twelve large community houses and numerous small sites bespeak a highly organized social structure and religious life and a complex community architecture of the highest type to be found anywhere in the country. Energy that was not spent in the production of food quite evidently went into religious ceremonies, ceramic manufacture, and building. Millions of pieces of stone were carefully laid in thousands of tons of mortar to build walls; thousands more of logs, poles, and slabs were cut in the distant forests, transported by man power, prepared with stone tools, and built into the roofs.

Most completely excavated and best known of the large community apartments is Pueblo Bonito, the City Beautiful. Tree-ring dating shows that it was under construction as early as 919, that additions were made at various times during the eleventh century, and that it was occupied as late as 1130. Some of the rooms still have the original timbered ceilings that made the dating possible. Unlike most of the ruins, which are variations on an E shape, Pueblo Bonito is in the shape of a capital D. Without unity in design, the later additions show it to have been increased in size from time to time without any preconceived plan.

The straight, one-story side of the court is six hundred and sixty-seven feet long, the shorter arm three hundred and fifteen feet, while the sweep of the curving wall, more than eight hundred feet long, once rose to five stories and is still standing forty feet high in places. The eight hundred rooms could have sheltered twice that number of people. Within the court are the ruins of thirty-two kivas.

Of particular interest is the beauty of the masonry, which was laid in great variety. The sandstone blocks were not "cut stone" since the Indians had no metal tools, but they were carefully shaped and were laid on their natural bedding planes. The stone facings of the walls were laid in patterns of large and small stones that would do credit to the most meticulously designed garden wall.

Only seventy feet behind the high curving wall of the pueblo is a seemingly precariously balanced vertical mass of rock a hundred feet to the top of the first ledge, which has become detached and stands away from the main canyon wall. A masonry reinforcing wall under the face of the base shows that the danger existed for the Bonitians hundreds of years ago. It has been thought that their wall was a feeble, childish attempt to hold up the colossal cliff. It can hardly be supposed that such builders were so naïve as that. Constant erosion by water and sand and wind had undercut the soft base of the cliff. What more natural than for an engineer to try to prevent further erosion?

But a short distance away from Pueblo Bonito is a smaller apartment house known as Pueblo del Arroyo. The two may have constituted one town. Like the former, Pueblo del Arroyo has some beautiful masonry remaining, but, unlike Pueblo Bonito in plan, it is the more typical E shape with an undeveloped middle stem. The evolution of this plan was probably first a straight linear mass, the back of the letter, then the addition of one wing, making an L, then a U, then an E. A curving one-story section commonly connected the ends of the E and enclosed a spacious court, usually filled eventually with kivas.

Chetro Ketl, a quarter of a mile to the east, is comparable in size to Pueblo Bonito, occupying an area approximately equal to two average city blocks. It is noteworthy for a kiva more than sixty feet in diameter, and it is especially rich in the variety and beauty of its masonry walls. Courses of large stones alternate with layers of fine laminated blocks, to produce a striking banded effect.

Space does not permit mention here of other ruins, of which there are many, large and small. The most interesting thing about them all perhaps is that they were truly community houses, with apartments all essentially the same size, connoting a democratic domestic life. There were no kings' palaces, or governors' mansions, or independently tasteless creations of the *nouveaux riches.*

At some time, probably during the twelfth century, the people of Chaco Canyon moved out. There was no gradual decay or degeneration. Many openings were walled up and the buildings were sealed and closed, much as you might close up your summer cottage, expecting to return in the near future, air it out, and live there again. That is all. It was a long time ago.

These great community centers of Chaco Canyon were all built at approximately the same time, by people of the same religion, social structure, living habits, and architectural practices. They were all abandoned, at the full tide of life, at approximately the same time. They date back more than a thousand years. But recent excavations show that beneath many of these ruins, buried under the soil, are the ruins of earlier towns which, in architecture, far surpass those which have so recently been brought to light and given a place in the mysterious early history of America.

For the amateur archaeologist who likes to travel "soft," the Aztec Ruin is ready made, just at the edge of town and complete with attractive garden entrance, museum, National Park ranger for guide, and completely restored kiva. He can in perfect comfort and with a minimum of effort wander over the walls of the once-great pueblo and, aided by a little imagination, project himself back into life on the American continent eight hundred years ago.

On the Animas River, which flows southeast into the San Juan, the Aztec Ruin lies about halfway between Chaco Canyon and Mesa Verde and shows cultural connections with both. The name has no significance. Like all of the Montezumas in that part of the country, it was just a mistake.

One of the interesting things about this large community village, one of several in the vicinity, is the comparatively short time occupied in its construction. Unlike the rather hit-or-miss and gradual growth of Pueblo Bonito, Aztec was planned and built within twenty years (1101–1121), ready for more than a thousand people to move in, leases all signed.

The pueblo, in the form of a rectangular U, measures approximately three hundred and sixty feet by two hundred and eighty feet and contains five hundred rooms and about twenty kivas. A former front row of one-story rooms enclosed a court a hundred and eighty feet by two hundred feet, in which there are two additional kivas, one typical but much larger than those incorporated in the building itself; the other a great, or superkiva. This great kiva was restored in 1934 under the direction of Earl H. Morris, who had carried out the excavation of the pueblo. Because of its completed condition and because it is so representative of that most interesting type of ceremonial structure found in the courts of the great community houses of the Classic Period it merits description in some detail.

But first a few words regarding the typical kiva. Not all kivas are circular. Farther west and south, in the Hopi villages and at Ácoma and Zuñi, they are rectangular. Evolved from the pit house, the kiva took its form therefrom. The typical Anasazi pit houses were circular; hence most of the kivas of the Anasazi sites took that shape. They are usually semisubterranean, but even where entirely above ground they are entered only through the roof, to retain the subterranean tradition. The kiva symbolized an earlier world which man passed through on his rise from a more primitive state and from which he emerged, always by means of a tall pine ladder symbolizing the trees which grow on the surface, into the world of the present. Directly under the hatchway is a firepit and in front of that is a shallow hole, the *sipapu* or symbolic entrance to the underworld. A bench runs around the wall, above which are niches for the safekeeping of objects used in ceremonial rites. Such a sanctuary, thought to be a "clan" kiva, is typical.

The great kiva, or superkiva, such as that restored at Aztec, is probably a tribal kiva and differs from the ordinary kiva in many details as well as in size. The circular chamber, more than forty feet in diameter at the floor and forty-eight feet above the benches (of which there are two, one above the other), is surrounded by an outer ring of arc-shaped rooms at a higher level. These rooms each have an outer door leading to the courtyard and an inner door with a ladder leading down to the floor of the kiva. One of these rooms is larger than the others and is thought to be an altar room, while directly opposite it is a large T-shaped doorway which was probably the main entrance.

Four square masonry columns support large timbers on which are placed layers of small poles and mortar to form a roof. The firepit is in this instance not an actual pit at all but a raised masonry box five feet square, and on either side of it is a rectangular vault eight and a half feet long, three and a half feet wide, and about three feet deep. The function of these vaults is not known. The walls are plastered with adobe and painted white with a red dado. As a restoration accurately carried out through careful study of excavations, this great kiva gives a fascinating picture of a ceremonial setting of the twelfth century. One cannot do as well today. Great kivas belong only to a more glorious past and the smaller kivas of today are not open to the public.

The cliff dwellers abandoned their fortress homes on the Mesa Verde about the end of the thirteenth century or shortly thereafter. The great apartment-house builders in Chaco Canyon locked their doors and left about a hundred years earlier. None of them just vanished. They must have gone somewhere. The answer appears to be the Rio Grande. There is indication that some of them moved in with the Hopis in their picturesque but wild and rugged country; others no doubt migrated to the Zuñi River; and still others continued on down to southern Arizona and to Chihuahua. But, evidenced by the situation as found later, the Rio Grande seems to have been the principal magnet.

U.S. 85, the main north-south highway in New Mexico, follows the Rio Grande from below El Paso for about two thirds the length of the state, to a point some twenty miles above Albuquerque. It is a natural route to travel. The Indians used it to travel south. The Spaniards used it to travel north. And the Americans use it to travel back and forth—on pavement.

But just a few miles beyond Bernalillo, which is seventeen miles north of Albuquerque, the highway leaves the swift river of the north and heads to the northeast to Santa Fe. It does not join the river again for more than fifty miles of its course, until a point a little north of Española on the way to Taos. That section of the river is not a good place for highways. Or Spaniards. But it was an excellent place for Indian nomads. And later Indian refugees.

Between that section of narrow, almost-impassable canyon of the Rio Grande and the Jemez Mountains to the west is the largest volcanic crater on earth, the "Great Jemez Crater." An oval bowl eighteen miles long and twelve miles wide, it is known locally as the "Valle Grande." The material ejected from it built up around it a plateau fifty miles in diameter. The layer of volcanic tufa which covers this plateau to a depth varying from one hundred to one thousand feet is cut by many canyons made by tributaries of the Rio Grande.

During the fourteenth and fifteenth centuries this plateau was the most densely populated area in the Southwest. The many natural caves had invited early nomadic tribes and they were joined by later tribes who brought agriculture and filled that country with cliff houses and valley pueblos.

Puyé, to the west of Española, where an elongated mesa reaches out into a wooded valley, was one closely packed center of populalation and consisted of many small houses, cave dwellings carved out of the soft rock of the cliff, and a large terraced pueblo built around a court on top of the mesa. Rooms were built against the cliffs in front of the caves and the holes for their roof beams are still visible. A network of trails and stairways connecting these various types of dwellings indicates that they were all occupied at the same time.

A little to the south, where the Rito de los Frijoles has carved its way through the Pajaritan Plateau to the Rio Grande, are many remains of both cliff houses and valley pueblos. The region is now a national monument named for Adolf F. Bandelier, the tireless explorer and archaeologist whose novel *The Delight Makers* brings to life the people who lived there in days long gone by.

The bases of the cliffs were lined with community houses with rows of holes, as at Puyé, showing where floor and ceiling timbers once rested. Some of them contained as many as seventy-five rooms. The largest was a continuous house varying from one to four stories in height and extending along the cliff for a distance of seven hundred feet.

The chief center of population was the great community house of Tyuonyi, the "place of council or treaty making." A terraced structure roughly circular in plan, it was probably three stories high. Unlike many such apartment houses which were added to as families increased, indications point to a preconceived plan executed at one time. A single passageway led to an inner court which contained three ceremonial kivas and from which the apartments were entered by means of ladders and hatchways. Near by is the largest kiva in the Rio Grande valley, forty-two feet in diameter, lined with a double row of tufa blocks.

Evidence points to a not uncommon drying up of the region and to the fact that this once thickly populated center was abandoned for lack of water. It is probable that the children of the cliff dwellers and community-house builders who lived near the Little River of the Beans moved closer to the Rio Grande.

Drought, progressive desiccation, and the raids of warlike nomads had combined to drive the Pueblo Indians out of their strongholds in the north and in the south. Gradually they settled along that river which, though seasonally dry, could be counted upon year after year to produce a flood of water for their crops and where they were as far away as they could get from the savage tribes which surrounded them. By the beginning of the sixteenth century they were concentrated in sixty or seventy villages in the valley of the Rio Grande, with but one extension westward, through Ácoma and Zuñi to the Hopi villages of Arizona. In most locations there was little stone and houses were built of adobe, not as large as those of several hundred years earlier but still rising as high as five stories.

Although pushed around many times, these people who had learned to build so well were not beaten. In the valley of the Rio Grande there was promise for the first time of the unity they had always lacked. Their culture had survived well. Their arts had developed. Concentrated in a dependable river valley, with the possibility of unity, the advance should continue. There was nothing to stop it. Nothing?

In 1540 the Spaniards came.

4

The Mythical Vale of Aztlán

THE AREA occupied by the ancient permanent-home-building Indians can for the sake of approximate visualization be thought of as a series of eccentric circles (see map, page oo), the smallest of which has its center at the Four Corners, with the line of centers extending south and the peripheries of the circles almost meeting on the north. The smallest circle represents the San Juan River valley with its concentration of cliff villages and valley pueblos. It includes principally Mesa Verde, with its adjacent sites in each of the states forming the Four Corners, and Chaco Canyon with its concentration of ancient communities. The second circle includes the more outlying sites in the valley of the Little Colorado and the later sites in the valley of the Rio Grande. These have been briefly described.

A much larger, third circle embraces in one direction the Gila and

Salt River valleys of southern Arizona and in another the pent-up river valleys of southern New Mexico and northern Chihuahua. This outer circle can be thought of as tangent on the south to a much larger outer circle in a series of *concentric* circles of a different group of ancient cultures whose center is Tenochtitlán, which is now Mexico City. The gear teeth in the peripheries of both outer circles are only faintly enmeshed and we are not directly concerned here with the Mexican circles, but in the area of the outermost Southwest circle are remains of two early cultures which are of interest to us. As was the case in the two smaller circles to the north, they are based on the river valleys which that large circle encloses. To distinguish them from the Anasazi or "Plateau" culture of the Four Corners, they are called the Hohokam or "Desert" culture and the Mogollon or "Mountain" culture.

The Gila River is notable today for what has been accomplished by irrigation. It was as notable for the same thing a thousand years ago. Indeed the Hohokam people, meaning "the ancient ones" or "those who have departed," are often referred to as the Canal Builders. The area which they occupied in southern and central Arizona had its center at the junction of the Gila and Salt Rivers, a little to the west and south of the modern city of Phoenix. Those rivers flow through a semiarid plain without canyons or rapids and supporting principally mesquite, salt bush, and many varieties of cacti. But irrigation makes it a fertile agricultural country and advantage was taken of this by the early Indian inhabitants. Theirs is, in fact, the only known instance of canal irrigation in pre-Columbian North America. Some of their canals, twenty-five miles long and thirty feet wide by seven feet deep with carefully-shaped and well-plastered sides, have been put to modern use. Reservoirs were also built for domestic water supply.

Their earliest dwellings, as with the Anasazi people, were pit houses. Evidences of these from before the beginning of the Christian Era show development from scattered, shallow pits dug out of the earth, with roofs of twigs and grass supported by poles, to large, carefully-built structures of adobe. Because of the scarcity of stone in that area adobe (mud) came to be almost universally employed for building. In that warm, dry climate sun-baked mud would harden and last almost as well as stone.

Sometime between 1100 and 1400 the Salado people moved into

the area from the north and east. They were cousins of the Pueblo builders who, because of probable pressure from the north, had followed the natural route of migration southward. They lived peacefully with the Hohokam for many years. But even before the newcomers moved in, the houses and villages of the Hohokam had undergone considerable change and now, with the pooling of efforts, an architecture developed which was quite unlike anything else in the Southwest.

With the continued use of adobe, houses were built in compounds with a dozen or more contiguous one-story rooms, the compound wall serving as one wall for the outer tier. The next development was to build even larger compounds divided into small plazas and room clusters until, in the final stage, the villages were built with houses of several stories with a compound wall making a walled village.

The method of wall construction was an interesting forerunner of our modern method of building with concrete. A typical specification of the period might read somewhat as follows:

SPECIFICATIONS FOR GILA RESIDENCE

HOHOKAM & SALADO · ARCHITECTS

October 12, 1392

FOUNDATIONS AND WALLS

First dig a shallow trench in the ground, using a well-pointed digging stick and piling all excavated material inside of trench. After trench has been dug to a level bottom, fill with a 3:1 mix of mud and broken stone, or river pebbles, tamping thoroughly to fill all interstices. Dampen mix only as necessary, using only enough water to soften mud to a stiff plastic consistency. A penalty will be imposed for using more than the minimum amount of water required.

After foundation has been allowed to set for a period of one (1) month, place forms, three (3) feet high, in six (6) foot lengths, around entire structure, inside and out, held eighteen (18) inches apart, forms to be made up of twigs woven on a framework of mesquite poles, plastered with mud and allowed to dry thoroughly. Fill forms with mud which has been moistened only sufficiently to form a plastic mass as in foundation, puddling thoroughly but using water sparingly. Tamp until form has been solidly filled.

Do not mold mud into bricks. This method of construction has not yet been introduced by the Spaniards.

Since time is not yet the essence, allow plenty for solidification of each course before removing forms and placing them to prepare for the next course. Six months should suffice. When mud has entirely dried and hardened, raise forms and repeat process as above until the desired height has been reached.

As far as extant remains are concerned, the period reached its climax in the ruins known as Casa Grande, now a national monument. The "Great House" is the dominating feature in the ruins of a village containing twelve or fifteen houses and covering two acres of land. It was one of several such villages in the area and was surrounded by a wall ten feet high. The principal building is forty feet wide by sixty feet long, is four stories high at the center, and rises about forty feet above the level of the desert. The lowest story was filled in, leaving five rooms each on two floors and one on the central top floor, which may have served as a watchtower. Wooden poles extending through the structure at the various floor levels were covered with sticks and filled with mud smoothed to a fine finish to form the floors. Low doorways were the only openings, except for small holes used either for ventilation or possibly for shooting arrows at marauders.

There is evidence of other similar structures in the vicinity, but today little remains of that distinctive culture except the one ruin now carefully but not too beautifully roofed over to protect it from the elements. What became of the Hohokam? Their walled villages had been deserted long before the coming of the Spaniards. They may have reverted to pit houses. The present-day Pima Indians, of relatively simple culture, gave to their predecessors in the Gila River valley the name by which they are known today.

The Salado? They probably continued migrating southward.

Just one more point. An interesting discovery, which proves nothing, is that evidence of ball courts similar to that recently found in the old Toltec capital of Tula, and to those which the Toltecs later introduced among the Mayas in Yucatán, has been found in the early Hohokam culture. So have rubber balls. The largest court was a hundred and eighty feet by sixty-one feet with walls of adobe. They date from the so-called Colonial Period, which lasted between the years 500 and 900. Nobody knows when Tula was built and occupied—probably sometime between the years 500 and 1200. During the following, or Sedentary, period of Hohokam culture of the next two hundred years the ball courts found were smaller. And then there were none.

The Gila River rises in the southwestern part of New Mexico, not very far away from that part of the country from which the Salado people came. In fact the Continental Divide obligingly makes quite a jog to the east so that the Salado people did not have far to go from their original home to the source of the river which was to be their new home for perhaps three hundred years before they crossed the Divide and moved on.

One would expect the rivers directly to the south of the jog to empty into the Rio Grande, but a ridge of mountains encloses a basin, bottling up the Mimbres River and forcing it to carry its waters into Chihuahua where, in common with other rivers in that area, it drains into the lakes of Guzmán. Thus is formed the great Mimbres-Chihuahua inland valley, which drains neither into the Atlantic nor the Pacific but is withal a well-watered basin where numerous rivers flow into a series of lagoons and thence into the high inland lake which is a paradise for large waterfowl. Spurs of the Mogollon Mountains which form the Divide to the north give the culture of that whole area its name. To the south the valley extends to the high watershed of the Conchos River, which flows into the Rio Grande just opposite the town of Presidio, a little above Big Bend National Park.

Pit houses similar to those of the Anasazi were characteristic of all the early periods of culture in the valley. At a later date influences from various directions made themselves felt. Ruins of pueblos from the Anasazi are found; individual one-story houses of adobe reinforced with stone and multistoried houses of many rooms indicate the presence of the Salado people; while on the slopes of the Sierra Madre, in which there are great caves of unknown extent, the ruins of many adobe cliff villages go back even farther to establish an ancestry. The Anasazi influence is dominant in many places. Ceremonial pit houses gave way to kivalike rooms with equipment pointing to the probability of ceremonies similar to those still practiced among the Pueblo Indians of today, in which they impersonate the spirits of their ancestors who are considered divine.

Curiously there have also been found in the high inland basin of Chihuahua great urn-shaped structures, twelve feet in diameter, made of ropes of grass and adobe in coils as in a basket and plastered inside and out—obviously granaries. They closely resemble the *cuezcomate* of the Aztecs more than a thousand miles to the south.

The mountain slopes were carefully terraced and irrigated by means of small trenches, resulting in the fine forests of the Sierra Madre in western Chihuahua. The same system of terracing for irrigation was used by the Aztecs.

Perforated stone disks two feet in diameter and six inches thick have been found in the vicinity. They are like the rings used in the ball game of the Aztecs and at an earlier date introduced into the cities of the Mayas by the Toltecs.

By the time the Spaniards reached that part of the country the cliff dwellings and the Great Houses of adobe were deserted and their builders had disappeared. It is possible that the Tarahumare of today, who speak an entirely different language, descended from them. Nobody knows.

When the Spaniards arrived in Mexico the center of that country was dominated by the Aztecs. Theirs was not an empire, as it has sometimes been termed; they just happened to be the most powerful tribe at the time. They were not in fact an ancient tribe like the Toltecs and the Mayas; they were latecomers to the Valley of Anáhuac, the last of seven principal Nahua tribes all speaking that language (which is of the Uto-Aztecan group spoken by most of the Pueblo tribes) and all coming down from the North. Earlier tribes had taken the choice locations, and when the straggling band of Aztecs arrived all that was left for them was a group of low, swampy islands on which to build huts of rushes, where they lived on fish, birds, and such seeds and roots as grew in the swamps.

That they came from an ancestry that knew how to rise above such handicaps is clear from the remarkable development they underwent. Within two hundred years they had built a beautiful city of palaces, temples, canals, and broad plazas and were exacting tribute from the surrounding tribes which had preceded them. It was their misfortune (and, thinking of their beautiful capital city, ours too) that they happened to be the people who stood in the way of the Spaniards bent on conquest. They were proud of their rise from such simple beginnings and to their conquerors they told the legends of their wanderings before they arrived, a sorry band, in the Valley of Mexico.

They had come down from the north, having migrated for a long time, and somewhere up there they, with the other Nahua tribes— but at long intervals—had issued from seven caves. They were the last to come. The name of their legendary ancestral home was Aztlán, which means "place of herons"; and they referred to it also as a "place of lagoons." Another legendary land, even farther to the north, was called Teocalhuacán, which is to say "a land of such whose ancestors are divine." There is nothing more definite than that. Whatever may have been their exact point of origin—and it is a matter which is entirely conjectural—their legends were to be heard by the Spaniards who, weaving them into their own, were to carry them back to the north whence the Aztecs had come.

PART TWO: *EL DORADO*

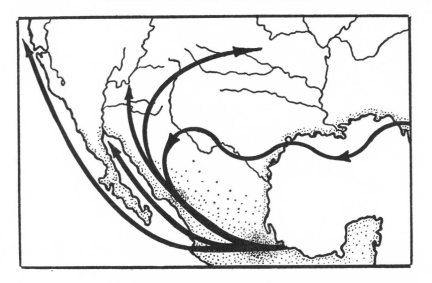

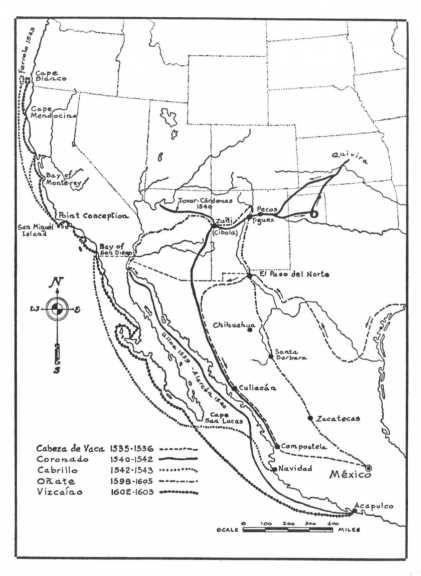

Cabeza de Vaca 1535-1536 -------
Coronado   1540-1542 ————
Cabrillo   1542-1543 ....
Oñate   1598-1605 —·—·—·
Vizcaíno   1602-1603 •••••••••

EARLY SPANISH EXPLORATION

5

Spices, Gold, and Amazons

THE FIRST STEP in the conquest of Mexico, the capture and enforced destruction of the Aztec capital Tenochtitlán, was achieved in August of 1521. Almost immediately the attention of the conquistadors began to be directed toward exploration in the Northwest. This thought was ever uppermost in the mind of Cortés. The capital must be rebuilt into a magnificent Spanish city even more beautiful than that which had been destroyed, revolts in the provinces must be quelled, a government must be established which was adapted to the needs of Spain, and missions must be built as centers for the conversion and instruction of the Indians. With these ends in view, Cortés and his captains built homes there. But they had no intention of settling down for long; that city was merely to be their headquarters for future operations. Discovery, exploration, and conquest must go on.

Spices were still all important—pepper was worth almost its weight in gold—as they had been when Columbus made his first voyage, and a short and direct route between the spice region and the kingdom of Spain was still a principal aim which prompted continued exploration. A direct sea passage to Cathay was thought to exist, as it still was in the minds of the French a hundred years later when Jean Nicollet paddled his canoe onto Lake Michigan dressed in robes suitable for his reception by the oriental monarch he expected to find on the farther shore.

The voyages of Columbus had proved that there was no opening along the Central American coast and continued exploration of South

45

America had shown that land to be a continent. But North America was thought to be less extensive than the southern continent, particularly in the distance from east to west; so somewhere to the north, it was argued, must be that strait which provided a short passage from Europe to Asia.

Cortés in a letter to Charles V presented his arguments for the building of a fleet on the "south sea" for further exploration and stressed the importance to His Majesty of the discovery of such a passage, writing: "to add this service to the others I have done, because I deem it the greatest, if, as I say, the strait be found"; but he qualified his confidence by adding: "and if it be not found, it is not possible that there should not be discovered very large and rich lands where your Caesarean Majesty may be much served, and the kingdoms and seigneuries of your royal crown be greatly extended."

That brings up a second objective, which was of even more immediate interest to the leaders of the expeditions which poured forth to that northern land of mystery: gold. He who had gold had magic powers; more than that, he had celestial keys. It had ever been thus, from the voyages of Jason in quest of the Golden Fleece and Hercules in search of the golden apples of the Hesperides to the bringing of gold by Portuguese sailors from the west coast of Africa in the fifteenth century and the discovery of golden ornaments in the noses of the natives seen by Columbus in October of 1492, the first trace of gold in America. During the first few years of its occupation Santo Domingo furnished to the crown of Spain five hundred thousand ducats in gold, and when Pizarro's conquest of Peru yielded riches that far eclipsed the meager booty of Tenochtitlán the fever for gold was intensified. The early Spanish explorers may be criticized for their aims and their methods, but the greed for treasure (the acquisition of great wealth being a universal dream) played a large part in the expansion to the northwest and the opening up of what is now our Southwest.

Another force that drove the Spaniards on was the power of legends, and most of these too were inevitably linked with gold. There were a number of these legends which played prominent parts in Spanish exploration and which grew as the explorers encountered Indians on their frontiers who would gladly nourish a germ implanted in their minds, sometimes even with a slight seasoning of truth, in order to get rid of their unwanted guests, and who often fabricated shells of fancy (in which they received no discouragement); but almost universally the kernel came from Europe. It is questionable how much of the Indian legend of that period remained unadulterated Indian legend. In many instances certainly the Indians supplied the basic information only; the Spaniards supplied the imagination. European legends always fitted very readily into Indian recollections. Such were the fables of the Seven Cities and of the Amazons. No myth of the Indians had a stronger influence on the Spanish mind than that of the Seven Cities, not even the one the name of which became synonymous with fabulous wealth and which, according to good authority, has a basis in fact.

Very shortly after the north coast of South America was first occupied by the Spaniards the natives began to tell of the ceremonies performed by a tribe of Indians who lived among the many lakes of the highlands about where the city of Bogotá now stands. Whenever a new chief was chosen the men of the tribe marched in procession wearing ornaments of gold and emeralds, the nobles and the priests following at the rear bearing the newly elected chief on a litter hung with disks of gold. His naked body was anointed with resinous gums and covered with gold dust. Upon arriving at the shore of the lake the gilded chief stepped onto a float and proceeded to the middle of the lake, where he plunged in and washed off his shining cloak while the people, with shouts and the beating of drums, threw into the water their gold and jewels. Thus grew the legend of *El Dorado*, the gilded man. The myth was encountered in varying versions throughout early explorations in South America.

When Pizarro's "king's ransom," drawn up by the royal (Spanish) notary in 1533, was found to amount to millions of ducats of gold and silver there was not only a rush for Peru but new hopes arose in Mexico for similar riches in that land of mystery to the north. There the Seven Golden Cities came to be the goal.

A globe had been constructed for the Portuguese service, while Columbus was still searching for new lands on his first voyage, which shows to the west of the Canaries an island called Antillia. On it there is a note telling of how in the eighth century, when the Iberian Goths were defeated by the Moors, two archbishops of Portugal, with five bishops, had taken their flock and sailed to the west and founded seven noble cities there. Some of the first discoverers thought they had found this place, wherefore the name of Antilles remained and was applied to the whole chain of islands that separate the Caribbean Sea from the Atlantic Ocean.

But in the rapid expansion the seven cities were forgotten until after the conquest of Mexico, when a Tejas Indian slave recalled that he had gone with his father to trade feathered plumes for gold and silver. Their journey had taken them across a great desert to the north and at the end of forty days he had seen with his own eyes cities as large as Mexico and its suburbs. There were seven of these cities and the streets were lined with houses in which men worked in gold and silver.

Then the Spaniards remembered the legend of the Aztecs and how they were thought to have originated in seven caves. Spanish writers changed that to read seven tribes and the tribes finally grew into seven towns or cities. Thus were the Spaniards prepared for any further allusion to the ever-mystical number "seven." Search for *El Dorado* had resulted in enormous riches from South America. Should not the northern land produce as much? After Cortés and Pizarro there had to be a Narváez and a Coronado. After Tenochtitlán and Cuzco it was inevitable that there should be the Seven Cities of Cíbola and Gran Quivira. The lure of those myths has lasted almost to the present day.

The Amazons were more quickly disposed of. Their legend was doubtless brought to America by the Spaniards and its embellishment by the Indians was readily misunderstood by them. Returning from his first voyage, Columbus spoke of an island inhabited only by women who used bows and arrows of cane and covered and armed themselves with brazen plates. Cortés in 1524 wrote to the Emperor of the account brought to him by his faithful lieutenant Sandoval of an island to the northwest of Mexico "inhabited only by women without any men, and that from time to time men went out to them from the mainland . . . when they bore daughters they kept them, but the sons were put away." Then in the same letter he adds, not too incidentally: "I was also told that they were rich in pearls and gold." In South America the myth of the Amazons became associated with that of *El Dorado* and still later that fable of classical antiquity was destined to endure in the great river which almost cuts the continent in two parts. How the Amazon bubble burst in the early days of northwestern exploration will be mentioned in later chapters.

But the influence of legends and the search for gold and for a passage to Asia continued. How they led to our Southwest is a story or rather a series of stories, of hopes and disappointments, of rivalry and intrigue, of hardships and cruelties, of myths and disillusionment but ultimately also a story of conquest and settlement and of the founding of missions and cities which remain to this day.

6

The Journey of Cabeza de Vaca

IN HIS expedition in 1520 to thwart Cortés, the red-bearded captain Pánfilo de Narváez, deserted by most of his men, fought desperately until he was heard to cry: "Holy Mary protect me, they have killed me and put out my eye!"

Narváez never forgave Cortés. Sent by Diego Velásquez, governor of Cuba, to enforce the governor's authority over the bold and presumptuous conqueror of Mexico, and with twice as many ships and three times as many men, he had seen his agents bribed with gifts of gold and almost his entire army corrupted by promises. He was kept a prisoner for three years and when in 1522 he was taken on a very thoroughly conducted tour of the splendid cities of the interior, which should have been his to rule, Narváez wept.

The following year he was released and, in spite of gifts of gold from Cortés and a promise to his acknowledged master to remain always a faithful servant, he returned to Spain in 1525 to appear before the Council of the Indies as a principal witness in the investigation of the deeds and alleged misdeeds of the great conqueror. As a reward, Narváez was given a grant by Charles V to conquer and colonize Florida, which then meant everything north of Mexico. It cost the Emperor little, and for a kingdom richer in golden cities than the Mexico of Cortés, Narváez was ready to risk the other eye.

Thus it came about that the discovery and exploration of what is now the Southwest of the United States began in the Southeast. Ponce de León, in quest of the Fountain of Youth, landed on the mainland of Florida in 1513 and, returning later to establish a colony, was killed by an Indian arrow. In 1518 Juan de Grijalva sailed as far north as Pánuco on the Gulf Coast of Mexico, which is about where the city of Tampico now lies; and the following year Alonso Alvarez de Pineda explored the coast of the Gulf from the tip of Florida to Pánuco. On his voyage he discovered the mouth of the Mississippi, which he named the Rio del Espíritu Santo, twenty-two years before De Soto crossed the Father of Waters. He then skirted the islands and sand bars off the coast of Texas and sailed into the mouth of the Rio de las Palmas, which we know now as the Rio Grande.

The next approach to the border of Texas was made by Francisco Garay, who first sent envoys to try to find a good harbor on the Gulf Coast and establish a colony there and who in 1523 arrived in person with a governor's commission. Disappointed at the lack of gold, Garay's men plundered the native villages and it was necessary for Cortés to come to the rescue to quell the revolt which ensued.

Cortés had still other enemies jealous of his glory and position and always ready to knife him in the back. Bitterest of these was Nuño de Guzmán, of whom history can recall hardly a decent act. He followed Garay as governor of Pánuco. Equally disappointed in the poverty of the country, he established a systematic slave trade, even raiding Las Palmas—which by then formed part of the territory assigned to Narváez—and sending his victims by the shipload to the islands until the country was almost depopulated.

By that time the weight of false evidence on the part of the enemies of Cortés had at least half convinced the Emperor that the conqueror should be removed. An *audiencia* was established to assume the government of New Spain and Nuño de Guzmán, a shrewd-enough lawyer to have his acts misconstrued as being for the good of Spain, instead of being hanged—as he richly deserved—was made its president! We shall hear of him soon enough again.

But to return to Narváez, in Spain assembling his men, his ships, and his supplies. It was not hard to find men because strange tales of mysterious wealth had been coming out of Florida ever since Ponce de León landed on the mainland in 1513, and there were many restless hidalgos in Spain itching for a share of the riches. By the summer of 1527 the expedition was ready to start. Five caravels, carrying six hundred men, made up the fleet. Accompanying it were five Franciscan friars. They set sail from the mouth of the Guadalquivír in

June, having been joined en route from Seville by Álvar Nuñez Cabeza de Vaca, who had ridden the fifteen miles from his home at Jerez de la Frontera to fulfill his appointment as treasurer of the expedition.

Cabeza de Vaca was born about 1490, the son of an alderman of Jerez and the grandson of the illustrious Pedro de Vera Mendoza, conqueror of the Grand Canary. The origin of the family name dates back to a time during the Reconquest when the Christians, about to abandon their pursuit of the Moors, were shown a secret mountain pass by a shepherd who had marked its entrance with a cow's skull. By following this route the Spaniards were able to surprise the infidel from the rear. The shepherd was ennobled, and his name changed to the glorious "Cow's Head." Young Cabeza de Vaca had served his country well both at home and in the wars of Italy. He must have given a good account of his ability to handle men and money for in his new capacity he was directly responsible to the king.

Misfortune seems to have pursued the expedition almost from the beginning. On landing at Santo Domingo one hundred and forty men deserted. The fleet encountered a hurricane off the coast of Cuba, two of the ships were lost, and sixty men and twenty horses were never seen again. It was not until February of 1528 that the expedition sailed for Florida. Beset by storms most of the way, the little fleet entered Tampa Bay on Holy Thursday and on the following day, Good Friday, the tenth of April, just fifteen years after Ponce de León had discovered the mainland and christened it Florida, the band of men was ready to begin its adventures in a new land. Of the four hundred who made that landing only four were destined to survive.

We must not dwell in detail on those dismal days that followed. After solemnly reading the King's Summons to the Indians to an audience consisting principally of live oaks, Narváez started on a tour of exploration. A golden ornament had been found in the deserted village of round thatched huts which they had sighted from the ships, and on later capturing four Indians and inquiring of them the source of the gold they were greeted with cries of "Apalachen!"

Against the advice of Cabeza de Vaca, Narváez decided to lead his men on a march inland while his ships followed the coast. They never met again. Apalachen proved to be a miserable village of forty thatched huts. Returning to the coast and finding no trace of their ships, they built rafts to take once more to the sea. Nails and tools they made from their stirrups and spurs, pine logs calked with palmetto and pitch formed the hulls, while their shirts provided the sails and the tails and manes of horses the rigging. The slain horses also provided food to supplement the dwindling supply of maize taken from the Indians, and the skins from the horses' legs were made into canteens for water. Well-aimed arrows of the Indians, hunger, and disease all took their toll of lives but on the twenty-second day of September—the last horse eaten—two hundred and forty Spaniards commended their souls to God and set sail in their leaky craft headed, they hoped, for Pánuco. That northernmost settlement of New Spain, more than a thousand miles away, they thought might be around the next headland.

The weeks which followed were filled with days of burning thirst, hunger, and exposure, and attempts to land for food were met with attacks by hostile Indians. Off the mouth of the Mississippi a storm was encountered, the fleet was scattered, and most of the vessels were blown out to sea. Narváez succeeded in reaching land farther along the coast, but while asleep in his boat he was carried out to sea and never heard of again.

Finally two boats, one of them commanded by Cabeza de Vaca, reached an island off the coast of Texas, near Galveston, and the men, exhausted and half starved, crawled on hands and knees to the shore. Building a fire and drinking rain water which they found, life began to flow back into their veins and they gave thanks to God for preserving their lives.

It was not long before Indians approached and, given beads and bells which some of the men still carried, were persuaded to bring food. After several days the Spaniards had regained sufficient strength to move, and at their suggestion they were led, tottering, to the Indian village where a house was prepared with many fires. It was doubtless the first human habitation ever seen by white men in Texas or the whole Southwest.

With the approach of winter food became scarce; it was bitterly cold and a native plague did its work so that it was not long before the eighty men who had landed in the two boatloads were reduced to fifteen. Fifteen Spanish slaves who had set out on a tour of great conquest spent their days digging roots and shellfish, which formed their principal diet when they were not reduced to spiders and rats, and carrying loads of driftwood on their bare backs to the campfires of their Indian masters.

Nuño de Guzmán governed Mexico in very much the same manner as he had ruled Pánuco. He made slaves of the Indians, exacted tribute from their chiefs, and kidnaped their women. At the same time he was careful to see that news of his activities did not reach Spain. But when he overrode the protestations of Zumárraga, newly appointed bishop of Mexico (whose office included that of "protector of the Indians"), even to the extent of causing one of the friars to be dragged down from his pulpit for denouncing him, Guzmán had gone too far. The bishop's famous letter, buried in a cake of wax and dropped into a barrel of oil, reached Spain and a new and honest *audiencia* was appointed.

Guzmán had already decided that the best place for him was the unexplored country to the northwest. In this land of mystery he might not only redeem himself from disgrace but might also gain wealth and win power and fame in a new and mighty realm. In December of 1529 he marched from the capital at the head of four hundred Spanish soldiers and ten thousand Indian allies. Plunder and murder followed in his wake through Michoacán and Jalisco, and on reaching the country farther north he gave it the name of Greater Spain, in a grandiose gesture to outdo the New Spain of Cortés. In November of 1530 he reached Sinaloa, and the following summer founded the town of Culiacán. Disappointed in the search for gold and for the cities of the Amazons, which proved to be villages that the men had fled to avoid the newcomers, the Spaniards were forced to settle down and live on the supplies which they had brought. When those gave out they went back to plundering the natives and seizing them as slaves.

Through the next five years explorations to the north continued, the Spaniards penetrating as far as the present state of Sonora, which borders on Arizona. One day in March of 1536 a party of slave raiders under the leadership of its captain, Diego de Alcaraz, was on an expedition along the Rio Petatlán, which flows from the Sierra Madre through the northern part of the state of Sinaloa. Discouraged because for some time they had been unable to find either Indians or food, the advance guard suddenly stopped. Ahead of them in the bushes were two men, a white man and a black, wearing only girdles and beards. On seeing the Spaniards on horseback the white man advanced and spoke to them in Spanish; then when the leader had dismounted the naked man clung to him and wept.

Back in Culiacán, where they were met by Melchior Díaz, alcalde

of the garrison and vice-governor of the district, Cabeza de Vaca
told his story.

The surviving castaways managed somehow to get through the
winter of 1528–29. Then as season followed season the white slaves
followed their Indian masters in search of food. Sometimes they
lived solely on shellfish, and when Cabeza de Vaca was not grubbing
for food his time was spent in setting up mat houses on mounds of
shells for a dry foundation. When the dewberries were ripe they ate
those; in midsummer they migrated to the cactus country and filled
their bellies with the prickly pear.

When the plague had overtaken both Indians and white men,
the whites were made to perform as healers. They followed the
practice of the native witch doctors, blowing upon the patients and
passing their hands over them, and to the native rites they added a
prayer. The results were remarkable. Cabeza de Vaca later was permitted to engage in trade, taking sea shells to a near-by tribe to be
used as knives. Thus for six years he lived among the Indians as trader,
medicine man, and slave, journeying along the coast forty or fifty
leagues and as far inland, learning the character of the country and
the languages of the Indian tribes. During his wanderings he ran
across three other survivors of the ill-fated expedition: Andrés
Dorantes, Alonso del Castillo, and the former's black Moorish slave,
Estebanico. The four were all that were still alive.

Several times the four met to plan an escape, and each time they
would be caught and dragged back to their masters. Finally they
did escape to another tribe, where they were welcomed as healers
and given food. Continuing their journey southward, they came to
a river as broad as the Guadalquivír at Seville. It was the Rio Grande.
By that time their fame as miracle men had spread before them from
tribe to tribe and their journey became a triumphal march, with a
retinue of Indians following in their train.

Thus they progressed to the west and northwest, crossing the Rio
Grande again just below the Big Bend and then again near El Paso.
As they marched west from there, always with their followers—
numbering sometimes thousands—to deliver them to the next tribe
to perform their miraculous healing, they noticed a marked change
in the Indians and in their habitations. These Indians were farmers;
they raised maize and wore cotton clothes and the huts of thatch or

mud gave way to more permanent homes. The medicine men were given ceremonial rattles made of gourds, painted and filled with seeds or pebbles and decorated with feathers, symbols of the magician.

It is doubtful that the wanderers entered New Mexico, as has been claimed, but they were fed piñon nuts and they probably saw the buffalo during their travels. They were also told of populous cities and tall houses among the high mountains to the north, where there were "emeralds." Repeated in Mexico and in Spain, that story grew as the imagination of the listener permitted.

The travelers turned again to the southwest, and on reaching the Rio Sonora they turned to the south, where signs of devastated villages told them only too well that they were approaching the country of the Spaniards.

Dorantes and Castillo soon caught up with Cabeza de Vaca and Estebanico, who had marched on ahead to meet the slave raiders, and it was difficult to persuade the latter not to take the six hundred Indian followers of the four Children of the Sun as slaves. At a signal from Cabeza de Vaca the Indians disappeared and returned bearing quantities of food.

At Compostela, which is near Tepic, capital of the present state of Nayarit, the Spanish wanderers were graciously received by Nuño de Guzmán, but when Cabeza de Vaca dared to remonstrate with the governor for his slave raiding they were sent on their way, after a warning had been sent to the viceroy that long years of exposure had affected the minds of the four. They arrived in Mexico City on July 23, where they were presented to Antonio de Mendoza, who had come to Mexico as viceroy the year before. The three hidalgos were dressed in gold-laced brocades which they accepted with gracious discomfort, while Estebanico marched around among the Negroes of the capital, an admiring throng at his heels.

Declining the offers of Mendoza to head an exploring expedition to the north, Cabeza de Vaca returned to Spain the following spring to seek, too late, the governorship of Florida, which had already been given to De Soto, and to return evenings to his room where he could in comfort pace up and down the tile floor in his bare feet and dream of what he might have done for the Indians of that great country to the north.

As for the denouement, Nuño de Guzmán finally got what he deserved, except that he did not get it soon enough or severely enough. In 1537 the Spanish authorities finally caught up with him and he was arrested and sent back to Spain, where his ill-gotten gains were confiscated and he died in poverty.

Andrés Dorantes was rewarded by Mendoza with a wealthy widow who bore him eleven children and whose descendants probably still proudly tell of the part their name played in Spanish exploration. Alonso del Castillo suffered a similar fate, except that his children were all girls.

Misfortune seemed to continue to follow Cabeza de Vaca. Appointed governor of La Plata in South America, he made other great marches but, through the jealousies of his rivals, he was sent to Spain in chains. He spent several years trying to clear his good name of the taint of misconduct in office while the authorities of the Church wrangled over the propriety of the arts of magic being practiced by a layman. The successful discovery and exploration of the Southwest by one who lived to tell the tale was of decidedly secondary interest to them. Cabeza de Vaca apparently managed to survive the ordeal, however. There is no record of his demise, but he is known to have been living in Spain twenty years later.

The only one of the survivors of that harrowing odyssey who played any part in the subsequent exploration of the Southwest was Little Black Stephen. But he did *not* live to tell that tale.

7

The Seven Cities of Cíbola

THE FIRST MAN from Europe to penetrate what is now the state of Arizona and to enter New Mexico was not a European at all but an African, a black slave from Azamor on the Atlantic coast of Morocco. He was closely followed by a Franciscan friar, an Italian who was a native of Nice in France.

Although Dorantes too declined the insistent request of the viceroy Mendoza to head an expedition back into the country to the north, he did part with Estebanico, who, back in civilization, unquestioningly resumed his status as a slave. Actually, after having attempted to sail to Spain and having been forced to return to Vera Cruz because of a leaky ship, Dorantes did accede to Mendoza's suggestion. Troops and horses were raised for an expedition; but it came to nothing.

Mendoza's next move was to induce the Franciscans to send a representative on an exploring journey in the interest of the Church and the Emperor. Fray Marcos of Nice and a companion, Fray Onorato, answered the call. Estebanico was to accompany them as their servant and guide, leading the way but obeying them in all things.

On March 7, 1539, the little band started on the march northward from Culiacán. With an arrogance born of the realization that he alone knew the road and that he alone knew the Indians, the Moroccan slave swaggered in the lead of his masters, decorated with plumes and bells and waving his magic gourd while Indians on the way begged for the healing touch of his hands. Fray Onorato soon became ill and had to be left behind. Fray Marcos then dispatched Estebanico on ahead with instructions that if he learned of a fair country he was to send back to the friar a white cross of "one handful long," if it were a great country a cross of two handsful long, and if he should hear tidings of a country richer than New Spain he was to send a great cross.

Four days later Indian messengers returned bearing a cross as tall as a man and a message urging Fray Marcos to come at once. Estebanico, he was told, was now at a town which was but thirty days' journey from the turquoise-studded gates of the Seven Cities which were called Cíbola. The houses in these cities were made of stone and lime, were very great in size, all joined together, and of two and three stories in height, and that of the Lord of the Province was four stories high. The gates of the principal houses, the messengers said, were set with turquoise stones, there were many such, the people wore rich clothes of cotton cloth; and beyond, toward the rising sun, there were other provinces that were much greater than these seven cities.

So on the second day after Easter the good friar, tense with excitement, marched on, humbly planting crosses on the way. But his proud servant was far in advance, gathering rich gifts and beautiful women as he marched. Out on the desert with an adoring retinue he was no longer a Moorish slave; he was a proud oriental chieftain. Robes of the colors of the rainbow flowed from his dusky body, bright feathers and jingling bells dangled from his arms and legs, and two Spanish greyhounds followed at his heels. Flutes of reeds, fifes of shell, and drums of fishskin played his march as he crossed the white desert and skirted the sunlit mesas. Gayly dressed young women swelled his harem, two dozen Indian servants carried his surplus gifts and his provisions, and his meals were served with pomp on green dinner plates.

Every day he sent back word to Fray Marcos or planted a cross on his path, but he moved on apace, careful not to be overtaken. He would have no interference in his new-found role. Out of the Sonora Valley he followed the San Pedro River to its junction with the Gila, then struck northeast across the desert and on across what is now the border between Arizona and New Mexico. Within a day's journey of his destination he halted and sent a messenger ahead with his rattling gourd decorated with feathers and hung with bells to say that the Child of the Sun had come.

Rebuffed by the chief, Estebanico only laughed and marched to the city where he was courteously met on the outskirts and shown to quarters for the night. On the demand that he be brought gold and their most beautiful women, the elders were sorely offended. Meeting in council that night they discussed their problem. The black man who claimed to be the agent of a white prince who lived across the sea might be a demon in disguise. The verdict was death.

In the morning Estebanico, calling upon the city to surrender, was greeted with a shower of arrows. Quickly forsaking his recent role, he took to his heels; but an arrow overtook him, and of his three hundred followers only three escaped to take the news to Fray Marcos. The body of the erstwhile Child of the Sun was cut in pieces and distributed among the elders as proof of his death. The chief kept the greyhounds and the four green dinner plates.

On learning of the fate of the black slave, Fray Marcos hesitated but a moment. His Indian guides were ready to flee, and it was only by offering them presents which had been prepared for the Lord of Cíbola that he was able to persuade two of them to lead him to a spot where he might see the city from a safe distance. So from a mesa the Franciscan friar looked to the north to where he could see spread out on the plain what looked to him, in the rarefied air abetted by a receptive imagination, like a great city of multistoried buildings behind whose walls were riches of gold and silver, "for they have no other metal." He raised a mound of stones and set up a wooden cross as proof that he had been there and as a sign that he would some day return.

Fray Marcos has been criticized in later times for having gone thus far and not entering the city, even at the risk of death, which would have been a glorious martyrdom. The friar himself answers his critics adequately: "I was tempted to go thither, because I knew I could but hazard my life, and that I had offered unto God the first day that I began my journey; in the end I began to be afraid, considering in what danger I should put myself, and that if I should die, the knowledge of this country should be lost, which in my judgment is the greatest and the best that hitherto hath been discovered." With one long fond look he gazed down upon that group of buildings, which he thought to be greater than any city of New Spain, and then turned and "with much more fear than victuals" fled to Mexico.

In the western part of New Mexico on Highway 66 is the busy trading center of Gallup. From here are shipped cattle and sheep from the grazing lands near by; it is the buying center for the Navaho wool clip; and piñon nuts are brought in by the Indians in trade. On busy trading days the streets are crowded with Indians and in the trading posts one can buy the turquoise jewelry for which the Indians to the southward are famous.

From Gallup a winding road leads over hills and through woods carpeted with pine cones to the peaceful and seemingly deserted red sandstone and adobe pueblo of Zuñi forty miles to the south. Its low-lying buildings spread out over the sand and on down to the river which flows, when it flows, through the village and on through the fertile fields of the valley to join the Little Colorado farther to the west over the Arizona line. Scattered among the houses are beehive ovens, clustered along the banks are corrals, and across the river are carefully fenced vegetable gardens. In the midst of the houses stand the crumbling ruins of the mission church built under the direction of the Franciscan friars in 1705. The bases of the massive red adobe towers flank what remains of a deep and shadowed loggia, and over it is what is left of a balcony once crowded with Indians gathered to watch the dances on the square below.

This pueblo is all that remains of what at one time were seven villages, most of them scattered over the plain farther south. It lies in fact on a comparatively new site, having been built there at the end of the seventeenth century. The older ones, which were greater than this, being of several stories in height, and even Háwikuh, the largest of the pueblos, are now but ruins. But the descendants of the people of those older pueblos farm and tend their sheep and gather in Zuñi for their dances, and there they make their famous turquoise jewelry. And on long winter nights, when the high precipitous buttes to the north are only vaguely outlined against a dark sky, when even the steep and streaked cliffs of Towayalane to the south blend into the darkness, and the pungent scent of piñon fills the air, the boys gather around to listen to the old ones tell the tale of the black sorcerer who claimed to be an emissary of a great king across the sea and who, taking undue advantage of his alleged position, was summarily put to death.

8

Coronado and the Quest of Quivira

WHEN Nuño de Guzmán had been relieved of his post as governor of Nueva Galicia, to which that truculent tyrant's Greater Spain had been reduced in name, his place was filled by Diego Perez de la Torre. Conditions in that outpost of the empire began to improve almost immediately, in spite of the great damage that had already been done and the storm clouds of revolt that seemed to be gathering constantly. Two years later, while engaged in a campaign against a revolting tribe and after winning a hard-fought battle, Torre was accidentally killed. In view of the increasing possibilities of the land to the north as reported by Cabeza de Vaca, the viceroy was careful to see that just the right man be appointed to act as the new governor and to carry on the exploration of that golden land of promise. That man was found in the person of Francisco Vásquez de Coronado.

The report of Fray Marcos on his return caused a furor in the City of Mexico. The discovery of the golden cities was proclaimed from every pulpit, among the idle cavaliers the story was on every tongue, and the tale lost nothing in the telling. For the conquest of Cíbola Mendoza at first wished to take command in person but, his duties in the capital making this impracticable, he appointed the loyal aristocrat Coronado captain-general of the proposed expedition.

Within a few weeks a company was enlisted and assembled at Compostela in New Galicia. The viceroy accompanied it there, and in February of 1540 cheered the army by a parting address. It was the most brilliant company yet assembled in New Spain. Three hundred cavaliers, many of them gentlemen of good family and high rank, in polished mail, lances held erect, were astride the best horses to be found in the country, trailing brilliantly colored blankets and wearing silver-mounted harness. Behind them marched the foot soldiers, armed with crossbow and harquebus, and bringing up the rear were eight hundred Indian allies, gayly painted and wearing the green, yellow, and crimson plumage of parrots. Indian servants and camp followers led a thousand horses, as many pack mules, and dragged the cannon; and to provide food there were droves of cattle, sheep, goats, and swine. At the head of all this display rode Coronado in golden armor, and contrasting with his brilliance were Fray Marcos and the other Franciscan friars in their gray robes. Amid the cheers of the people trumpets were blown, banners flew, and the expedition started on its march.

At the same time a maritime expedition under Hernando de Alarcón was sent up the coast to carry additional supplies and to cooperate with the army. Alarcón, with three ships, sailed to the head of the Gulf of California and then, crossing the Colorado delta with some difficulty, sailed up that river for a distance of eighty-five leagues, perhaps as far as the mouth of the Gila.

Coronado, dividing his forces, marched on ahead with Fray Marcos and a picked force of fifty horse and twenty-five foot soldiers. Crossing the Sonora Valley into Arizona, they soon reached the Gila River and Chichilicale, the "red house" ruin, which may have been the ancient Casa Grande. Continuing on to the northeast, they crossed the Little Colorado and about the tenth of July the band of soldiers came in sight of the famous Cíbola.

The disappointment of the men at first sight of that much-heralded city of Fray Marcos—their mental pictures having been aided no little by the ever more colorful descriptions of the imaginative friar —can well be imagined; and the curses hurled at the much-embarrassed Franciscan must have been adequate, to cause Castañeda, historian of the expedition, to enter in his report a prayer that God might protect him from them. As for Fray Marcos, he wisely decided to return to Mexico with the first messengers.

Háwikuh was not taken without a struggle. Stones hurled from the roof tops by the Zuñi warriors felled even the golden-armored Coronado, who would have been killed but for the heroism of one of his officers. Entering the village, the soldiers found food but no gold, no silver, no precious stones.

Forcing the remainder of the Seven Cities into submission, Coronado stayed at Cíbola until December to recover from his wounds and to send out exploring parties. Melchior Díaz he sent to try to make junction with Alarcón's ships while Pedro de Tovar was sent to the northwest to explore the newly reported province of Tusayan. While in the villages of that desert province Tovar learned of a great river which flowed far down between red mountain walls. When this news had been reported to Coronado, López de Cárdenas, that same gallant knight who had saved his commander's life, was sent to find the river. So high were its banks, he found, that the stream, which the Indians said was more than half a league wide, looked like a mere rivulet three or four leagues below; and some huge rocks on the sides, which from above looked to be about as tall as a man, were sworn by those who succeeded in climbing about one third of the way down to be taller than the great tower of the cathedral in Seville. It was the first view by white men of the Grand Canyon of the Colorado.

In the meantime the detachment at Zuñi was visited by some Indians from the east, led by a chief whom the Spaniards nicknamed Bigotes (Whiskers), who told them of great towns and of buffaloes in his country. So, with instructions to return within eight days, Hernando de Alvarado was sent east, where after a march of eight days he reached a large river flowing from north to south which was said to be well settled for fifty leagues or more. In the midst of the towns along the river was the province of Tiguex, or country of the Tiguas, with twelve towns in a broad valley. So well impressed was Alvarado that he sent back to Coronado a recommendation that he establish his winter quarters there. A week's journey beyond the Rio Grande Alvarado came to the town of Cicuyé, or Pecos, in the valley of the Pecos River. Bigotes and his Pecos Indians gave the visitors a warm welcome and urged on them presents of cloth and turquoises. Alvarado then made a trip out onto the plains where he saw great herds of buffalo, after which he returned to Tiguex where he found that Cárdenas had arrived from Zuñi to prepare winter quarters for the army.

In December, having been joined by the main army under Tristan de Arellano, Coronado proceeded to Tiguex where, despite the instructions of the viceroy, the soldiers helped themselves to such houses as they wanted, turning out the natives without ceremony.

The winter proved to be an unusually severe one. As far as the heavy snow and intense cold would permit, it was spent in trying to conquer the pueblos which were in a perpetual state of revolt. There was not enough food for all; the Spaniards labored under the assumption that they should be fed whether the Indians had food or not; and the soldiers complained that the officers took the best of everything for themselves. It was a winter of hunger and bloodshed and disillusionment. How often must the men have renewed the curses which they had hurled at Fray Marcos with his tales of golden cities!

But the imagination of Fray Marcos was exceeded by that of an Indian slave who had been picked up in Cicuyé by Alvarado. He was a prisoner from one of the plains tribes, and was named by the Spaniards El Turco (The Turk) "because he looked like one." This gifted liar told of a new El Dorado far to the east called Quivira, where there was a river two leagues wide in which the fish were as big as horses and where golden galleons were rowed each by forty oarsmen. Even the common people ate from golden bowls and the emperor had his couch under a tree on which were hung golden bells that played a tune in the wind to lull him to sleep.

If only he could recover the beautiful golden bracelets that had been taken from him by the Indians of Cicuyé! He then could prove his story by taking the Spaniards to this province. Coronado sent Alvarado to Cicuyé to demand that the bracelets be returned. The indignant citizens of that town bluntly called The Turk a liar, which he certainly was; whereupon Alvarado clapped Whiskers in chains. This enraged the Indians who had treated Alvarado with such friendliness and trust, and they took up their bows and arrows and drove out the Spaniards.

Coronado followed up the arrest of Whiskers with a demand for a large quantity of clothing for his army, and because it was not immediately forthcoming proceeded to take it off the Indians' backs. One Spanish officer called to an Indian to hold his horse and then, climbing up a ladder to enter an upper apartment, violated the Indian's wife. In the melee that ensued the natives proved no match for their unwanted guests and from the roofs they made the cross sign of the evening and morning star. The Spaniards replied by crossing their spears, and when the Indians threw down their arms they were seized and two hundred of them burned at the stake.

So, on April 23, 1541, it was only by leaving behind bitter enemies that Coronado took up the march for the Golden Quivira. Crossing the Pecos River and entering upon the Great Plains, he soon reached Texas, where great heards of buffalo provided plenty of meat. It was almost impossible to mark a trail. Fifteen hundred Indian servants, a thousand horses, five hundred cows, and five thousand sheep made no more lasting impression on the prairie than does a ship on the surface of the sea. The short grass straightened up as though it had never been trodden upon. Bones and cow dung had to be piled at intervals so the rear guard could follow the army.

The Tejas Indians who had joined the march told Coronado that the cities they sought were north, not east. Coronado then ordered the main body of his army to return to Tiguex, and when the soldiers reluctantly turned to recross the monotonous stretches of prairie they had to send Indians on ahead to shoot arrows each morning at sunrise in the direction of the line of march and then, by shooting others in the line which the arrows determined, they could keep a straight course.

Coronado, with thirty picked horsemen and six foot soldiers, marched to the north. (Had he continued to the east he might have helped bury De Soto in the Mississippi.) Into Kansas and then on to the Arkansas River the little band finally reached a village of the Wichita Indians. Coronado saw no dripping oars on golden boats, no golden bells murmuring in the breeze, no golden bowls; the water pitchers that the women carried as they stooped to enter their grass-thatched huts were of clay. He saw no great cities, no wide rivers bearing proud galleons; except for the grass huts all he had seen was more grass—grass on a prairie as flat and endless as the sea in a calm—and great bellowing herds of buffalo and sky—plenty of sky.

The Turk then confessed that he had been induced to tell his tall tales in order to get the Spaniards out on the plains and lose them. After having El Turco strangled in his sleep, Coronado set up a cross to mark the limit of his march and turned back toward Tiguex.

Another hard winter and an injury due to a fall from his horse made the conqueror resolve to give up his quest. The pleas of his officers were of no avail; Coronado, on remembering a prediction that a brilliant career in a distant land would be ended by a fall, became despondent. His only thoughts were to return home so that he might die near his wife and children. So in April of 1542 the ragged remnants of the once-proud army painfully made their way back to Mexico.

Unlike most of the Spanish conquest of America, which was carried through by private initiative, the Coronado expedition was financed with public funds. Only Columbus, for whom Queen Isabella was supposed to have pawned her jewels, had hitherto received any help from the Crown. Coronado was the last. When the results were known, an order came from the Emperor that no more of the Crown's money should be wasted on such nonsense. The rose-colored glasses of Fray Marcos had proved to be among the most expensive instruments in history.

The immediate significance of Coronado's expedition, however, lay not in what he succeeded in finding but in what he failed to find. It was fifty years before any attempt was made to settle in New Mexico. In territory covered and in new lands discovered—in sheer boldness—it was one of the great expeditions of all time. Arizona and New Mexico and parts of Texas, Oklahoma, and Kansas had been thoroughly explored, the pueblos of the Rio Grande had all been seen, the mouth of the Colorado River had been entered, and the Grand Canyon had first appeared to white men. Even more important, Coronado had pierced the illusion and learned the truth. But the expedition was considered to be a colossal failure. No trace of gold had been found, the shining silver and jewels of Cíbola had been reduced in truth to sandstone and adobe, and the golden bells of Quivira had proved to be only a figment of an accomplished liar's imagination.

But it is often amazing how a name or a myth, once fabricated, can in spite of the record cling tenaciously to receptive minds and even when almost dead be brought to life again. How the name of Gran Quivira lasted through the years, always misunderstood and misapplied, until even today it occupies a place on all maps of New Mexico, will be told in a later chapter.

9

Search for the Strait of Anián

"KNOW THAT on the right hand of the Indies there is an island called California, very close to the side of the Terrestrial Paradise; and it was peopled by black women, without any men among them, for they live in the fashion of Amazons. They were of strong and hardy bodies, of ardent courage and great force. Their island was the strongest in all the world, with its steep cliffs and rocky shores. Their arms were all of gold, and so was the harness of the wild beasts which they tamed to ride; for in the whole island there was no metal but gold."

The author of these words, Garcí Ordóñez de Montalvo, had never seen this land of which he wrote; they appeared in a romance, *Las Sergas de Esplandián*, which was first published in Spain about 1510 and rapidly became a "best seller." After many theories had been advanced as to the origin of the name "California," the Latin *calida fornax* or "hot furnace" being the favorite, it was Edward Everett Hale who in 1862 came across the novel which settled the dispute. It still is not definitely known by whom it was first applied. It may have been Cortés, but he is not known ever to have used the name.

As early as 1524 the conqueror of Mexico had sent his nephew Francisco along the coast from Colima to search for the island of Amazons which had been reported to him, and, although it was not found, the belief in its existence persisted. Ten years later, while Nuño de Guzmán was wreaking havoc in Nueva Galicia and while Cabeza de Vaca was grubbing for roots for his Indian masters off the coast of Texas, Fortún Jiménez, one of Cortés's pilots, discovered the peninsula of Lower California, which he thought to be an island. He too found no Amazons and was killed in the search, but the survivors of the voyage reported pearls. The following year Cortés attempted to establish a colony there, which he named Santa Cruz. A failure almost from the start, it was soon abandoned.

About that same time Cabeza de Vaca arrived at Culiacán and Mendoza began laying his plans for exploration in the north. In order to get ahead of his rival Cortés rushed an expedition to the north under Francisco de Ulloa. Sailing from Acapulco July 8, 1539, almost a year before Alarcón started on his voyage up the Gulf, Ulloa found that the low, sandy shores of Sonora and Santa Cruz united. The Amazons were not given up entirely but at least the mysterious strait was not to be found in that direction!

In the diary of that voyage the new name for the peninsula was used. The Emperor Charles V had banned fiction from New Spain, probably feeling that the dice-rolling adventures in that new land needed nothing to stimulate the imagination; but some copies of Montalvo's tale had undoubtedly breached the blockade, for his *California* was applied between 1534 and 1539, perhaps at first in derision to that abandoned colony which had failed so miserably to produce either gold or Amazons and later to include a land which was to produce more gold, literally and figuratively, than the Spanish author had ever pictured in his wildest dreams.

That last desperate attempt on the part of Cortés to beat Mendoza to the solution of the "northern mystery," which he felt was his sole prerogative, closed his career in Mexico. When he returned to Spain the following year to plead his cause with the Emperor, a deaf ear was turned to him and the greatest conqueror of them all found a place only in American history. His right-hand man, Pedro de Alvarado, then appeared on the scene with a dozen vessels, but instead of quarreling with him Mendoza took him into partnership instead. So when that conquistador took a leave of absence to show the acting governor of Nueva Galicia how to quell an Indian revolt, and was fallen on by a companion's horse during a retreat, Mendoza not only had rid himself of his two bitterest rivals but also had inherited Alvarado's fleet!

Coronado's reception in Mexico City was cold. He must have given, for the time being at least, a satisfactory explanation of his failure, for he was permitted to return to Nueva Galicia as governor. But the viceroy's interest in exploration in the north by land had waned, and he set about making plans for the use of the fleet to which he had fallen heir.

To explore the outer coast of the California peninsula and to continue northward in search of the Strait of Anián, he sent Juan Rodríguez Cabrillo with the two small vessels *San Salvador* and *La Victoria*. Sailing from the port of Navidad in Jalisco on June 27, 1542, this Portuguese mariner progressed slowly across the mouth of the Gulf and up the west coast and on the tenth of August, with his tiny ships, had passed the most northerly point reached by Ulloa.

On the twenty-eighth of September they "discovered a port, closed and very good, which they named San Miguel." While a gale blew without, the ships rode at anchor for several days, safely sheltered in this bay, the beautiful Bay of San Diego.

Continuing northward, Cabrillo passed the islands of San Clemente and Santa Catalina and then, sailing on to the west, passed through the Santa Barbara Channel. On the eighteenth day of October the two ships reached Point Conception. Driven then by a northwest wind to the island of San Miguel, they remained for a week in the shelter of the harbor there. During that time the master of the expedition fell and broke his arm near the shoulder. Nevertheless, when the wind had abated temporarily they sailed on and for a month encountered severe storms.

Sighting land again about opposite Fort Ross, a shift in the wind drove them south, and on November 23 they again landed on the island of San Miguel. The bold and rugged coast, combined with heavy winds, had prevented their landing at any place beyond Point Conception, and both the Bay of Monterey and the Golden Gate remained hidden from their sight.

On January 3, 1543, the exposure and the weakness suffered because of his broken arm were more than the courageous captain could bear and, charging his men with his dying words to go on "exploring as much as possible of that coast," Juan Rodríguez Cabrillo "departed from this life."

The command was taken over by the pilot Bartolomé Ferrelo who, obeying his master's dying order, continued north beyond what is now the northern boundary of California to a point about opposite the Rogue River in Oregon. Encountering storms even more severe than before, "they commended themselves to Our Lady of Guadalupe" and through "great fear and travail" turned back to the south. On April 14, 1543, they reached their home port of Navidad.

The net results of the expedition were the knowledge of more than a thousand miles more of coast, and its northwesterly trend toward Asia, and the pushing of the yet-undiscovered strait to the north and farther away from New Spain. To Americans of today it meant the discovery by Cabrillo and Ferrelo of California.

A few months after Cabrillo had started on his hazardous voyage another part of Alvarado's fleet sailed west across the Pacific and took possession of the Philippine Islands. Some twenty years later the first successful eastward voyage across the Pacific was made, opening up the trade route from Manila across that wide ocean to a point off Cape Mendocino in California and down the coast to Acapulco. The Philippines became the rendezvous of Chinese junks and other oriental craft bringing the products of their countries. Chinese goods thus found their way in quantities to Spain, and to this day Madrid is an excellent place to buy silken "Spanish shawls" of oriental make.

To protect the ships that plied that route, and to have a place for repairs after the long ocean voyage, a port along the California coast was considered necessary. This should also serve as a fortified haven because of the danger of interception by ships of other countries, for the English sea rovers especially were a constant menace.

In 1579 Francis Drake, after rounding Cape Horn, anchored the *Golden Hind* off the coast of California in what became known as Drake's Bay and named the region New Albion. Friendly Indians came to the shore in great numbers. Drake established his crew on land, putting up tents for the men, and when a procession of natives arrived bearing gifts in woven baskets Drake had a service solemnized according to the Church of England. That was probably the first Christian service held in Alta California.

Drake's voyage was strictly a business enterprise and the Spanish galleons his objective. Plunder of Spanish ports had attended his voyage northward. In addition he was believed by the Spaniards to have discovered the Strait of Anián and to have sailed homeward through it. When a few years later a Spanish galleon had been waylaid and plundered by another English pirate, Thomas Cavendish, the necessity for further exploration and the establishment of a fortified port became more than ever apparent. One Spanish galleon, on the return voyage in 1595, made extensive explorations of the California coast but was wrecked in the process, so it was decided that any future exploration should be made from the south, without risking valuable cargoes.

By now Russia had become a threat in the north and even Dutch and French freebooters on the Atlantic, it was feared, might discover the Strait of Anián; so toward the end of the sixteenth century Philip II ordered the Count of Monterey, then viceroy of New Spain, to proceed immediately to make new settlements in California and to continue the search for the ever-elusive strait.

At that time Sebastián Vizcaíno, a prosperous merchant in the Manila trade, was granted permission to establish pearl fisheries in the Californias provided he colonize that coast with a view to its use as a defensive outpost. For the purpose of establishing missions four Franciscans accompanied his expedition. They settled in that part of Lower California where Cortés had attempted to establish a colony and named it "La Paz," by which name the site has been known ever since. According to the records, the Indians liked the friars but objected to the soldiers, who paid too little attention to the native customs and too much to the native women! Storms interfered with the pearl-fishing operations and the country was unsuited to the needs of the new occupants, so the colony was abandoned after two months.

Undaunted however, Vizcaíno made plans for another expedition. Fresh interference in the Pacific, this time by the Dutch, delayed preparations and it was not until 1602 that the voyage got under way. Detailed instructions called for a thorough exploration of the coast from Cape San Lucas, at the extreme southern tip of the peninsula of Lower California, to Cape Mendocino, the westernmost tip of the Upper California bulge. An expert map maker was included in the carefully picked personnel and on May 5, Vizcaíno's expedition, with three ships, set sail from Acapulco.

Storms impeded their progress and several times the ships lost sight of each other, but on November 12, the day of Saint James (San Diego), they arrived "at a port which must be the best to be found in all the South Sea." It was San Miguel of Cabrillo. Mass was celebrated and the port was renamed in honor of the saint—which also happened to be the name of the fleet's flagship—the name which the port bears to this day.

Passing through the Santa Barbara Channel, the name of which they also bestowed, they rounded Point Conception and sailed along the coast beneath the peaks of the Santa Lucia Range, both of which they so named, and entered a large bay "sheltered from all winds, with many pines for masts and yards, and live oaks and white oaks, and water in great quantity, all near the shore." On the next day, December 17, a hut and an arbor were built on shore in which to say Mass and the bay was named in honor of the viceroy.

The expedition continued northward, reaching Cape Mendocino a little less than a month later; but then, suffering the same experience with storms as had Ferrelo sixty years earlier, and with "the sick crying aloud," they limped into Acapulco on March 21 "in the greatest affliction and travail ever experienced by Spaniards."

The Count of Monterey was delighted with the discovery of the bay bearing his name and made immediate plans to occupy the port, with Vizcaíno leading the enterprise. But before the plans could be carried out a new viceroy succeeded Monterey and, instead of establishing a port on the coast of California, Vizcaíno was sent out into the mid-Pacific to found a port on one or the other of two islands which existed only in the imagination of a sailor-friar who had made a voyage across the Pacific forty years earlier. Suggestively enough, the mythical islands were called Rica de Oro and Rica de Plata— Rich in Gold and Rich in Silver.

As the inflamed imagination of Fray Marcos had been responsible for the thorough but expensive expedition of Coronado, thus delaying the occupation of New Mexico, so now did the credulity of another friar a generation later change the course of the history of California.

Although both Cabrillo and Vizcaíno had passed the Golden Gate without finding it, the former had discovered Upper California and the latter had found the Bay of Monterey. But the immediate and negative results of both expeditions were even more decisive than those of Coronado's. For almost a century and three quarters the native sons and daughters of California were permitted to continue gathering and grinding acorns undisturbed.

10

The Moving Frontier

AS THE sixteenth century progressed it gradually became apparent to those men seeking wealth in New Spain that immediate riches were not to be had for the finding. The Amazons were fairly well relegated to their proper place in mythology and, although hopes of finding gold by plunder were not given up entirely—the conquistadors continuing at least in their spare moments to engage in dreams—it began to be realized by colonists whose ambitions did not necessarily preclude industry that surer results could be obtained by a little honest toil, provided most of the toiling was done by Indians.

The real problem of conquering northern Mexico came to be appreciated as the much greater breadth of that part of the country became known and what has been called the "aggressive aggressive" gave way to an "aggressive defensive." Except for occasional conquests to avert perils which threatened the security of the Spanish advance, the adventurers settled down. With Indian labor they began to gain slower but surer profits from mining and cattle raising.

It was while Coronado was chasing rainbows on the plains of Kansas that there occurred the most widespread struggle for liberty ever made by the Indians in Mexico. It began in the mountains of Zacatecas, where those independent tribes who had managed to escape being crushed under the heel of Nuño de Guzmán persuaded their less fortunate brethren to join them in rebellion. The *encomienda* Indians, resenting that system whereby they performed all of the manual labor in return for the acceptance by their masters of the responsibility for the Indian's soul in the hereafter, burned the churches, killed the *encomenderos*, and fled to the hills. Establishing themselves on these rocky heights called *peñoles*, from which they conducted raids on the Spanish settlements, the Indians came very near to bringing about the extinction of the Spaniards in New Galicia, weakened as they were by the exodus for the current El Dorado in the north. It was in this revolt that the great Alvarado suffered his first defeat by the Indians and lost his life in the bargain. It was finally necessary for Mendoza to take to the field himself, and after a long and bloody campaign an end was put to the uprising. Thousands of Indians had been killed, and those who were captured were made slaves and distributed among the soldiers as booty. Many others escaped and took refuge in the hills of Zacatecas; but the spirit of rebellion had been broken.

This revolt (known as the Mixton War from the *peñol* where the final siege occurred) and its results, curiously enough, brought about the first great mining rush in North America. Realizing the necessity of conquering Zacatecas, peacefully if possible, Mendoza sent a party of friars into the mountains to preach the gospel. The result was the discovery by the soldiers and prospectors who accompanied the party of veins of silver which far outvalued the plunder of Tenochtitlán. The pioneers all made fortunes, and when the news had spread the rush was on. This was in 1548, almost exactly three hundred years before another rush—for a more precious metal—occurred in a land which the Spaniards first settled but the riches of which they missed—a gold rush they would have loved.

From that date silver flowed in a steady stream to Spain and much of the remainder was poured into churches in Mexico. From that date also the subjugation of all the north central part of the country followed quickly. Trails were opened to the capital to transport the silver and new trails were made in the hopes of finding more silver. An even richer lode was discovered in Guanajuato and very shortly afterward another at San Luís Potosí. El Dorado had been found nearer home than the plains of Kansas.

In the meantime the Franciscans and Jesuits were at work in the northwestern territories of Durango, Sinaloa, Sonora, and Chihuahua, but slave-raiding expeditions to secure workers for the mines made their progress difficult. In 1554 Francisco de Ibarra, the sixteen-year-old nephew of Diego de Ibarra, one of the founders of the Zacatecas mines, was financed by his uncle to undertake the conquest of the Northwest. For twenty years the younger Ibarra marched across that country searching for silver mines and mythical kingdoms. About 1561 he was made governor of the immense area, which he named Nueva Vizcaya for his native province in Spain. His province was supposed to be confined to the territory east of the main sierra, but Ibarra extended his authority over the coast provinces as well, on the grounds that they were mostly unoccupied. It is barely possible that in his explorations he entered what is now New Mexico; at least on his return he boasted that he had discovered a "new Mexico" as well as a new Vizcaya. The name soon was applied to a country that Don Francisco may never have seen.

In Durango and Chihuahua there were no mines as rich as those in Zacatecas and agriculture was not possible without irrigation, but the grassy uplands proved to be ideal for cattle and sheep and large ranches were established. The herds originally taken north by Coronado formed the basis of what was one day to become one of the greatest cattle-grazing centers in the world. But the horses, taken as allies in the exploration and conquest of the north, were left to roam wild and, multiplying rapidly, were to be a powerful influence in retarding the Spanish advance.

Toward the end of the sixteenth century settlements and missions had been established as far up as Santa Bárbara on the Conchos River, which flows through the southern part of the present state of Chihuahua into the Rio Grande, and a new highway was soon to be opened up from there, leading over the sand hills straight to the north.

In 1573 an ordinance was passed forbidding military expeditions among the Indians; any future entries were required to go in missionary guise. Three Franciscan friars of the Coronado expedition had stayed behind to do missionary work among the Indians. One of them, Fray Juan de Padilla, returned with native guides to Quivira in Kansas and, although winning the affection of the Indians there, he was murdered on attempting to extend his work among neighboring enemy tribes. The two who stayed in New Mexico eventually suffered the same fate. Thus we have in the names of Juan de Padilla, Luís de Escalona, and Juan de la Cruz the first Christian martyrs in the Southwest, a fate which Fray Marcos had avoided and later may have wished he had accepted.

In the advance into Chihuahua new stories were heard of the pueblos to the north. With the success of the mines in northern Mexico and the possibility of a fertile field for friars, the trials and tribulations of Coronado and even the fate of the pioneer Franciscans were forgotten after forty years and interest in the north was again aroused. Among those whose imagination had been stirred was Fray Agustín Rodríguez, stationed at Santa Bárbara on the new frontier. On June 5, 1581, accompanied by two other friars, Fray Francisco López and Fray Juan de Santa María, nine soldiers, and a dozen or so Indian servants, the little band followed the Conchos River to its junction with the Rio Grande. After marching up this river for twenty days they came to the country of the Tiguas, visited by Coronado forty years before.

From there Fray Juan set out alone to return to Mexico with reports of the progress of the expedition; but on reaching the foot of the Sandía Mountains he was killed by Indians. The other two friars, with their party, continued their explorations, going north to Taos, east onto the buffalo plains, and west as far as Zuñi.

The soldiers then returned to Santa Bárbara, and the two Franciscans, with a few servants, settled in Puaray on the Rio Grande (near the present city of Bernalillo), where they established a mission. Within a few months one of the servants appeared in Mexico with the news that Fray Francisco López had been killed at a moment when he was in prayer.

In the hope that Fray Agustín might still be alive, a rescue expedition was hastened to the north under the leadership of a wealthy mineowner, Antonio de Espejo, accompanied by a Franciscan friar, Bernardino Beltrán. But it was too late; by the time they arrived at their destination Fray Agustín also had been killed.

After exploring a large part of the country Espejo returned to Santa Bárbara with reports of great mineral wealth, good grazing country, and "land suitable for fields and gardens." His report noticeably did not include Amazons, silver cities, or golden bells. The time had come for settlement.

In March of 1583 a royal order was issued calling for a contract with some suitable person to undertake the settlement of New Mexico, without cost to the royal treasury. Several aspirants presented their names, with lists of their proposals and their demands, some of which included everything from titles for themselves and their descendants to the right to build ships on either ocean and to use them for trade without paying duty. Among the claimants to recognition, naturally enough, was Antonio de Espejo, who had just returned from that country. Another claimant, however, was favored by the viceroy and was given a contract, but before he could begin operations he was arrested on a charge of poisoning his wife. Consideration of the claims had to begin all over again.

When the chief constable of the city of Puebla was called upon to investigate the various claims, he made a study of what had already been done in the field and, coming to the conclusion that no one so far had found anything worth keeping, he made the remarkable recommendation that what was needed was an expedition not of colonization and conquest but of exploration! In view not only of his own patriotic zeal, that worthy's report concluded, but also of that of his father he offered to command the exploring party in person. And should the preliminary survey prove satisfactory he himself, accepting all titles and emoluments in such cases provided, would take charge of colonizing New Mexico.

While all of these claims were being presented, investigated, and coming to naught—one of them even demanded the rights to distribute as *encomienda* all the natives of the conquered towns and provinces for ten generations (the rights would just about have expired by now)—there was one man who felt that time was a-wasting; so he decided to just go ahead and settle New Mexico himself.

Gaspar Castaño de Sosa had been alcalde at San Luís Potosí for a while and in 1590 was acting lieutenant-governor of the province of Nuevo León to the northeast of Zacatecas. In the little frontier mining settlement where he lived he spent most of his time digging for silver in the barren mountains, without finding his efforts very lucrative. Being ambitious, Castaño conceived the idea of taking advantage of the political standstill to take a short cut to glory, his thought being simply to move his whole settlement to the north country where it would become a great colony and he would be the governor. In order to persuade people to go with him he hinted that he had some rich silver ore from the north; and to prove it he had some rocks smelted to show his constituents, surreptitiously throwing a couple of large silver mugs into the brew.

The law permitted a governor to settle lands already discovered, provided he complied with all requirements, which among other things gave directions as to how to lay out towns, how wide the streets should be, and where the church should be built. He must, however, first notify the viceroy of his intention and then send complete reports of his movements. In this Don Gaspar was most meticulous, including even such details as the exact day and hour Juan Perez's dog died as the result of the kick of an ox but skipping such generalities as the course or the distance of a day's journey.

With one hundred and seventy men, women, and children and a wagon train laden with supplies, Castaño started out on the twenty-seventh of July from the villa de Almaden (his report neglected to state where that is). After crossing the Rio Grande the caravan wandered into the state of Texas and eventually reached a deep gorge, evidently that of the Pecos River. Enduring untold hardships on the trek northward, in which their supplies became exhausted, it was the end of December when the party reached the pueblo of Pecos in northern New Mexico.

Greeted at first with hostility, Castaño took a bold stand in one of the plazas of the town and made overtures of peace. It proved necessary, however, to employ two brass cannons to be convincing, and when the Indians had laid down their bows and arrows Sosa and his party camped for the night near by, determined to complete their work of civilizing the Indians the next day.

On returning to the pueblo in the morning the Spaniards found it completely deserted. The Indians had fled to the mountains during the night. The would-be settlers remained several days, admiring the massive adobe structures rising to a height of three or four stories. They were built in a number of units enclosing five plazas in which there were sixteen kivas and, best of all in the eyes of the hungry Spaniards, immense stores of maize.

Throughout the winter the party marched through the snow across northern New Mexico and up and down the Rio Grande, visiting pueblos and setting up a cross in each one they visited. They returned to Pecos just as their stores of food were again almost exhausted. This time they found the Indians back in their homes and entirely submissive and Castaño, feeling they had seen the light and were now ready to be good Christians, conferred the blessings of God upon them.

Eager for personal power as he may have been, and deceptive in trying to gain it, one cannot help admiring this bold man who heedlessly entered strange towns where through sheer weight of numbers his whole party might have been annihilated and who was solemnly convinced that he had accomplished in a few weeks what after more than three hundred and fifty years has not yet been accomplished. When his followers, tired of the privations they had suffered and little interested in his Christian preaching, plotted to kill their leader, the kindhearted Castaño forgave them and by generously inviting all who wished to return to Mexico to do so (but he would go on alone, even to death) regained their loyalty.

While encamped on the Rio Grande and once more almost facing starvation, Castaño was delighted to hear of the arrival of a new party of Spaniards. Expecting to find reinforcements and official approval by the viceroy of his conquest, Don Gaspar rode forward to meet the leader. At this point his elaborate report of the expedition comes abruptly to an end. Informed that he was being arrested for entering the country without license, the bold and peaceful conqueror was put in chains. Evidently his followers meekly returned with him to Mexico.

Tried and convicted, Castaño was exiled to China. Later, on reconsideration of his case, the decision was reversed and it was ruled that not only was he within his rights according to the law but that in so courageously and peacefully opening up for settlement the province of New Mexico he had done a great service for his country and his king. Messengers were sent to bring him back as governor of the new province.

But in the meantime he had been killed trying to help quell a mutiny on a Chinese junk.

There was nothing unofficial about the next major step in the settlement of New Mexico. But first there was a minor *entrada* which can be skipped over quickly. In 1594 or in the following year, there being no record of the exact date, one Francisco Leiva Bonilla, a Portuguese, was sent out from Nueva Vizcaya with a companion, Juan de Humaña, and a few native guides on a raid against rebellious Indians. The leader, unable to resist the temptation of northern wealth, led his men into New Mexico and then set out over the buffalo plains to find the real Quivira. In a quarrel he was killed by

Humaña, who assumed command only to be killed by the Indians later. The only survivor to return was a Mexican Indian deserter who tells the tale.

At last, in September of 1595, a choice was made of a leader for the expedition to found a permanent colony in New Mexico. The honor fell to Juan de Oñate, the scion of a distinguished family and son of Cristóbal de Oñate, another of the discoverers of the mines of Zacatecas and one of the wealthiest men in New Spain. The younger Oñate had made his social position the more secure by his marriage to Doña Isabel Tolosa Cortés Montezuma, daughter of Juan de Tolosa (the leader of the expedition which had subdued the Indians of Zacatecas and discovered silver there), granddaughter of Hernando Cortés, and great-granddaughter of Montezuma II.

With these impressive connections Don Juan had no trouble in securing the support of the most influential men in New Spain, and as little in recruiting an army. When, with an artillery salute, his enlistment banner was unfurled in the grand plaza of Mexico City the scenes of 1540 were repeated and the ranks were soon filled. It was then that Oñate's troubles began. What with a change of viceroys, jealousies of rivals who seemed to have more influence with Monterey than they had had with Velasco, annoying inspections, and consequent threats of desertion, it was not until January 26, 1598, more than two years after the award of the contract, that Oñate and his following actually started north from Santa Bárbara.

Four days later they crossed the Conchos and camped on the far side of the stream, where they remained a week making final preparations for the difficult march over the new route directly north across the desert of northern Chihuahua. There they got rid of the unwelcome *visitador*, who is said to have departed without bidding the colonists good-by, and were joined by ten Franciscan friars under the leadership of Padre Alonso Martínez, who were to look after the spiritual needs of the party and found permanent missions in New Mexico.

The expedition had been almost feudal in its preparations. Colonists were promised the rank of hidalgo, men of means were made captains, all had sworn homage to their leader, and each company had its standard. The equipment of the *caballeros* was in character. The wardrobe and impedimenta of Captain Luís de Velasco, for example, included:

1 *suit of blue Italian velvet trimmed with gold braid*
1 *suit of rose satin*
1 *suit of straw-colored satin*
1 *suit of purple Castilian cloth*
1 *suit of chestnut-colored cloth*
1 *suit of Chinese flowered silk*
1 *doublet of blue Italian velvet*
1 *doublet of royal lion skin trimmed with gold*
2 *doublets of Castilian dressed kid*
40 *pairs of boots, shoes, and gaiters*
1 *black hat trimmed with silver cord and black, purple, and white feathers*
1 *gray hat trimmed with gold cord and yellow and purple feathers*
1 *purple taffeta hat trimmed with gold and silver braid and blue, purple, and yellow feathers*
4 *saddles of blue flowered Spanish cloth bound with Córdovan leather*
3 *suits of armor*
3 *suits of horse armor*
1 *silver-handled lance with gold and purple tassels*
1 *sword and gilded dagger with belts stitched in purple and yellow silk*
1 *broadsword*
   and
2 *shields*

In addition, he took velvet and linen breeches, linen shirts, silk stockings and garters, linen handkerchiefs, and a raincoat. For his comfort at night he was equipped with a bedstead and two mattresses with coverlet, sheets, pillows and pillow cases, and a canvas mattress-bag bound with leather. Thirty horses and mules carried him, his wardrobe, and his equipment, several servants attended his wants, and a silken banner led the way.

On the seventh of February the caravan of colonists left the Conchos. Ahead of them stretched miles of desert hemmed in by jagged mountains in the distance to the right and to the left. One hundred and thirty soldier-settlers, most of them taking their families, made up the nucleus of the expedition. Eighty-three wagons and carts transported the women and children and carried the supplies, a large retinue of Negro and Indian servants busied themselves in attendance, while seven thousand head of stock—horses, cattle, sheep, and goats—were driven beside the train. For the benefit of those who are inclined to abuse the word by applying it to their own peregrinations, *this* was a trek.

In the second week of April, a little more than two months after leaving the Conchos, they reached the Médanos, some forty miles south of El Paso, where clean, white sand dunes roll and blow over the country for miles. The march had been hard; the provisions had given out and the party was reduced to edible weeds and roots. It was even worse when the water supply had vanished. A scouting party went on ahead to find the river which was their goal, the horses almost frantic with thirst and the men seeing lakes which on arrival proved to be only more expanse of desert shimmering in the haze. When finally they reached the long-sought waters of the Rio del Norte, the horses plunged in and almost burst their bellies, two of them, blinded by thirst, going so far that they were caught in the swift current and drowned; and the men, drinking as though the river could not hold enough to satisfy their thirst, finally flung themselves upon the sand, deformed and swollen, looking, according to the chronicler of the expedition, more like toads than men.

When Oñate, with the main body, had overtaken them it was a joyful meeting. On the thirtieth of April the leader took formal possession "of all the Kingdoms and provinces of New Mexico, on the Rio del Norte, in the name of Our Lord King Philip." A chapel was built under a grove of trees, Solemn High Mass was read, and the horsemen, in their most gala attire, lined up at attention while artillery salutes were fired. The day ended with the presentation of a comedy written for the occasion by one of the officers, depicting the old favorite subject of victory, through the aid of Santiago, of the Christians over the Moors.

On the fourth day of May the long train crossed the Rio Grande.

PART THREE: *NUEVO MÉXICO*

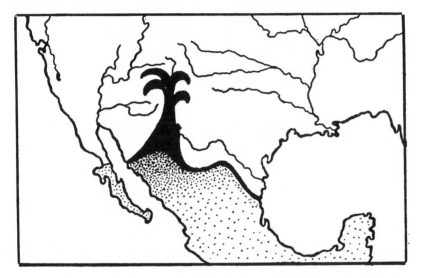

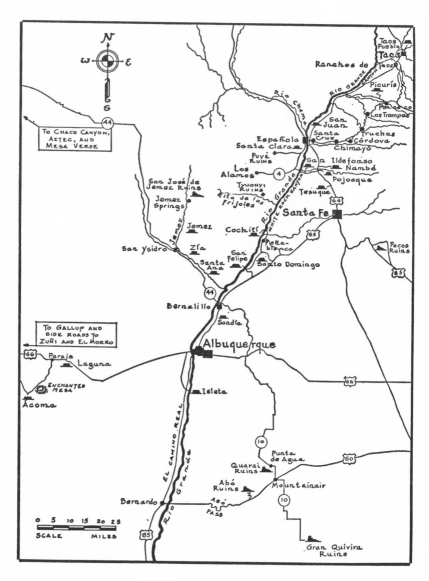

UPPER RIO GRANDE

PART THREE

11

The Royal City of the Holy Faith of Saint Francis of Assisi

IN THE beautiful Italian land of Umbria, spreading up the slopes of a hill which rises some six or eight hundred feet above the surrounding broad valley, stands the ancient city of Assisi. Built on the site of an early Roman town, it overlooks a mountain stream which flows into the Tiber, and facing its narrow streets are buildings which date back nearly two thousand years. But it is dominated now by a great monastery church which climbs the hillside at the west edge of the city. Occupying two levels, it is the earliest Gothic church in Italy.

Here in the year 1182 was born Giovanni, son of Pietro Bernardone, a wealthy cloth merchant of the city, and of Pica, his wife, daughter of a noble family of Provence. Not untypical of his station in life, the boy's youth was spent in pleasure and gaiety. Fine clothes and a love of show absorbed his thoughts and the desire for personal fame guided his steps.

Although baptized John, he came to be known as Francis for one of three possible reasons given by his various biographers: his father's fondness for France where business often led him, as a compliment to his French mother, or because of the boy's facility with the French tongue. In any event the youth had traveled widely, making one long visit to France, the language of which land became dear to him because of its poetic associations—it was the language of the troubadours. So Francesco he became, and by that name he has been known ever since.

Rich, popular, and carefree, Francesco was no mere man of fash-ion. He took up the sword in the wars between Perugia and Assisi when his native town joined the struggle for freedom from German rule. After being captured and imprisoned in Perugia he returned to Assisi, only to be struck down by a severe illness. On recovering he started out again to fight, and again was struck down with fever.

Convalescence gave him much time for thought, and there was much food for it in those troublous times. Pondering over his wasted youth, Francis decided to cast aside his worldly possessions and to pattern his life after that of Christ. He began by helping the poor and the sick and by rebuilding with his own hands the churches of Assisi which had fallen into disrepair. Close by one of them he took up his abode and, when he was not out visiting the unfortunate or preaching to the growing crowds, he spent his time there in prayer, dressed always in the poorest of garments. Although disinherited by his father and at first ridiculed by his pleasure-loving friends, he began to attract a following which soon grew to great numbers willing to adopt his rule of poverty, chastity, and obedience. His influence and that of his followers spread throughout Italy and not long afterward throughout the world, even to the Far East, long before the time of Columbus.

The Friars Minor, or Lesser Brothers as they called themselves, were soon joined in their vows and their work by Clare, the beautiful daughter of a wealthy family of Assisi, and shortly thereafter by her younger sister Agnes. Thus was founded the Second Order of St. Francis—the Sisters of Clare or Poor Clares. A Third Order of Franciscans was established for the benefit of the many people who wanted to follow a plan of religious life but without restrictions which would prohibit their working for pay, owning property, and raising families. This order grew to include people from all walks of life and numbered in its ranks kings and queens, scientists and artists, discoverers and explorers.

Francis died in 1226 and less than two years later he was canonized, the one saint whom all succeeding generations have agreed deserved the distinction. His tomb is in that double monastery church, the foundations of which are said to have been laid the day after his death. In this church, which now crowns the end of the long hill on which Assisi lies, are some of the finest frescoes in all Italy, illustrating the life of the saint.

Among the followers of Saint Francis to be canonized are to be found the well-known names of Clara of Assisi, Antonio of Padua, Diego (James) of Alcalá, Francisco of Solano, Juan of Capistrano, Fernando, Rey of Castile, and Luís, Rey (King Louis IX) of France.

After the discovery of America by a member of the Third Order of St. Francis the work of the Franciscans was taken to the Western Hemisphere. Friars accompanied Columbus on his second voyage and celebrated Mass on the island of Haiti in 1493, and not long after that Franciscan missions were established throughout the West Indies. The first group of Franciscans came to Mexico in 1524 and within seventy-five years there were more than four hundred missions in that country, almost half of which had been built by the followers of Saint Francis.

When the work of exploration and settlement moved north the Franciscans were always in the lead, and the pioneering in what is now the southwestern United States was almost exclusively theirs. One cannot travel anywhere in the Southwest without being conscious of the influence of that self-denying saint born in the ancient Umbrian town. Both the oldest city in the Southwest and the second-largest city and most glamorous port in America were named in his honor. Not only cities and villages but, throughout that part of the country, counties and townships, city streets and country highways, churches and schools, hospitals and homes, parks and forests, rivers and bays, mountains and valleys bear his name.

The first permanent settlement in the north to be named for him lies on the banks of a small stream at the base of the southern end of the Sangre de Cristo Mountains. A long way from Assisi, it was also a long way from Mexico and a heartbreaking journey for those earliest settlers. But we are getting ahead of our story; so let us return to the Rio Grande, which Juan de Oñate and his followers have just crossed to establish homes in the still somewhat mysterious, yet beckoning New Mexico.

Once across the Rio Grande, Oñate with sixty men marched on ahead "to pacify the land." The main caravan followed slowly, suffering hunger and thirst as ox carts became stalled in the sand and food supplies ran low. When the advance party reached the first group of pueblos they were welcomed by the natives and given supplies of maize, which they sent back to the slowly starving train far in the rear. From this rescue Socorro got its name. When the main body had reached that place and resumed its march to the north, two friars remained behind to serve the Indians, and built a small church there. This structure burned shortly afterward, but in 1629, under the direction of Fray García de San Francisco Zuñiga, it was replaced by a new church which stands today, much renovated, in the once-booming mining town of Socorro.

Continuing up the Rio Grande the expedition passed through several villages, pausing at Kihwa (Santo Domingo) to receive the allegiance of the chieftains of thirty-four pueblos gathered there in a great council. Finally, near a spot where the Rio Chama flows into the Rio Grande, the party came to a halt. The inhabitants of the Pueblo of Ohke were persuaded to give up their village to the Spaniards and move to the east bank of the Rio Grande. The new pueblo of the Indians Oñate named San Juan de los Caballeros; it is said by some as a reward for the gracious generosity of the Indians (which they could hardly have avoided), but according to Villagrá, who wrote an epic poem describing the conquest and settlement, it was in honor of the Spanish knights who had made the great march. The pueblo bears that name to this day. The Spaniards called their settlement San Gabriel. It is now the village of Chamita.

With the help of the Indians irrigation ditches were dug to ensure a supply of water. After water came God; a small chapel was soon built. Following its dedication the sham battle between the Moors and the Christians was re-enacted, to the great glee of the Indian guests. The Indians expressed joy too at being told they were to receive the friars as their spiritual masters, such expression being partly induced perhaps by the cheering assurance by the soldiers that if they refused to obey the friars implicitly they would be burned alive as well as burned later in hell.

This was in the late summer of 1598. Thus was founded the second permanent white settlement in the country (after St. Augustine, Florida, in 1565). The pueblos were apportioned into working districts, friars were assigned to their posts, and the work of building missions began.

Oñate was a restless caballero, always in a rush. Having invested a substantial sum in his expedition and having established his followers in a permanent settlement near the banks of the Rio Grande, he was ready to do something about recouping his fortune. Water and souls had been provided for; now it was time for gold. He started out again, dispatching his scouts in various directions. Hardly stopping to rest between trips, he covered all of the near-by territory and then plunged across the plains to try to find the real Quivira. As on his earlier journeys and as was true of Coronado, he found only adobe or thatched villages—and disappointment.

Six years after the founding of San Gabriel Oñate set out for the South Sea, reaching the Gulf of California in January of 1605. Vizcaíno's voyage had focused attention on that part of the country and this was a final, desperate move to regain lost fortunes. But no gold and no pearls were found—just more tall tales—and starvation again almost overtook the explorers, only horse meat saving their lives.

On the return the party camped one night at a spot some thirty-five miles east of Zuñi where a great gray sandstone rock rises perpendicularly for two hundred feet out of the cedar-dotted valley and where shelter, wood, and a water hole—the first water in a hard day's march—provided a natural camping site. It has continued to be that almost to this day. But it is much more than that. The rock is doubtless the largest and most valuable single historical document in the country.

In 1849, while on a military reconnaissance, Lieutenant James Henry Simpson, accompanied by an artist, R. H. Kern, camped at that spot and copied inscriptions which had been carved on the rock by hundreds of Spanish explorers. Called by the Spaniards El Morro and known now to Americans as Inscription Rock, the rock's carvings, beginning with prehistoric petroglyphs, continue for several hundred feet around the base. Oñate's is the oldest dated record and, translated, reads: "Passed by here the Governor Don Juan de Oñate, from the discovery of the Sea of the South, the 16th of April, of 1605." (See Plate 9.) Not far from the inscription of Lieutenant Simpson a huge pile of fallen rocks lies below a cliff so creamy white and clean that one is involuntarily stopped—it appears to have happened yesterday. It could happen again. A seventeenth-century date carved on the creamy surface is reassuring.

The little colony of San Gabriel had not prospered during the governor's various absences. Drought and discouragement had resulted in wholesale desertions. Among those to withdraw to Santa Bárbara in Mexico was Captain Luís de Velasco, though it is not recorded whether he took with him all his doublets, tassels, and plumes. Oñate sent urgent requests to Mexico for reinforcements but they arrived in such dribbles that the commander too became discouraged and asked to be relieved of his post unless more help was forthcoming. Whether it was desperation or a bluff, his resignation was accepted and he was recalled to Mexico City where, charged with a long list of crimes, he was forced to stand trial. His sentence included a heavy fine and perpetual banishment from New Mexico, where he had founded the first settlement, organized the first mission system, and explored far more thoroughly than Coronado.

To succeed Oñate the viceroy appointed Don Pedro de Peralta governor, with instructions to found a new capital more centrally located among the pueblos. Early in 1609 Peralta arrived in San Gabriel and some time during the following winter a new site was chosen some thirty miles to the south and east. Most of the colonists from San Gabriel moved thither and the new capital was called La Villa Real de la Santa Fé de San Francisco de Asís. Saint Francis has continued to be the city's patron saint but the large mouthful of name has been cut to Santa Fe.

Its situation is a beautiful one. Away from the Rio Grande, which in that vicinity cuts its way through a canyon and is relatively inaccessible, the city lies on a sunny but breezy plain seven thousand feet above the sea. Through the middle of the city flows the Rito de Santa Fe, which issues from the foothills of the often-snow-covered Sangre de Cristo Mountains to the east.

Detailed plans for the city were sent from Spain and work was begun accordingly. There was to be a large plaza at the center on one side of which was to be built a *palacio*, to serve also as a fortress; the church was to be located on an adjacent side; and the surrounding walls were to be built far enough away from the center of the city so that "no matter how much it might expand there would still be room."

The plaza was laid out much larger than it is now (occupying the site of the post office and the buildings which line the east side of the present plaza, the first church being built on the east side of the original plaza, on the site of the present Cathedral of Saint Francis) and work was soon begun on a palace for the governor facing the plaza on the north. Built of adobe, this single-storied structure, the most important part of the royal presidio, was four hundred feet long on the side facing the plaza and a walled area extended to the north for a much greater distance. Within the enclosure thus formed were the palace proper, including the governor's offices and his residence, other buildings for governmental use, quarters for soldiers, woodsheds, and outhouses. At either end of the palace, on the side facing the plaza, was a low tower, the one to the west serving as an arsenal and the one to the east as a chapel for the garrison. Adjoining the west tower were the dungeons. Extending the length of the south front was a *portal*, or covered walk, appearing much as it does today.

This venerable building has withstood much from sieges, decay, attempted destruction, and ill-considered renovation. At some time during the latter part of the eighteenth century it was shortened and the towers were removed. At a still later date a wood-molded cornice was applied the length of the façade, supported by spindly, square-paneled columns, and a discordant balustrade crowned the flat roof. About the turn of this century, the building having fallen into disrepair, the proposal was made to tear it down and replace it with a many-storied office building. Fortunately the palace was restored instead as nearly as possible to its original appearance. There was neither sufficient data nor room to rebuild the towers where they had been, but the balustrade was torn off and the projecting *vigas* (beams) were replaced so that today the façade has much the character of the original structure. Since 1909, when this restoration was accomplished, the building has been used as the Museum of New Mexico, serving also as headquarters for the School of American Research and for the New Mexico Historical Society.

The Palace of the Governor, in its restored state, is an excellent exhibit of what has quite properly been called the Spanish-Pueblo style, where Spanish ideas and methods have been applied to an indigenous architecture of local materials put in place by Indian labor. It is peculiar in that it is the only architectural style in the country where native influence continued to be strongly felt.

As has been pointed out in an earlier chapter, this was the only part of the country where the Indians had developed a culture to a degree that included the building of permanent homes, which they continued to build up to the time of the arrival of the Spaniards and which they still do. Naturally the materials they employed were those that were readily available and the type of construction was that which was imposed by the limitations of those materials. Where stone was available it was used for walls; in localities where stone was not readily available walls were constructed of adobe, which was puddled into place in layers. The molding of adobe into square blocks was an art not known until the advent of the Spaniards.

Room sizes were dictated by the spans permitted by the logs, or vigas, placed at regularly spaced intervals to form roofs. The vigas were usually six or eight inches in diameter and their limitations resulted in narrow, rectangular rooms, such a room becoming the unit of the structure, often multiplied many times. Over the vigas were placed smaller poles at right angles on which in turn branches, rushes, or grasses were laid closely. On this a thick layer of mud was spread to form the finished roof, or floor above where the building was of more than one story.

The walls were finished with a smooth coating of adobe mud inside and out which on the outside, because of weathering, required periodic renewal. This, combined with a gentle slope of the wall inward, served to produce the soft contours so characteristic of the style.

With the coming of the Spaniards some changes were made, but, the materials and their limitations remaining the same, these changes consisted principally of certain improvements in practice due to new requirements, improved tools, and a broader background of construction experience. Imposed on the logical Indian style and with Indian labor, the blend was a harmonious one. The effect on churches will be discussed later, but the changes were felt throughout all subsequent work. The first major change was the introduction of adobes in the form of precast bricks mixed with straw and dried in the sun. This permitted thicker and consequently higher walls which in turn made it possible to increase the span of roofs once heavier timbers were employed. That brings up the second major improvement: the introduction of iron tools.

The Indians had to cut and trim their vigas with stone axes. The great labor involved limited them to logs relatively small in diameter, and resulted in the re-use wherever possible of old timbers. Where timbers so used did not fit, they were permitted to project beyond the exterior wall, a characteristic feature retained by the Spaniards. The iron ax and the adz made practicable the use of larger timbers for longer spans, and instead of being confined to the round form they could be made rectangular in section. Square columns, carved corbels to help support the vigas, and similarly carved postcaps to support lintels came to be other characteristic features of the style.

Last but not least, wooden doors and windows and frames for both came to be used. (They form the most conspicuous innovation in the present-day pueblos. During a recent fire in Zuñi the Indians busied themselves taking doors off their hinges and lifting windows out of their frames—their most valuable assets.) Wooden casings, however, are still generally omitted.

The houses of the early Spanish period were built in this style and on a smaller scale presented much the appearance of the Palace of the Governor. The typical Spanish plan, adopted for use in Mexico, was well suited to New Mexico because of the similarity in climates. Built around a patio, as protection both from attack and from sun and wind, the house was usually but one or two rooms wide with communication from room to room. Facing the patio were open corridors composed of wooden posts and postcaps supporting wooden beams. The materials employed precluded the use of the arch, so commonly found in Mexico. There was usually but one door on the street front and one at the rear leading to the corral. Doors were sometimes paneled and carved, but in the simpler houses were built up of hand-hewn planks. Iron being scarce, hinges were not used; the doors were operated on pivots extending into sockets above and below. Windows, without glass, were small and were covered with wooden grilles on the outside and provided with wooden shutters on the inside.

Floors were usually of earth or were covered with thin stone slabs. Fireplaces were quite commonly used, being built into corners to take advantage of two walls for the support of the chimney.

The houses varied considerably in size, depending upon the means of the occupant, and ranged from the house such as just described to the simple one- or two-room dwelling with no patio and no *portales*. But the character was the same in all: rectangular masses, flat roofs, and soft contours. They were usually but one story in height—even the more pretentious ones—although some were of two stories. One of the rare examples that can still be seen is the so-called oldest house in Santa Fe, across the *Rito* from the plaza, facing a narrow lane adjacent to the old Church of San Miguel.

This church was built about the middle of the seventeenth century, perhaps earlier, there being no record of the exact date (except that it is known to have been built some years before 1680, when the roof was destroyed). There is no support for the sometimes-made claim that it is the oldest church in the Southwest or in the United States, though it is the only remaining example of ecclesiastical architecture in Santa Fe dating from that early period. It originally served as a chapel for the Indian servants of the Spanish officials.

Having been changed in appearance many times, and not for the better, San Miguel is of much greater interest historically than architecturally. It was partially restored by De Vargas in 1693 and repairs were completed in 1710 by the Marqués de la Peñuela, the Spanish governor at the time. The church once boasted a three-storied tower, rather stubby in character, on the front. This crumbled and fell in 1872 and was never rebuilt. In 1888 stone buttresses were built on either side of the front to prevent a similar disaster to the church. The vigas supporting the ceiling were replaced in 1830. The reredos, carved by the Indians, contains old paintings, probably early copies of the masters.

In the Santa Fe of that period the day's business was conducted on the plaza, known as the Plaza Mayor, as in all proper Spanish cities (the Plaza de la Constitución during the Mexican regime). So was the evening's entertainment. Here too all political pronouncements were made, banners were raised, and parades were held. A market place by day, where produce was bought and sold and the craftsman's goods were traded, it was transformed by night for the benefit of the lighter things in life.

The plaza was the starting point for the regular caravan—loaded with blankets and buffalo skins—by way of Chihuahua to Mexico City and the terminus for the return caravan, loaded with ecclesiastical equipment and general supplies, missionaries, and occasionally a new governor. Three years were required for the round trip: a year and a half on the road, including the time spent in New Mexico, and the rest of the time preparing and loading in Mexico City. Since the supply train was the only regular means of transportation in and out of New Mexico and the only line of communication between Santa Fe and the rest of the civilized world, its arrival was always the big event in the monotonous life of the little colony. The dusty plaza hummed with activity and excitement. When finally the return caravan started back the Spaniards returned to their homes near the plaza, the soldiers went back to their barracks in the walled enclosure behind the palace, and the Indian servants crossed the *Rito* to the "Barrio de Analco," the "ward beyond the river," to their simple houses clustered around the Church of San Miguel. Another three years would pass before there would be any more news of the outside world.

If the plaza was the business and recreational center of the city, the place to trade and gossip and promenade, the Palace of the Governor was certainly the social and cultural center. For many years the only city in New Mexico—whatever there was in the way of intellectual expression and whatever there was of luxury and elegance —was to be found in Santa Fe, and it centered around the palace.

What library the city could boast was there, and books were eagerly borrowed from the governor who, except for the friars busy at their posts among the pueblos, was the one man of the colony with any pretense of cultural background. Soldiers gathered around him and listened eagerly to stories of other lands.

As a colony Santa Fe was never a success. No mineral wealth was found and the practice of agriculture was far from easy. Aridity to the extent of recurring drought many times almost resulted in near starvation. The same lack of rain and consequent lack of waterways that made farming difficult made the hardships of transportation from Mexico enormous. It is small wonder that there was almost constant talk of abandonment.

Only the Church took the colony seriously. The Franciscans would not give up; if this was a land of poverty for colonists it was a land of wealth in souls for God. So Santa Fe was maintained principally as a presidio and as a center for missionary endeavor. For seventy years after its founding the actual records of the capital city are meager, owing to subsequent events which will be described later. But during that time the greatest missions in New Mexico were established and the greatest mission churches were built there. Of these great structures only one remains more than an impressive and picturesque ruin.

12

The Forgotten Missions

FROM BERNARDO on the Rio Grande, about fifty miles south of Albuquerque, Highway 60 leaves El Camino Real, crosses the river, and traverses a flat plain toward the mountains which form a dim outline to the east. This is the Manzano Range, connected on

the north to the Sandías by wooded ridges and on the south to the
Gallinas by a series of mesas, also heavily wooded. The Manzano
Mountains provide a barrier formidable enough so that south of
Highway 66, the main east-west route through Albuquerque, there
is no ingress from the west until Highway 60 winds its way among
them through Abo Pass.

To the east of these mountains is the wide and treeless expanse of
the Estancia Valley, a region of salt and alkali lagoons. According to
Indian tradition these waters were once fresh, the home of fish and
waterfowl, the watering places of the buffalo and the antelope; but
because of the sins of an unfaithful wife they were accursed to be
salt forever. Bones of livestock that had perished for lack of water
attest the grimness of that lifeless stretch of salt plain, which has only
in recent years begun to be reclaimed.

Here on the wooded foothills of these mountains overlooking the
salt plain were the pueblos of a large group of Indians known as the
Piros, while stretching to the north were the southeasternmost
pueblos of the Tanoans, most of whom lived along the Rio Grande.
At the time the Spaniards came into the country this was the eastern
frontier of the Pueblo Indians. With that barrier between them and
the river they lived with their backs to a wall and faced the grim
stretch of the salt plain. They were thus almost constant prey for the
Apaches and Comanches who roamed the land which melts on the
horizon to the east and the south.

A few miles up from where the highway from the west begins to
wind through Abo Pass a side road on the north climbs up through a
wooded wilderness enlivened now by the screams of a little sawmill.
From the crest of the hill there can be seen spreading out a beautiful
valley, completely hemmed in by mountains. On a hillock in the
middle of the valley, and dominating its surroundings, gaunt and
jagged rise the red stone walls of what truly appears to be a castle in
Spain.

To the east and north, beyond the modern town of Mountainair
and just around the bend in the road (Highway 10) that leads to the
village of Punta de Agua, can be seen a similar pile, of browner stone
than the other but in a valley even more beautiful. The reddish-
brown walls outlined against the green mountains are visible a mile
away.

To the south the character of the country changes. The Arroyo
de Abo is the last flowing stream until the Rio Grande bends east

again not far above El Paso. Beyond the Gallinas Mountains it is a land so desolate that the Spaniards on their way north almost perished and significantly called the stretch the Jornada del Muerto—a land so desolate that it was chosen as the wisest place to explode the first atomic bomb. Traveling south from Mountainair a hint of this desolation beyond is given as one climbs the sandy hills sprinkled with scrubby trees. On one of the most desolate of these rises a third group of ruins, not red or ruddy brown like the others but ghostly gray, as if to add to the austerity of the landscape.

This is all that remains of what at one time were three of the greatest of all Spanish missions: Abó, Quarai, and what is now called Gran Quivira.

The whole center of the valley of Abó is covered with mounds and strewn with stone—evidence of a fair-sized pueblo; it is said that a hundred years ago three-story homes were still visible. Rising in the midst of this wide area of scattered grass-grown debris are the walls of the mission which the Spaniards founded in 1629 and dedicated to San Gregorio, patron saint of the old city of Åbo in Finland. The building was begun by Fray Francisco de Acevedo, who had just arrived in New Mexico with a group of twenty-nine new friars to aid the work of Father Estévan de Perea, custodian of the New Mexico missions.

All the walls, of the church and of the monastery which adjoins it on the east, are built of dark-red sandstone in narrow courses laid in adobe mortar. The walls of the church, especially on the west side, still rise to a considerable height. A narthex on a raised terrace at the south end of the church leads into the nave, off the southwest corner of which is the baptistry with remains of the sacrarium and font still in evidence. The plan of the church is that of a Latin cross, with a nave one hundred and fifteen feet long and forty-two feet wide and with shallow transepts each containing an altar of adobe. Near the south entrance of the nave are circular foundations which evidently once supported a choir loft, the slots for the beams of which are clearly visible in the walls. An opening in the east wall of the sanctuary leads into the sacristy and two storage rooms.

The extensive monastery comprises two courtyards, with a corridor along the south front extending the length of the building. Corridors on the other three sides of the western court open into living quarters, kitchen, and rooms for storage. The living rooms were along the south side and within one of them, in the northwest corner, is a small fireplace. A small court in the center of the maze of rooms contains the remains of a circular kiva into which refuse from the kitchen was thrown. The easternmost court, at a lower level, was used for corrals in which sheep, goats, and pigs were kept.

Time and pillage have dealt harshly with Abó but they have left a noble ruin. The walls provide a fascinating study in stonework and nowhere in the country is there greater richness of color.

While Abó was a pueblo of the Piro Indians, Quarai, less than ten miles away as the crow flies but about twenty on the road, was the southernmost of the pueblos speaking the Tiwa language. Like Abó the village is now but a series of mounds, though their size indicates that the houses were terraced and rose to a height of three or four stories. It has also been discovered that it was a completely walled town.

The walls of the ruined mission do not rise as high as the west wall of Abó, nor is the stone of which it is built as rich a red in color, but more of the church has survived the depredations of time and treasure hunters. With part of the walls on each of the four sides of the church rising as high as thirty or forty feet, the plan of the nave, a hundred feet long, is clearly outlined. Lintels over the entrance to the nave and over a window above, where the walls had given way, have been replaced to stabilize the structure. The monastery which adjoins the church contains in addition to the remains of two kivas, one round and one square, a small circular structure which was doubtless a *torreón* or watchtower.

The Quarai mission, dedicated to the Immaculate Conception, was begun at the same time as the mission at Abó and by the same Franciscan friar. Even as the stately ruins stand today, adjoining an ancient grove of cottonwoods in a beautiful valley, it is evident that Quarai, with two towers rising on the front, was once one of the most imposing of all the missions of the Southwest.

Farthest to the south are the ruins which are called Gran Quivira. Like the others, extensive mounds indicate the presence of a village of considerable size and rising in their midst are the ruins of not one but two churches. Both are of gray limestone. The smaller of the churches probably was begun shortly after 1628 and the larger church was erected some twenty or thirty years later and was never completed. The larger and newer church is about the same size as those at Abó and Quarai, but the adjoining monastery is much larger. The whole group has the appearance of never having been completed, as if the work had suddenly been interrupted and never resumed.

The pueblo in the midst of which this mission was built—the largest of the abandoned pueblos of the Piro Indians—has never been satisfactorily identified. It was thought by Bandelier to be Tabirá and until recently that identification has been accepted; now evidence has been presented to identify it with the pueblo of Humanas. Until its identity is definitely established it might as well be called by its misnomer, the name by which it will probably continue to be incorrectly known.

At some time a hundred years or so ago a prospector who had grown weary of his vain search for gold was approached by an Indian who told him he knew the secret of the Gran Quivira. The search of Coronado had been in the wrong direction, the searches of all his many Spanish followers had not taken them to the right place, but *he* knew where to go. The prospector, eager to take the chance of a change in his luck, was led to these hills, to this great pile of gray limestone beyond the Manzano Range. He was followed for many years by others who dug among the ruins searching for treasure which was thought to have been buried there by the last of the Piros retreating from the place, treasure which included gold and jewels brought from Mexico by the Franciscans, ignoring the truth that Franciscan wealth was limited to the riches to be found in the teachings of Christ. None of course was ever found, but the name clung. The myth of the Quivira had come to this place to stay. The Quivira of Coronado is forgotten—it never amounted to anything anyway—and in its place is this new Quivira, grown to *Gran* Quivira by now. Governments had to step in to save it from its despoilers and it is now both a state and a national monument.

Much farther to the north, only some twenty-five miles southeast of Santa Fe, was the pueblo of Pecos, also called Cicuyé, which had first been visited in 1540 by some of Coronado's men and again fifty years later by Castaño de Sosa in his premature attempt to colonize New Mexico. At that time it was one of the largest and strongest of the pueblos. On the eastern frontier, it was the starting point for the tribal buffalo hunts when the Indians from the pueblos along the Rio Grande brought their families while the hunters set out to gain a supply of meat; and it was from there that Coronado too set out to find the mythical Quivira.

The pueblo was begun about 1358, according to tree-ring dates which have been found, and consisted of two great communal dwellings each reaching in part four stories high and containing more than five hundred rooms. According to the early chroniclers, one could make the entire circuit of the village without setting foot on the ground.

In 1617, only seven years after the founding of Santa Fe, the mission of Nuestra Señora de los Angeles de Porciúncula was begun at Pecos and named for the little church in Assisi where Saint Francis so often knelt in prayer. The general plan of the church and monastery were typical of the mission churches in New Mexico: facing west, the church was cruciform in shape while adjoining it were the quarters of the resident friars and lay brothers, refectory, kitchens, living quarters for the neophytes and Indian servants, and rooms for storage. The structure was entirely of adobe with main walls five feet thick. A unique feature was that the church had six towers and another unusual feature was that the choir loft was not in the nave but in the south transept. No less interesting are the doorways in the north and south walls of the apse, leading to the two sacristies. They are true keystone arches built of adobe brick, still standing intact to belie the limitations of the material of which they are built.

Beautifully situated on an eminence in a valley entirely surrounded by wooded hills, this reddish-brown adobe pile is an indescribably picturesque ruin. Only the walls of the sanctuary and transepts are still standing, the nave having been leveled to the earth.

The pueblo of Pecos prospered until the middle of the eighteenth century. Attacks by Comanches, then smallpox, and finally mountain fever took their toll, greatly reducing the inhabitants and driving out the resident priests. Finally in 1838 seven men, seven women, and three children picked up their few personal belongings and marched to the west to join their cousins in Jemez.

The pueblo to which the last survivors of Pecos made their way is not the same as that which was in existence when the Spaniards first arrived but is the modern pueblo of Jemez, built as recently as the end of the seventeenth century. The ancient pueblo, known as Giusewá, was some twelve miles up the Jemez River where the hamlet of Jemez Springs now stands. The drive up the ever-narrowing canyon from Highway 44 is a beautiful one. Streaked cliffs rise higher and closer as the ascent is made until at Giusewá, "where water comes up," there is barely room for the mission church to butt its octagonal tower against the mountain in the rear.

The people of Jemez have had a turbulent history. Famine, pestilence, Navahos, and Spaniards caused them at various times to abandon their homes and flee to the mesa far above the canyon. The constant fear of attack was partially responsible for the six-foot walls of the Mission San José de Jemez, built almost entirely of stone on the floor of the canyon. The mission was begun in 1617 and work on it was continued for several years thereafter under the direction of Fray Gerónimo de Zárate Salmerón. The useful life of the mission was short, owing to the almost constant attacks of the Navahos, and both pueblo and mission were abandoned shortly after the latter was built.

Since both were abandoned at such an early date their history is little known, but that the church was built to serve also as a fortress is evidenced not only by the thickness of the walls (they are actually eight feet thick in some places) but by the fact that the walls were extended some five or six feet above the level of the roof, probably as bulwarks for defense. Of curious interest is the octagonal tower built directly behind the sanctuary, doubtless to serve as a watchtower. A doorway led from the adjacent sacristy to a stairway up to the roof of the church, from which a spiral staircase of hewn timber continued to the top of the tower. This tower still rises nearly fifty feet above the floor level of the church and, according to early settlers, it rose within their memory to a considerably greater height. A fortress monastery indeed!

Of the missions mentioned only Pecos was in use at the turn of the eighteenth century. San José de Jemez was abandoned well over three hundred years ago. The three missions facing the salt plains to the east and south, and the pueblos of the Indians they were designed to convert, suffered so severely at the hands of the Apaches that every village in the region was deserted before 1680. These missions had all been built, and all but Pecos abandoned and forgotten, a hundred years before the missions of California were begun.

This in brief is the story of five of the six great Spanish missions in New Mexico: Abó, Quarai, Gran Quivira, Pecos, and Jemez. The sixth was Ácoma. It will be discussed in a later chapter.

13

Revolt and Reconquest

THE SEVENTEENTH century was the great mission-building period in New Mexico. The missions covered an area from Pecos on the east to Zuñi on the west and extended north up the Rio Grande as far as Taos. By 1617 there were said to be fourteen thousand Indian converts and eleven churches had been built. In 1630, according to Father Alonso de Benavides, there were fifty friars at work in twenty-five missions and the number of converts had increased to sixty thousand. His report, submitted in person to the king at the completion of his term as custodian, was considered so important that it was translated into French, Dutch, Latin, and German. It painted in glowing terms the work of the Franciscan friars in New Mexico and cited figures to show that conversion to Christianity was growing at a rapid rate.

But all was not as rosy as the statistics would seem to indicate, especially during the third quarter of the century. Difficulties began long before that, however.

According to the terms of Oñate's contract, the Crown was to supply the necessary funds and equipment for six Franciscan friars to accompany the expedition to colonize New Mexico. Because of delays in starting, four of the friars assigned to the task had either been recalled or had grown tired of waiting and had returned to Mexico City, leaving only two of the original force. In the meantime a petition to increase the number had been granted; so ten Franciscans finally made the trip. Within two years reinforcements had arrived to join the colony at San Gabriel and with them were eight new friars; but by the following year about two thirds of the Franciscans, having become discouraged, had returned to Mexico with the deserting colonists.

The appointment of only Franciscans to accompany the expedition and to establish missions in New Mexico had not been made without some dispute at the outset, especially between the secular and regular clergy. The bishop of Guadalajara claimed that religious jurisdiction over the new territory should be his and that he had a right to exclude the friars from administering the sacraments. The viceroy, feeling that it would be unwise to have both secular and regular clergy working independently in the same field, submitted the question to the Council of the Indies. The verdict is not a matter of record, but presumably the bishop was overruled, for New Mexico was made a *prelature nullius*—a territory belonging to no diocese but under the jurisdiction of a prelate who had much the same functions as a bishop, though he was appointed for a limited term, usually three years. Because of the unrest and desertions, Oñate in asking for reinforcements in 1601 had requested that missionaries of all the orders be permitted to enter New Mexico; but the request was refused and the missionary work in the new province was left in the hands of the Franciscans exclusively.

Although the work of establishing missions was slow in getting under way, when Peralta came to the province as governor and the capital was moved to Santa Fe things took a turn for the better. Reinforcements arrived under the leadership of Fray Alonso Peinado, an extremely zealous missionary, and the work among the pueblos was undertaken in earnest. About the same time the prelate's church was moved from San Gabriel to Santo Domingo, which remained the ecclesiastical capital of New Mexico throughout the seventeenth century.

In 1612 Juan de Salas, who had come with a new group of reinforcements, began the church and monastery at Isleta, said to have been the finest church in New Mexico in its day. In January of 1617 the supply caravan arrived in New Mexico with word that because of the success in conversions New Mexico had been elevated to a custody. With the caravan came Fray Estévan de Perea as the first custodian. He had already served in New Mexico for several years and had built the church and monastery at Sandía Pueblo. At the completion of his three-year term Father Perea must have given a good account of the expansion in which he had engaged, for he was again elected custodian in 1628 and came once more to New Mexico the following year with twenty-nine new friars, the largest number yet to arrive with the caravan. It was during his first term that the great churches at Pecos and Jemez were built, and almost immediately on taking office the second time he sent Fray Acevedo to establish the missions at Abó and Quarai, he himself supervising much of the work on the latter mission.

In 1631 the number of friars to be supported in New Mexico from the royal treasury was set at sixty-six, a quota which remained fixed for almost fifty years although it was not always filled. When Father Perea died at Sandía in 1639 the mission program had reached its peak. Forty missions had been established.

Not the least of the problems of maintaining the missions in New Mexico was that of the supply service. For almost thirty years, beginning in 1627, the management of that service was in the hands of Friar Tomás Manso, who during his many terms as procurator-general made nine round trips between Mexico City and Santa Fe. During that time he also served a term as custodian of New Mexico. That he was an executive and manager of rare ability and honesty is shown by what happened to the supply service when he left it. The Perea-Manso team was in large measure responsible for the success of the whole mission program during one of the most trying periods in its history.

When in 1655, as a reward for his service, Manso was made bishop of Nicaragua the mission supply service almost immediately ran into trouble. After ten years of inefficient management the service was taken out of the hands of the friars, the wagons were sold, and contracts were let to the lowest competitive bidder. The result was that adequate supplies simply did not reach New Mexico, the successful bidder's pockets bulged, and finally, in 1673, another change of operations had to be made. The wagons, which had at first belonged to the royal treasury, were bought by the Franciscan Order, which again took over the operation of the supply service. But when in 1675 Friar Francisco de Ayeta, a worthy successor of Tomás Manso, arrived with his first caravan he found the situation in New Mexico desperate. All of the pueblos east of the Manzanos had been abandoned, the great new church at Tabirá (or Humanas?) having been left unfinished; the Navahos to the west had burned the church at Háwikuh and beaten out the brains of the resident priest, Father Pedro de Ávila, with a bell while he clung to a cross; and the Apaches had descended upon Senecu to the south, murdering Father Alonzo Gil de Ávila and most of the inhabitants there. Two more names had been added to the list of martyrs of New Mexico.

Recent studies of tree rings show that the first half of the seventeenth century was an abnormally fat period; that is, according to the tree-ring calendar set up for northern New Mexico the width of the annual rings was increasingly great during that period, indicating a rainfall throughout those fifty years that was not only well above the average but was getting better from year to year. A decrease began to be apparent between 1650 and 1660, but it was still above normal until about 1665. At that time a rapid decline began, culminating in extreme drought some ten years later which lasted for several years.

The remarkable mission-building program which began about the time of the founding of Santa Fe and continued unabated for at least a full generation was accomplished, of course, with Indian labor. The Pueblo Indians had had centuries of building experience behind them and, quick to learn, they soon caught hold of the improvements in the building arts taught them by the Spaniards. They acquired the use of metal tools and learned the rudiments of measurement. They learned how to mold adobe into bricks and how to cut and to carve the vigas and corbels used for the support of ceilings. Under the supervision of the friars, who for generations had been competent building superintendents, they constructed chapels, churches, monastery buildings, living quarters for the priests and for the neophytes, kitchens, granaries, and wine cellars.

Under Spanish tutelage they learned other arts: spinning and weaving, cooking in the Spanish way, improved methods of agriculture and of irrigation, the care of domestic animals—especially of the horse, for they soon learned "to ride on horseback and to salute the Spaniards with an Ave María." They learned to speak Spanish; so for the first time they had a common language. They learned to sing the Catholic chants and the boys were taught to serve the priests at the altar. According to Father Benavides, "these Indians are very dexterous in reading, writing, and playing on all kinds of instruments, and are skilled in all the crafts, thanks to the great industry of the friars who converted them."

Their contact was chiefly with the friars. The Spanish settlements were small and far apart, extending along the Rio Grande from Socorro to Taos. Throughout the seventeenth century there were never more than two or three thousand Spaniards in the country. Almost half of them lived in or near Santa Fe, which was the only incorporated town and the center of such civil and military power as existed. Grouped about the plaza, it was a village of adobe houses with cornfields and orchards between. The governor had his headquarters in the palace and behind it a few soldiers, clad in armor and carrying harquebuses, were supported by a couple of brass cannon. The Pueblo Indians rarely saw them.

Along with the instructions they gave, and the labor they exacted in the construction of the mission buildings, the friars attempted to convert the Indians to Christianity. That was fundamental. They made the Indians attend church services and they preached to them, pointing to the image of Christ, promising heaven and threatening hell if they did not give up their ancestral worship of the rain gods. They baptized Indian babies, giving them Spanish names; they married couples, heard confessions, and granted absolutions. The Indians accepted it all stoically; they had no objection whatever to adding Christ and the Virgin Mary to their pantheon. Then they went to their kivas and emerged, their drums rumbling, to dance naked in the sun. The friars fumed and called on the civil authorities.

The situation was very much the same as the first Franciscans had encountered in Mexico a hundred years earlier, with one essential difference: the friars in New Mexico did not have the military organization necessary to back up their demands. At no time did they have that; so the Indians kept their kivas and continued their supplications to the rain gods. They still do.

For a long time it did not greatly matter if the Indians felt themselves persecuted; the rain gods had been good to them, crops were plentiful, and they were well fed. They conducted their rites more or less surreptitiously; there were enough Indians so that the Spaniards could not maintain constant surveillance—they outnumbered the Spaniards ten to one. As long as the food stocks were ample they were content to unite with the Spaniards against the common enemy, the Apache and the Navaho.

But there came a time when the rain gods became inactive and the crops suffered accordingly. Things grew worse year by year. The Apaches and Navahos, facing starvation, swooped down upon the Pueblo villages, stole their reserve supplies, and carried off whole herds of livestock. The outlying villages, especially to the east, were deserted, their people moving in with the Pueblos along the Rio Grande. There was not enough food for all. The Indians reverted boldly to their animistic practices. Drums rolled and incantations to the rain gods sounded from every pueblo. The civil authorities stepped in and arrested the elders of the pueblos and tore down the kivas, which to the Indians were the symbols of those powers which controlled the very sources of life. Bonfires were made of pagan masks and images. The Indians were enraged at the sacrilege but the Spaniards kept up their work of destruction, never doubting the sanction of God.

This was the state of affairs in 1675 when Ayeta arrived with the caravan from Mexico City.

The situation was especially aggravated when on one occasion forty-seven Pueblo medicine men were arrested and taken to Santa Fe for trial. Four of them were found guilty and hanged for witchcraft; the rest were sentenced to be whipped and sold into slavery. The whippings were carried out, but a few days later seventy Indians dressed in full war regalia surrounded the governor's palace and demanded that the prisoners be released. The governor, having his mere handful of guard and fearing rebellion, opened the doors of the jail. Among those who had been imprisoned and whipped was a San Juan Indian called Popé.

On his return to Mexico City Ayeta appealed to the viceroy for aid for New Mexico, not for the missions this time but for military protection. When the seriousness of the situation was made clear to him the viceroy acceded to the procurator-general's requests. When he returned to New Mexico in 1677 Ayeta was accompanied by fifty soldiers and one thousand horses fully equipped. All of the facilities of the Franciscan supply caravan were put at their disposal. With the caravan was Don Antonio de Otermín, the newly appointed governor.

The Indian by nature, and by centuries of his own peculiar development, is rarely an individualist. In their successful communal living the Pueblo Indians did not produce leaders. Even the medicine men learned their arts from the lips of the elders and contributed little, if anything, of their own. Tradition was so strong that it tolerated little of innovation from any single individual; and leadership and entrenched tradition do not mix. Only in time of crisis—and that crisis has to be sufficiently acute to mean *war*—does the name of an individual stand out. That is true of all American Indians, as it is of all primitive peoples. Popé was one of these.

Forty-two of the medicine men who were released from prison

in Santa Fe doubtless went back to their homes only glad to be free. But Popé brooded over his imprisonment and came out of the experience an inspired man. When he was not too well received in his own pueblo of San Juan he went to Taos, often the headquarters of troublemakers for the Spaniards. He conferred there with the elders in the kivas, claiming that he was endowed with supernatural powers. He found ready listeners and plans were laid to strike. Their gods had been insulted; this was to be a holy war. Only the chosen leaders in each of the pueblos were informed of the details of the plot until it was time for the blow to fall. The time was set for August 13, 1680. At a given signal all were to act simultaneously. Not a Spaniard was to be left alive.

Popé had planned the attack well. Santa Fe was to be cut off from the pueblos to the south by holding the roads between while the warriors from the northern pueblos were to converge at the capital, from which there could be no escape. For some reason the date was changed to the eleventh, but news of the plot leaked out on the ninth so the Pueblos struck the next morning. The friars in the northern pueblos were the first to feel the fury of the Indians. Very few escaped alive. Among those killed was the Franciscan friar who for thirty years had served as priest at the beautiful, six-towered church at Pecos. At Santo Domingo, the ecclesiastical capital, three priests were killed and their bodies were piled on the altar. In all, twenty-one friars went to their deaths that summer morning. The Indians then looted the churches and set fire to them; and, tearing the rosaries and crosses from the friars' necks, they threw them into the flames.

The news first reached Santa Fe when the priest at Tesuque was about to celebrate Mass and was beaten to death with clubs. A soldier who had accompanied the priest to the church galloped to the capital to give the alarm. In addition to the friars four hundred Spaniards had been slaughtered, seventy of them in the valleys of Taos and Picurís where the revolt began. The few who escaped in the north ran for Santa Fe while those in the south gathered in Isleta, which had not joined the revolt.

A thousand people—men, women, and children—were crowded into the walled enclosure behind the governor's palace, only about a hundred of them capable of bearing arms. On August 14 scouts who had been sent out returned and reported that five hundred Indians were approaching from Pecos. They were moving slowly, stopping to loot and burn every house in their path. The next morning they appeared before the palace, the leader bearing two crosses, one red as a token of war and the other white. If the Spanish governor chose the white cross, his people might leave the country in peace; but they must leave. If he chose the red, the Indians would massacre them all.

Otermín replied by sending out a force to attack the enemy before reinforcements could arrive. By the end of the day, when the Spaniards seemed on the point of victory, the northern army from Taos appeared and the Spaniards were forced to retire to protect the palace.

The siege lasted five days. Reinforcements of Indians continued to arrive until there were several thousand Pueblos surrounding the palace, showering the Spaniards with arrows and waiting for them to starve.

Finally conditions in the palace became unbearable. The water supply had been cut off, food supplies were getting low, and the stench of dead animals permeated the place. What little water they had would soon be gone, so the Spaniards prepared for a desperate sortie. Outside, the Indians were already celebrating their victory, shouting that God and the Virgin Mary were dead. Charging in their midst and invoking the name of the Virgin, the Spaniards fought furiously, killing hundreds of the Indians and driving the others back until they fled to the hills.

The next day it was decided to abandon the city, so the governor, the soldiers, women and children, and three friars began the march on foot, each carrying his own luggage. There were barely enough horses for the sick and wounded. From the hilltops the Indians watched them go.

A few miles below Isleta they joined the refugees from the southern pueblos and the whole party marched slowly and painfully to the south. By the end of September the whole force was encamped near the site of the modern city of El Paso, where they were fed and clothed and their wounds were dressed by Father Ayeta who had arrived but a few days before from Mexico City with the mission supply caravan. Not a living Spaniard was left in New Mexico.

Popé was conspicuous by his absence during the siege of Santa Fe. He was a prophet, not a fighter. The actual fighting he had left to his chosen captains. But when the Spaniards were well out of sight he appeared in full Indian costume, wearing a bull's horn on his forehead. The Christian God was dead, he said, having been made of rotten wood, but their gods were still potent and would make them a prosperous people. His visit was followed by an orgy of destruction. Churches were looted and burned; the vestments, fixtures, and archives were all destroyed. The Church of San Miguel was the only church in Santa Fe that was not leveled to the ground.

Mounted on a black mule and followed by a retinue, Popé made a tour of all the pueblos with all the pomp and dignity of the governor whom he mimicked. He knew no other way and there was nothing in his tradition to teach him. Everywhere he was received with great acclaim, which he acknowledged by scattering corn meal on the people as a token of his blessing. At his orders the Indians all went to the streams and "washed off" their baptisms with soapweed. They dropped their Christian names and were forbidden to speak a word of Spanish or to mention the names of Jesus and the Virgin Mary. Marriages made by the priests were annulled and the men took new wives. Since the land of the Pueblos was to be purged of everything Spanish, only native crops could be raised.

For twelve years the Indians had the country to themselves. Popé followed up his orders with the death penalty for disobedience. He taxed the Indians' contributions of corn for the support of his government and took all of the prettiest girls of the pueblos for himself and his captains. The first summer after the revolt was marked by the worst drought that even the oldest men of the pueblos had ever experienced. Crops failed and game was scarce. The Apaches conducted raids worse than ever before. Still Popé went on prophesying while crops continued to fail. The Indians of the pueblos in anger deposed him and fought among themselves. All unity which they had found for the first time in their history was destroyed. Barbarism settled down upon the land.

Several attempts were made during the next decade to reconquer the country. Having been too feebly prepared, they were all unsuccessful. In 1691 Diego de Vargas Zapata Luján Ponce de León was appointed governor and captain-general for the purpose of regaining New Mexico. Troubles with the Indians near El Paso delayed his departure for the north, but by September of 1692 de Vargas was at the gates of Santa Fe. The city had been taken over by the Indians of several abandoned pueblos. Don Diego de Vargas was a courageous fighter when necessary, but he was also a diplomat of patience and tact. The complete demoralization of the Indians helped. Santa Fe was taken without a blow.

When the news reached Mexico City there was a great victory celebration in the capital of New Spain in which, by the viceroy's order, the cathedral was illuminated. And every year in Santa Fe on the second Sunday after Trinity there is a procession in honor of "Our Lady of Victory," who led de Vargas to the peaceful recapture of the city.

In 1693 the recolonization of New Mexico was begun. Unlike the submission of Santa Fe, it was not accomplished without bloodshed. For the next five years new settlers continued to arrive in the north, devastated areas were rebuilt, and the missions were re-established. Sporadic uprisings required the constant attention of the soldiers of de Vargas and of his successor Cubero, and it was not until 1698 that Spanish rule was made secure. Exactly a hundred years had passed since Don Juan de Oñate first took his colonists into New Mexico.

14

The Desert Province of Tusayan

BETWEEN THE Little Colorado and the San Juan and traversed by canyons whose stream beds are dignified only as "washes" lies a desert country, wind swept and bare of grass or trees. In geographical terms it is a part of the great Colorado Plateau. It is a land of weird shapes: broad mesas rise suddenly out of it, jagged stone spires thrust themselves through the sand, stone ships sail full rigged across the silica sea, and naked, sawed-off buttes project irregular dumpy shapes out of their eroded shavings like stunted giants clad only in petticoats.

Bare as it is, and fantastic in its geological formations, it is a colorful land. Highway 66 skirts its southern edge and from the highway may be seen a sample of the Painted Desert which extends for many miles beyond. Out of a background of buff, broad bands of pink and yellow, with occasionally a band of lavender or green, melt into a horizon of purple. In the midst of this three mesas jut southward from a great plateau like long irregular fingers of a giant hand. They are separated one from another by miles of sage-grown valleys suddenly bounded by the steep, rocky walls of the mesas.

This is the center of the province of Tusayan, the people of which have sometimes been called Moqui, which means "dead" and is not considered complimentary to the people who prefer to be known as Hopi, that name being a contraction of their own name for themselves: "Hopituh"—People of Peace. They are an ancient tribe, speaking the Shoshonean language, who long ago pre-empted the three mesas and have lived on or near them ever since, probably for fifteen hundred years. They now live in six principal pueblos atop the mesas; and in addition there are four new settlements, three of them near by and another some fifty miles to the west. There is a seventh pueblo on one of the mesas too, but it is occupied by people who speak a different language.

On the first or easternmost mesa are the pueblos of Walpi, Sichomovi, and Hano. The first of these is perched precariously on the southern tip of the rocky cliff, looking out over the desert. When the Castilians first saw that cliff the pueblo did not occupy the top of the mesa but was built at the foot, the present village having been founded about 1700. Its flat-roofed, terraced stone houses, two or three stories in height, crowded together and blending with the stone of the mesa, give the appearance of a medieval fortress. Sichomovi is hardly more than a suburb of Walpi, but Hano, at the opposite end of the mesa and less than a mile away, has had a distinctive history quite different from the others.

About two hundred and fifty years ago the ancestors of the people of Hano lived in the Rio Grande Valley near the pueblo of Santa Clara. Chafing over the treatment they had received at the hands of the Spaniards, the old men of the village were one day visited by some Hopis from Walpi who invited them to move up to their mesa to live. If they would bring their people to fight the Navahos for them, the messengers said, the Hopis would give them corn and would help them to build a pueblo of their own. Tempted by the location far away from the Spaniards, those Tewa Indians from the

Rio Grande made the long march to Tusayan, where they built their pueblo on the mesa near Walpi and have lived ever since.

The people of Hano have adopted Hopi customs but they still speak their own Tewa language. According to legend it was agreed that they would spit in each other's mouth, so the Hopis could speak Tewa and the newcomers could speak Hopi. The Tewa Indians permitted the experiment, so it is said, but the Hopis reneged and thus never could understand that language of the Rio Grande.

The people of Hano say too that the very night they arrived the Navahos came and, while the Hopis ran away, they killed thirty of the enemy, leaving only two alive, whom they tied with rawhide ropes. They told the Hopis that they were going to turn them loose so they could go back and tell their people that fighters from the Great River toward the Rising Sun had come there to live; and then the Navahos would not bother them any more. When the Hopis suggested killing one of them and letting just the other go back to his people, they said, "No, the Navahos are all such liars that they will not believe one alone, for our people always say it takes two Navahos to tell the truth."

On the second or middle mesa are the pueblos of Shongopovi, Shipaulovi, and Mishongnovi. The first, after occupying two known sites at the base of the mesa, moved to the present site about 1700, while part of the group moved a little farther away to found the village of Shipaulovi. Mishongnovi too was at first located below the present pueblo, which was founded about the same time as the others.

Farthest to the west, on the third mesa, is the pueblo of Oraibi, which has been there since about 1150 and is quite probably the oldest continuously occupied town in the United States. Until 1906 it was the largest of the Hopi pueblos. At that time a quarrel between conservative and liberal factions was settled by a "push-of-war," with the agreement that the losers would leave by nightfall. The "conservatives" lost and marched with their food, bedding, and personal belongings to a site seven miles away where there was an excellent spring, the principal requirement for locating a Hopi pueblo. Thus was founded the pueblo of Hotevilla, which has since outgrown its parent. The villages of Bakavi and New Oraibi near by and that of Moenkopi to the west were somewhat similarly begotten.

In one of the houses of Oraibi, abandoned in 1906, a beam was found which had been cut in 1370. It is quite possible that this house had been continuously occupied for more than five hundred years, thus giving it a substantial claim for the oft-disputed honor of being "the oldest house in the United States."

Because of its isolated position the province of Tusayan was never as thoroughly penetrated by the Spaniards as were the pueblos in what is now New Mexico. Nevertheless the Franciscan friars were there building missions. At the time of the Pueblo Revolt of 1680 the Hopis entered enthusiastically into the alliance proposed by Popé and his captains. The missions were destroyed and all of the resident friars were killed. It has also been said (but one should be permitted to doubt it because it has never been proved) that when the other Hopis learned that one of their pueblos was practicing forbidden Christian rites they trapped them in a kiva, set fire to it, and poured chile on the flames. The Hopis may have had their Christian martyrs too. At least an end was put to the domination of Tusayan by the Spaniards. None ever came back, with the exception perhaps of one or two; but they did not stay. The Hopis had moved up to the tops of the mesas for better protection from intruders.

On the fourth of July, 1776, Father Francisco Garcés arrived at the pueblo of Oraibi. He had ridden alone, except for Indian guides, from the Mohave Desert to the Grand Canyon—which he was the first white man to see from the west, perhaps from the spot where El Tovar now stands—thence east into the Painted Desert and Tusayan. Weary and hungry, he descended from his mule, offering gifts and salvation and expecting to be offered in return food and shelter. The Hopis would accept nothing and Father Garcés was offered nothing. They asked him only to leave. They have thus asserted their aloofness and independence ever since.

9. (*Top*) EL MORRO NATIONAL MONUMENT, New Mexico. (*Middle*) INSCRIPTION OF DON JUAN DE OÑATE, El Morro. (*Bottom*) INSCRIPTION OF LT. SIMPSON, El Morro

10. (*Top*) RUINS OF ABÓ MISSION, New Mexico. (*Bottom*) RUINS OF
SAN JOSÉ DE JEMEZ MISSION, New Mexico

11. (*Top*) RUINS OF QUARAI MISSION, New Mexico. (*Bottom*) RUINS
OF PECOS MISSION, New Mexico

12. (*Top*) THE GREAT CHURCH AT ÁCOMA, New Mexico. (*Middle*)
THE APSE OF THE CHURCH, Ácoma. (*Bottom*) THE PATH UP THE
ROCK, Ácoma

13. (*Top*) CHURCH AT ISLETA PUEBLO, New Mexico. (*Middle*)
CHURCH AT TESUQUE PUEBLO, New Mexico. (*Bottom*) CHILE PEP-
PERS, Tesuque Pueblo

14. (*Top*) THE CHURCH OF SAN JOSÉ, Laguna Pueblo. (*Bottom*) LA-GUNA PUEBLO, New Mexico

15. THE ALTAR AND REREDOS, San José de Laguna

16. (*Top*) OVENS AT TAOS PUEBLO. (*Bottom*) HOUSES ATOP THE ROCK, Ácoma

17. (*Top*) OLD HOUSE AT SANTA FE. (*Bottom*) THE GOVERNOR'S PALACE, Santa Fe

18. THE CHURCH OF SAN MIGUEL, Santa Fe

19. INTERIOR OF THE CHURCH OF SAN MIGUEL

20. (*Top*) THE PUEBLO OF PICURÍS, New Mexico. (*Bottom*) SANTU-
ARIO DE CHIMAYÓ, New Mexico

21. (*Top*) THE CHURCH AT SANTA CRUZ, New Mexico. (*Bottom*) THE
CHURCH OF THE TWELVE APOSTLES, Trampas, New Mexico

22. THE CHURCH AT RANCHOS DE TAOS

23. (*Top*) THE CHURCH AT TAOS PUEBLO. (*Bottom*) APSE OF THE
CHURCH, Ranchos de Taos

24.   THE PUEBLO OF TAOS

15

Mission on the Mesa

FROM HIGHWAY 66, about fifty miles west of Albuquerque, a side road turns off to the south at Paraje, distinguished only by an inconspicuous road sign, and winds over a sandy plain covered with rabbit brush and dotted here and there with juniper trees. In the distance ahead the colored rock formations so characteristic of the New Mexico landscape form a sky line of irregular horizontal lines extending around to the right and to the left and after a few miles dominated by the golden-brown sandstone butte known as the Enchanted Mesa. The road passes close by its base, where a fringe of juniper surrounds the great piles of loose rock spilled from the sheer formation rising four hundred and thirty feet above the plain.

According to tradition the Indians once dwelt upon Katzimo, as they call it because it is "haunted," when one day a great storm arose and swept away the upper part of the steep, rocky trail; so the people could never again reach their homes. Most of them were working in the fields below, but the old people who had stayed behind were left stranded, to die of starvation. The village was abandoned and the survivors moved to the top of another mesa three miles away. Katzimo has been climbed and a few cultural remains have been found on its top—indicating that it had at least been visited in ancient times—but no trace of building walls has been found.

Three miles beyond one comes upon another rock rising vertically out of the sand, almost as high as Katzimo and extending for some distance to the left. The escarpment has been cut into grotesque shapes by the sand blowing against it for ages; gigantic pillars and slender pinnacles alternate with dark caverns gouged deeply into the surface. The great crag is reached almost before one can distinguish the long, even lines on the summit as blocks of terraced houses, three hundred and fifty-seven feet up, so much the same color that they appear to be a part of the natural cliff. High up to the left can be seen a wide wall built on top of the rock, and behind it a much higher wall with towers rising above either end. This is Ácoma, the "City in the Sky."

From an Indian guide Fray Marcos heard in 1539 of the "great city built on the rock," but on learning of the fate of Estebanico he hurried so fast to get back to Mexico that he never got beyond Zuñi. Captain Hernando de Alvarado, dispatched from Zuñi a year later by Coronado to explore to the east, was the first Spaniard to see Ácoma, described by one of the party as "a rock with a village on top, the strongest position that ever was seen in the world." The following winter, on his march to Tiguex, Coronado and his men stopped at the rock where they found the Indians friendly and ready to give them presents and provisions. Forty years later Fray Agustín Rodríguez visited Ácoma and the following year Espejo spent several days there. The Indians were still friendly and generous with both entertainment and gifts.

With the advent of Oñate the Indians of Ácoma seemed to have undergone a change of disposition. He was received there with apparent cordiality and with gifts but, being naturally wary, he forbade his men to separate from each other while on the mesa. He also declined the all-too-insistent invitation of the chief to descend into a kiva; and the company went safely on its way.

The next Spanish visitors were not as fortunate. On his way west with thirty soldiers to join Oñate at Zuñi, Don Juan de Zaldívar was met at Ácoma by the chief and escorted, with sixteen of his men, up the steep path in the rocks. Not as cautious as his captain, Zaldívar permitted his men to become separated when all at once, with a war cry, the Indians fell on the Spaniards with clubs. When twelve of them, including Zaldívar, had been killed in the massacre, the remaining five, having been pushed to the edge of the cliff and deciding that some other death would be preferable to having their brains beaten out with clubs, leaped off the rock. At one place along the circling cliffs, somewhat lower than most of the table top, great soft sand drifts have piled up to about half the height of the rock. It must have been there that the soldiers landed, for only one was killed. When the four who survived the miraculous leap had been nursed back to health by the men who had been left below with the horses, the little company divided into groups, some of them going on to warn Oñate and the others returning to San Gabriel to make provisions for the defense of the women and children there.

Oñate quickly decided that punishment was necessary or New Mexico would have to be abandoned. Don Vicente de Zaldívar, who had been left in command at San Gabriel during Oñate's absence, insisted on the right to avenge his brother's death. With seven officers and seventy soldiers, he arrived at Ácoma on the twenty-first of January, 1599. A summons to surrender was greeted with shouts of derision, supplemented by a shower of stones and arrows, and the Spaniards spent that night encamped below the mesa listening to the din of an Indian war dance.

The assault began on the morning of the twenty-second. During the night twelve picked men had dragged the only cannon the company possessed around to the top of the south mesa and, while the rest of the soldiers distracted the Indians by a feinted assault, they established themselves and their one piece of artillery across a narrow but dizzy gulf separating them from the pueblo. That night the rest of the company, with the exception of a few left behind to guard the horses, dragged up logs to where the twelve were stationed. At daybreak, while the cannon held back the onrushing Indians, the Spaniards rushed from their hiding place and, with a log bridging the gap, crossed in single file. From then on it was hand-to-hand fighting, while the little howitzer battered away at the blocks of houses. For two days the struggle lasted until finally the Indians, feeling that these were no mortal foes, sued for mercy.

The houses were so nearly destroyed that they had to be rebuilt. How long they had been there nobody knows, for Ácoma vies with Oraibi for the title of the oldest continuously-occupied town in the United States. The inhabitants may have come from Mesa Verde when the cliff dwellings there were abandoned at the end of the thirteenth century. The houses today, built on the old foundations, extend in three roughly parallel lines of stone and adobe one thousand feet long. Each row consists of three terraced stories, each house separated from the next by a substantial dividing wall. Between the rows are streets with the natural rock for pavement, widened at one place to provide a plaza for ceremonies and dotted occasionally with beehive-shaped ovens for baking bread.

Fewer and fewer people live the year round on top of the rock, most of them having moved to farming villages near by—more conveniently located for working in the fields—from which they go up to the mesa top only for ceremonies.

There are several foot trails leading to the village atop the rock and an ancient toe- and finger-hole trail leading through a crevice, but the trail used by visitors today leads up a wind-deposited sand hill at the back of the mesa to a series of stone steps.

On breathlessly reaching the top of the steps, instead of being met by a shower of stones and arrows one now encounters an Indian woman, probably carrying a child and being trailed by two or three more, ready to collect the tax of a dollar a head and another for a camera, plus an additional quarter if one wants to see the inside of the church the Spaniards caused the Indians to build. The Indians of Ácoma make a fair income from their visitors today, but the visit is well worth the fees.

After that battle in the sky the next major visit to Ácoma was of a very different nature. Missionaries were soon assigned to the village, but because of the hostility of the inhabitants little headway was made before 1629. At that time Fray Juan Ramírez came as the first permanent missionary. Born in Oaxaca and having taken holy orders in the monastery of San Francisco in Mexico City, he came to be so noted a religious teacher that he was chosen to go with that famous group of Franciscans who accompanied Estévan de Perea to New Mexico in 1629. Upon hearing that the most rebellious of all the Pueblo Indians were those who lived upon the rock at Ácoma, the zealous friar immediately besought the custodian to be sent thither.

Legend has it that Ramírez truuged the hundred and fifty miles from Santa Fe to Ácoma alone, declining an escort of soldiers and with no defense save his crucifix and his breviary. But for once history definitely disputes legend, for it is known that he was escorted there by Governor Silva and a company of thirty soldiers, along with other friars assigned to Zuñi and the Hopi villages. They set forth from Santa Fe on June 23, 1629. The governor stopped at El Morro on his way both to and from Zuñi, for his name is carved on the rock there with a verse telling of how his "indubitable arm and whose valor have now overcome the impossible . . ." together with the dates July 29 and August 9, 1629.

Once arrived at Ácoma, however, Father Ramírez was left to his own devices while the governor and his party continued west. Again legend steps into the picture to tell of his reception. Greeted with rocks and arrows, not one of which pierced his habit, he was climbing the steep, rocky trail when a little girl was accidentally pushed over the brink and fell upon a ledge of rock sixty feet below. The good friar picked her up unharmed and carried her in his arms to her astounded kinsfolk. He was received as one who was superhuman, and to this day the rocky trail which he climbed is known as El Camino del Padre.

Whatever the manner of his reception, Father Ramírez remained at Ácoma for twenty years, during which time he must have gained the love or at least the co-operation of his following. Not long after his arrival he went down from the great crag, attended by his flock, to visit some of the other friars at their posts. Amazed to find him still alive, they were even more amazed to see these warrior Indians ⸱ changed from "lions to meek sheep."

During these years Father Ramírez, with his multitude of Indian assistants, built a great mission and church there which was dedicated to San Estéban Rey (Saint Stephen, the king of Hungary, canonized by Pope Benedict IX because he had converted the Magyars to Christianity). There is nothing legendary about it; it is to be seen to this day, looking from the heights of the precipitous rock out over the valley and the Enchanted Mesa, the largest and finest mission church in New Mexico. In addition to uncommon zeal and a powerful personality on the part of the friar-architect, it must have required years of tremendous labor on the part of his helpers, hauling up material from the valley below and timbers from the distant mountains.

The church, of stone and adobe construction, is one hundred and fifty feet long and forty feet wide, with walls sixty feet high and ten feet thick. The vigas which support the roof are more than forty feet long and are fourteen inches square in cross section. All of them were carried by the Indians from the Cebolleta Mountains thirty miles away. The simple massive front is battered, like an Egyptian temple, and except for the large central doorway is pierced only by a square window above the entrance. Projecting from the front, a severely plain square tower rises on either side, a story above the flat top of the façade, and is pierced with openings on the four sides. The high side walls of the church, cut by but few openings high up, taper to a narrow apse without any openings.

On the interior the nave is severe and bare, enriched only by a carved and painted reredos and by elaborately carved corbels which help to support the heavy vigas. The half-dozen or so wooden benches placed in the nave near the chancel serve to emphasize the great scale of the interior and cause one to appreciate more greatly the tremendous labor involved in hauling all that material up onto the rock. Each ceiling beam, weighing more than a ton, had to be cut, trimmed, and carried on the shoulders of a small army of men for thirty miles to reach the base of the rock. The Indians say that after a viga for a church has been cut and smoothed it would be a sacrilege to let it touch the ground, so it must be carried all the way. The forty feet of each unwieldy timber had to be maneuvered up the steep crag three hundred and fifty-seven feet up and then hoisted sixty feet higher to the roof of the church.

An idea can be gained of the work involved by reading the figures in the report of the committee in charge of repairing the roof of the church in 1924. In addition to other materials, all water had to be brought up from springs in the plain below because at that time the water in the reservoirs on top of the rock was so low that there was barely enough to meet the needs of the few Indians who lived there. Materials required for that repair job included fifty thousand pounds of water, twenty-four thousand pounds of cement, seventy-two thousand pounds of sand, five thousand pounds of roofing felt, five thousand pounds of asphalt, and thirty-five thousand feet of boards for scaffolding.

Adjoining the church on the north is a cloister which encloses a large patio one story in height, except at the northeast corner where a loggia has been built above to serve as a lookout tower. From this loggia there is a magnificent view over the long lines of houses onto the valley far below.

No less remarkable than the church itself is the burial ground in front of the church. In order that the Indians might bury their dead in consecrated ground near by, a place had to be made for them in front. A high stone retaining wall was built up on the sloping ground, enclosing an area two hundred feet square; then earth was brought up from the plain below, a sackful at a time to fill the enclosure formed. It is probably the only cemetery of its kind in the world.

After twenty years of devoted service Fray Juan was reluctantly carried back to Old Mexico to end his days in an infirmary. But the old man could not be comforted and "rivulets of tears coursed his cheeks" as he thought of his children whom he had been forced to leave. He died on the twenty-fourth of July in 1664, truly one of the great builders of New Mexico.

At the time of the Pueblo Revolt in 1680, although remote from the center, Ácoma joined with most of the pueblos and killed the resident priest, Fray Lucas Maldonado, and burned all the emblems of Christianity. Just how much damage was done to the church at that time has never been ascertained, but that it was not destroyed is proved by the letters of de Vargas, who visited Ácoma in 1692. He mentions visiting the church of Saint Stephen after receiving the submission of the people and describes it as of great extent with thick walls "which stand firm in spite of the heavy rains that break the windows."

Some repair work was doubtless necessary after the Spaniards again took over in 1699; and in 1924 extensive repairs were made— on the roof, as already mentioned, and on the façade and towers. By that time the tops of the towers had disintegrated and the adobe surfacing had worn away, but in making the repairs great care was taken to retain the original character of the church.

In spite of the report of de Vargas, however, the idea persists that the church of Ramírez was completely destroyed in the revolt and that the one seen today dates in its entirety from 1699 or 1700. It hardly seems probable that the Indians of Ácoma would have taken the trouble to demolish the church between the time of the visit of de Vargas in 1692, when they again submitted to Spanish rule, and 1700; and there is no record of any church construction after the latter date.

Other arguments present themselves in favor of the earlier date, in addition to the testimony of de Vargas. Chief among them is the record that after the reconquest the Spaniards simply did not build churches like that in New Mexico. It is a product of the height of missionary fervor. A similar situation is evident in the churches of Old Mexico. It was only during the first hundred years, or somewhat less, that the friars there built the fortress monasteries that still stand as silent testimonials to early pioneering, the finest architectural monuments in Mexico. Such missionary and architectural pioneering reaches a peak which can last for a limited time only, after which a decline begins. Once a decline has begun, the peak cannot be reached again in the same field.

By the time the seventeenth century had dawned the pioneering of the Franciscans in Old Mexico was done. The secular church took over and the pioneers went farther afield. Some of the giants among them went to New Mexico, just as the pioneers of later periods—when the missionary architecture of New Mexico had settled down to mediocrity—found new fields in Texas and Sonora and then in California.

It is exceedingly doubtful that the missionary zeal and its architectural expression evident in the work of those first Franciscan friars in New Mexico could survive the revolt and reconquest. There is nothing there to show that it did. There are some very interesting postconquest churches in New Mexico, but they are all small.

Those friars who came to New Mexico in the first half of the seventeenth century, especially those who came with Benavides and Perea, were the intellectual and missionary-fervent descendants of the sixteenth-century Franciscans in Mexico. Owing to limitations of material and equipment the architectural expression of their zeal took an entirely different form, but the spirit is shown in the ruins of Abó, Quarai, and Jemez. San Estéban Rey at Ácoma belongs with them.

The site of the church at Ácoma is doubtless the most commanding of any church in the United States. The erection of a great church on that site under the adverse conditions that existed has an appeal for the imagination beyond that of any mission church ever built. But the church itself has in its huge simplicity a strength and dignity, a rugged power, to a degree seldom if ever exceeded. Here as in almost no other church can one appropriately say: "A mighty fortress is our God."

In 1699 Ácoma had a child. In that year, while on an expedition to Zuñi, Governor Pedro Rodríguez Cubero, who succeeded de Vargas after the reconquest, ordered the establishment of a pueblo some twenty miles to the northeast. Settlers came from Ácoma and from other Keres-speaking pueblos, and from Zuñi too, to establish the new village. It was called Laguna for a near-by lake which has since disappeared. The only pueblo established after the arrival of the Spaniards, it is now—including several satellites scattered within a radius of a few miles—the largest of all the pueblos.

Like Ácoma the Laguna pueblo is built upon a rock, but differs from the former in that it is merely a low outcropping which reaches the surface in irregular waves. Owing to its recent foundation (it is only a little over two hundred and fifty years old) it shows in its houses an interesting blend of Indian and Spanish architecture. The streets, built up here and there with retaining walls, rise and fall as the solid foundations of the village permit; and the stone and adobe houses, some flat roofed, some peaked, spill over the rock at various levels.

At the highest point stands the Church of San José de Laguna, built at the time of the founding of the pueblo by Fray Antonio de Miranda, the last of the early missions and the best preserved. Of stone covered with adobe, newly whitewashed each year, it is one hundred and five feet long by twenty-two feet wide. Entrance to the adobe-walled churchyard is through a gateway up a short flight of steps, from where a bevy of small children, upon being approached, will fly in all directions to find the custodian of the keys. The simple façade of the church has a window on the center line above the entrance and a belfry with two square openings in the false gable front surmounted by a glistening cross.

The small interior is one of the most delightful in New Mexico. The carved double corbels which support the vigas are more elaborate than most and the herringbone ceiling is of saplings painted in bright colors in bands of red, white, yellow, and black. The chancel is separated from the rest of the church by a railing of simple, rather crude but effective carved-wood balusters painted red and blue. The reredos is framed by twisted baroque columns and between them are painted decorations of charming primitive designs in rich but mellow colors. A painting of Saint Joseph done on elkskin occupies the center, while above it are the figures of the Trinity with triangular halos. On the ceiling immediately above are painted Indian symbols of the sun, moon, stars, and a rainbow. The side walls of the church also are covered with designs painted in bright colors.

An earlier painting of Saint Joseph was the subject of a bitter controversy between Ácoma and Laguna some years ago, a bone of discord which lasted for five years and had to be settled by court action. It seems that Ácoma was the proud possessor of a painting of Christ's foster father, said to have been presented to Fray Juan Ramírez by King Charles II of Spain. Because of the miraculous powers with which the painting was thought to have been endowed by Saint Joseph, it was held in great veneration and Ácoma prospered.

Now all of this time the neighboring pueblo of Laguna was not thriving. If they had such a painting it would surely be a boon to their crops and their childless women. So, after a meeting of the head men of the Pueblo, the people of Ácoma were asked to lend their painting to their neighbors. After an equally solemn council at Ácoma it was agreed that Laguna might borrow it, but for one month only. Laguna's fortunes immediately changed; the sick became well, the crops were good, and the women bore children.

But on the due date the picture was not returned. Ácoma sent messengers to Laguna to inquire the reason but they got no satisfaction. Months later, weary of waiting, Ácoma again sent messengers, but they were told by the people of Laguna that they could have the painting "only over their dead bodies," or words to that effect. The parish priest, Fray Mariano de Jesus López, last of the Franciscans at Ácoma, was consulted. A council was held of the elders of both pueblos and after a Solemn Mass it was agreed that lots should be drawn. Twelve slips were prepared, eleven of them blank and one bearing a rude sketch of San José. The slips were shaken up in a large pottery jar and two little girls dressed all in white, one from Ácoma and one from Laguna, did the drawing. On the fifth drawing the little girl from Ácoma drew the saint. "So," said the priest, "God has decided in favor of Ácoma."

One day, while Ácoma was still rejoicing over the return of its beloved saint and the people went to pray before him in the church, lo! the picture was gone. A war would have ensued had not Fray Mariano once more come to the rescue and suggested that the case be laid before the United States District Court in Santa Fe. Sitting as Chancellor was Judge Kirby Benedict, a close friend of Abraham Lincoln. The court decided in favor of Ácoma. Laguna appealed the case to the Supreme Court. The earlier decision was affirmed. This was in 1857.

With great rejoicing a delegation started from Ácoma to Laguna to recover the picture. Halfway there they found San José resting against a tree, his face toward Ácoma. To this day the people of Ácoma say that their beloved saint, having heard the final decision, could not wait and had started out by himself to return to his proper home in the great church of the mission on the mesa.

16

Upper Rio Grande

SEVEN YEARS after the pueblo of Laguna was founded Don Francisco Cuervo y Valdés, governor of the province of New Mexico, moved thirty Spanish families from Bernalillo on the Rio Grande to a new site seventeen miles to the south. At that location the valley is wide and green with cottonwoods, and a good ford in line with an easy pass through the Sandía Mountains to the east makes it a natural center for farming and for trade.

The records show that there were actually only twelve founding families but since, according to law, it took thirty to establish a *villa*, thirty there were according to the governor. They did not come riding on horseback, wearing armor; these people were farmers and artisans who walked beside their *carretas* piled high with household goods; and on arrival they set to work making adobes and cutting cedars in the mountains to build their own homes. Thus was founded, in 1706, San Francisco de Alburquerque, named in honor of the governor's patron saint and the viceroy of New Spain, Fernández de la Cueva Enriquez, Duke of Alburquerque. The latter diplomatically dropped the saint and substituted the king, making the villa officially San Felipe de Alburquerque. The passage of time has erased the prefix and one *r*.

It was the third villa to be established in the province of New Mexico (Santa Fe was the first and Santa Cruz, the second, will be reached in the next chapter) and it soon became an important trade center. The new villa was built around the typical Spanish plaza, wide and dusty, faced with one-story buildings and surrounded by an adobe wall. On one side of the plaza Father Manuel Moreno, who had accompanied Governor Cuervo and his "thirty families," built the Church of San Felipe de Nerí. It stands today, with its front re-modeled but with its four-foot-thick adobe walls and its windows built twenty feet from the ground for protection during uprisings still there. Parish records boast that not a Sunday service has been missed since the church was opened in 1706. The adjacent monastery where the Franciscan missionaries of the vicinity made their head-quarters has been altered too, but it is still in use as a parish house.

The villa, especially within the last few years, has grown into a thriving modern city, much the largest in the state and the only one of importance on the upper Rio Grande; but the modern city does not belong here, except to say that in so growing Albuquerque has done by far the best job of any city in the Southwest of leaving the old plaza alone. Enlivened at night by visitors patronizing a favorite restaurant in an old Spanish house, it is quiet and sleepy by day. No-where else in the Southwest is there as much unhampered inducement to picture life in a provincial villa of more than two hundred years ago.

As a center of trade routes Albuquerque soon surpassed neigh-boring settlements both in area and in population. As a military post it was a magnet for settlers seeking protection from attacks by marauding Indians. All of the settlers owned farming land along the river or reached by an irrigation ditch, and they shared grazing lands. Some of them were content to engage for the most part in trade or to operate their small farms, raising corn and beans, melons and grapes with also perhaps a few sheep and cattle for their wool and their hides. Others, with special favor of blood or wealth, spread out along the Rio Grande, increasing their holdings and developing great haciendas over which they reigned as feudal lords.

The richest lands along the great river, where the valley is wide and fertile, were granted in great tracts by the Spanish king to men who claimed to be of pure Spanish blood. Their great houses were to be seen only a few miles apart, from Socorro to Bernalillo. Sheltered by huge cottonwoods, whose shade was a haven in the wide stretches of hot sun, these houses were built as forts. Long and low, they had porches, supported by wooden posts and carved post-caps, the length of the whitewashed adobe fronts. With walls three or four feet thick, the New Mexican country house of that day en-closed the inevitable courtyard, called a *placita*, into which the principal rooms opened directly. The house was entered through a high and wide passageway, or *zaguan*, through which a coach and team could drive—much as in the early mansions of Mexico.

Behind was another enclosed square where the peons were housed and carts and wagons were kept. Horses could be driven in there when there was danger of attack. Storerooms were filled with grain —bins of wheat and many-colored corn—and barrels of jerked buffalo meat while dried fruit, herbs, and strings of chile hung from the beams of the ceiling.

The rooms of these adobe houses were whitewashed every year and covered with colored cloth to a height of four or five feet to protect the clothes of the *ricos* and their guests. The furniture was scant and simple; all homemade, it included only a dining table, a few wooden chairs with seats of rawhide, and, in lieu of the bed there was the *colchón*, folded against the wall and covered with a bright-colored blanket to serve as a sofa by day. Luxury items all were shipped over the long and perilous trail from Mexico City through Chihuahua and included painted chests and embroidered shawls from China, laces and satins, metal- and leatherwork from Europe, and silver service from Mexico.

Such were the houses of the *gente de razon*, "the right people," as this aristocratic minority called themselves. They lived pleasant lives of well-nourished security, of isolated luxury, while small armies of peons, constantly in their master's debt, worked on and in the house and in the fields, tending the orchards, vineyards, gardens, and pastures; and scattered among them the Indians tilled the fields in their grants of land around the pueblos, maintaining a precarious economic independence while being subjected constantly to the teachings of the friars.

Nearly all that has changed now, partly because the dying gasps of the Spanish Empire severed the *ricos* from the source of feudal spirit, partly because new people were breaking down the wall to the east, but more recently and largely because of the Iron Horse. The houses of the *ricos* have crumbled and fallen, the haciendas have been broken up, the tracts are smaller, some of them operated by descendants of the pioneers and others by Americans moving west seeking health and sunshine. But throughout the length of that area and beyond to the north the Indian pueblos, though not as many, are still there, each with its own tract of land granted by the United States Government; and here the Pueblo Indians have their farms and live in their villages much as they used to do then and before the Spaniards came.

The sixty or seventy Indian pueblos which the Spaniards found in the valley of the upper Rio Grande have now been reduced to sixteen. Only one of these lies below Albuquerque and the others dot the valley for a hundred and fifty miles, up as far as Taos. Eight of them, south of Santa Fe, lie along the great river and its sometimes-turbulent branch, the Jemez, until White Rock Canyon stops them to turn a twenty-five-mile section of the Rio Grande over to the domain of archaeology. The other eight, conveniently divided from the first group to make Santa Fe the center of the pueblos—for which purpose it was located—begin again some eight miles north of the capital and find the river again farther north.

Most southerly of the present pueblos is Isleta, thirteen miles south of Albuquerque. Formerly on an island—hence its name—it is the largest of the Indian villages of the Rio Grande. When the village was founded or where the people came from is not known, although tradition says they came down from the north and the pueblo still occupies the same site as when Coronado spent the winter of 1540–41 near by.

Its one-story adobe houses sprawl over a large area and in the midst of them, facing a large, bare, sandy plaza, stands the church which was begun in the early part of the seventeenth century by Fray Juan de Salas. The church has been much restored and disfigured. Rising above the thick, whitewashed adobe walls is a peaked roof, the gabled front covered with clapboards, while a skinny American Gothic tower rises on either side, surmounted by a cross. Another large cross adorns the gable. Among the corbels helping to support the vigas of a modern ceiling are some old corbels with evidence of former painted decorations. A large bell hangs in each tower; another reposes in the attic.

An equal distance to the north of Albuquerque and only about a hundred yards east of the highway lies moribund little Sandía, once one of the largest and strongest of the pueblos. Its troubles began with Coronado. The center of the province of Tiguex, it was imposed upon to furnish houses, food, clothing, and women. When the inhabitants rebelled they were burned at the stake.

About the time of the founding of Santa Fe, Fray Estévan de Perea was sent to Sandía where he established a mission and built the

Church and Monastery of San Francisco. For a while things looked better for Sandía. After serving two terms as custodian of New Mexico Perea returned to Sandía as resident missionary, and there he died and is buried.

The church was destroyed during the Pueblo Revolt and the inhabitants of the pueblo later fled to the Hopi country to evade the wrath of the Spaniards. They established a pueblo there, on the middle mesa; but, unused to the difficulties of the sandy wastes of the desert, they had a hard time growing crops and were ready to be persuaded to return sixty years later to their green valley. Three thousand of them had gone to Tusayan; only four hundred were left to return.

Fray Juan Menchero built a new church for them in 1748, which stood until 1875, but in religion they were hopelessly muddled. The new generation which returned to the Rio Grande knew only the Hopi methods of farming and their crops failed. When they practiced the Hopi rites in order to aid the crops their Indian neighbors accused them of witchcraft, and when they would not go to church the priest punished them. When there was a plague of grasshoppers the other Indians blamed the Sandía witches, and when their food stores were low the other Pueblos banded together for their own protection and left the Sandíans to the mercy of the hungry Apaches and Comanches. So they grew vines and made wine and drank it by themselves. Now fewer than one hundred and fifty people live in "Nanfíat," or "dusty place," in a cluster of adobe houses around their uninteresting modern Church of Nuestra Señora de los Dolores— Our Lady of Sorrows.

When the people of Jemez finally abandoned Giusewá they moved down the Jemez River several miles to establish a new pueblo. Even then their new home could hardly be considered as established, because intermittent war with nomadic tribes, with other Pueblo Indians, and with Spaniards kept them on the move for many years. For a time after the Pueblo Revolt they moved up with their former enemies, the Navahos, with whom they intermarried, and it was not until about 1710 that they settled down in their present village. Since 1838 they have shared their pueblo with the survivors from Pecos, and today Jemez is among the largest of the Rio Grande pueblos. Northwesternmost of these pueblos, it is reached by turning off Highway 44 at San Ysidro and driving north on Highway 4 for a distance of about five miles. The pueblo is beautifully situated in a sloping valley at the mouth of a canyon. At the west edge of the village stands the modern Chapel of San Diego, replacing an earlier church which burned.

The people of the two southernmost Rio Grande pueblos, Isleta and Sandía, speak a dialect of Tanoan called Tiwa, or Tigua, as do also the people of the two northernmost pueblos, Picurís and Taos. The Indians of Jemez speak a distinctive dialect of the same language group, Towa, while all of the other pueblos north of Santa Fe speak a third dialect known as Tewa. But in the midst of the Tanoan villages is a group of five pueblos the people of which are related to the Indians of Ácoma and Laguna and speak Keres. Two of them, Zía and Santa Ana, are on the Jemez River below Jemez and the other three—San Felipe, Santo Domingo, and Cochití—are on the Rio Grande.

The average visitor can see no differences among the people who speak the various Tanoan dialects, but on a visit to any of the Keres pueblos an atmosphere different from the others is almost immediately sensed. Once noted as fighters, there has always been war in their organization, in their ceremonies, in their myths—and in their history. Perforce peaceful today, their background is still evident. It takes the form of a conservatism which borders on restrained hostility. People of the Tanoan pueblos welcome visitors or pay no attention to them. Photography is permitted with the permission of the governor—sometimes for a consideration; but it is permitted. In the Keres pueblos it is evaded or even refused. The governor is sure to be away—in the fields, in Albuquerque, or visiting a sick cousin in Laguna. No one else has authority or the keys to the church. Hence the lack of photographs herein of the pueblos just named. And some of them have the most interesting churches too.

The people of Laguna, because that pueblo lies at the edge of a cross-country highway and perhaps too because it is a comparatively recent mixture, are amenable to persuasion, at a fee, when the governor can be found at his woodpile. But prosperous Santo Domingo does not need the extra income and flatly says no.

The pueblo of Zía is visible from Highway 44, spreading over a rocky knoll on the northeast bank of the Jemez River some fifteen miles above its confluence with the Rio Grande. A side road winds through the sand to a bridge over the river immediately above which rises the small pueblo with a fine view of the valley and mountains to the south. The people claim that they have occupied the site since the time of Coronado, when their pueblo was much larger than now with a thousand terraced houses three or four stories high built around five plazas.

The church is a fine example of Franciscan mission architecture. Built on the foundations of an earlier church, which is said not to have been completely destroyed at the time of the revolt, the present church was begun in 1692, almost immediately after the reconquest by de Vargas and was dedicated to Nuestra Señora de la Asunción. It is a simple structure of whitewashed adobe, with a massive buttress on either side of the front and a single pierced and stepped belfry above the center of the façade. Above a recessed entrance a gallery is supported by carved corbels and huge beams on which rest projecting vigas. Other wooden beams, spanning the front over the gallery, support the roof and the belfry.

Halfway between Zía and the Rio Grande the pueblo of Santa Ana, built on the north bank of the Jemez River, looks so much like the sands out of which it grows that one is inclined to think it is a mirage. Like Zía, a sandy road winds from the highway for about a mile to the river; but, unlike Zía, there is no bridge. The guide-book says that even when the river bed is dry the sand is deep and treacherous, but I have never tried it when the river bed was dry. Low gear is advisable, without slowing down in the middle of the river and aiming as well as possible for wagon tracks emerging on the opposite bank. When one has safely crossed he feels that his car ought to shake, like the dog approaching from the cluster of deserted adobe houses.

Most of the inhabitants of Santa Ana have moved to a farming settlement on the Rio Grande, leaving the old pueblo in charge of a caretaker. He will be friendly but he will have no keys and no authority. The small mission church is charming. Like the church at Zía it was built after the reconquest, perhaps on the site of an earlier structure, though the records regarding that are not clear. An adobe-walled forecourt extends for some distance to the front and low, one-story buildings frame the sides, the one on the right extending to a line with the front wall of the court. Over the recessed entrance to the church is a wooden gallery wider than the entrance and with a projecting wooden railing. The flat roof above is partially supported by a wooden column at the center of the balcony. A small pierced belfry rises above the roof, on the right-hand side rather than over the center.

The other three Keres pueblos follow up the Rio Grande and can be reached separately from Highway 85 as it continues toward Santa Fe, or the northern two can be reached from San Felipe by means of a winding dirt road that connects the three. About twelve miles north of Bernalillo, at the foot of a long hill, a side road drops off the highway to the left and leads past a small suburb and store on the east bank of the Rio Grande over the bridge to San Felipe. The low, light-brown adobe houses spread over quite an area, for San Felipe is one of the larger pueblos and at the far end of the village, facing a plaza, stands the mission church. Built during the first quarter of the eighteenth century, after the vicissitudes of conquest, revolt, and reconquest shared by most of the pueblos, it is the finest of the extant Rio Grande pueblo churches.

Several visits found the governor of San Felipe always "away" so I had to be content with surreptitious sketches from the car (permission to sketch or paint, if one can get it, is usually several times the cost of photography).

In front of the church is an unusually large forecourt enclosed by a low adobe wall. The wide, recessed entrance portal is flanked by twin towers with open belfries terminating in four merlons projecting above the belfry roof. A gallery, supported on projecting vigas, has a lattice railing painted yellow and blue and the roof over the gallery is supported by a large wooden beam which rests on huge, decorative, pale-purple wooden corbels at either end. A small false pediment above the flat roof is crowned with a cross. The severity of the long side walls is relieved only by the projecting ends of the ceiling vigas.

Six miles north of San Felipe is Santo Domingo, largest of the Keres group and second in size of the Rio Grande pueblos. One of the most prosperous, it is also the most conservative. Having been destroyed several times by floodwaters of the Rio Grande, the pueblo has been moved from time to time during its history. The present village, which has suffered three disasters by flood, dates from the reconquest in 1692. The pueblo today comprises several parallel streets of one- and two-story brown adobe houses, with circular kivas among them, and is one of the tidiest of Indian pueblos with neatly-kept corrals well segregated from the village.

For a long time the ecclesiastical capital of New Mexico, Santo

Domingo has had several churches since the time of Fray Juan de Escalona, who came to New Mexico in 1600 as the first resident missionary. He died and was buried in Santo Domingo in 1607, probably the first Franciscan to live out his natural life in New Mexico. The present church is a replica of one which was destroyed by a flood in 1886 and has the typical recessed portal with a gallery and a pierced, stepped belfry above. It is unique in exterior decoration however. The gallery railing is painted to resemble tiles and above, on the gallery wall, a horse on either side guards the central window. One horse is black and white and the other is yellow.

The people of Cochití, seven miles north of Santo Domingo, claim, as do their neighbors, that they originally lived at Tyuonyi in the Canyon of the Rito de los Frijoles. After leaving the cliff dwellings there they settled in several different places before they founded the present village some years before the Spaniards found them.

The dirt road which goes from San Felipe to Santo Domingo continues north through the Spanish settlement of Peña Blanca, and on reaching the Rio Grande crosses the bridge and turns south again for a little more than a mile to Cochití, on the west side of the river.

Among the one-story houses are a few of two stories, one an exceptionally fine example of a type that is rapidly disappearing from the pueblos of the Rio Grande. The second story, set well back from the first, has a porch well protected by a roof supported by projecting vigas, while the stepped-up end walls project as far as the porch and terminate in round chimneys above. It is reminiscent of the lines of houses on the mesa of Ácoma.

Until 1910 Cochití had a church of the same period and much the same character as those at Zía and Santa Ana, with a pierced belfry above the flat roof as at Zía but with porch and gallery above divided into three bays by two wooden columns supporting beams resting on carved wooden postcaps. At that time the Church of San Buenaventura was "remodeled" and it now has a corrugated-iron pitched roof with pointed steeple and an arcaded porch of plaster columns on metal lath, the middle arch wider and higher than those on either side—a perfect example of what Carlos Vierra calls "benevolent vandalism."

North of Cochití the high cliffs of the narrow White Rock Canyon make the river uninhabitable almost to San Ildefonso. Since roads are out of the question, it is necessary to return to Highway 85, continue to Santa Fe, and then drive north on Route 64.

The Tewa settlement of Tesuque, one of the smallest pueblos but the most visited because of its proximity to Santa Fe, seems singularly drab and lifeless. Perhaps it is the color of the adobe, a dull gray instead of the more frequent golden brown. The pueblo is accustomed to visitors, but there is not much to photograph. The chile peppers are as colorful as in other pueblos but the old mission church of San Diego, built about the same time as that at San Felipe and similar in appearance, crumbled and fell in the late nineteenth century and all that is left is the sacristy, remodeled into the present small chapel.

I had visited all of the pueblos except Pojoaque. A friend of mine, who is with the Indian Bureau, assured me that there was nothing to see there; and the books all say (if they mention it at all) that it is extinct. But since the government recognizes its limited autonomy (I later learned that it was reduced a few years ago to one survivor but that some of the emigrants have returned), I started out one Sunday and climbed the hill, where a dirt road leaps up from Highway 64, and drove a few hundred yards. My friend was right. The modern brick church merited no lengthy visit and any resemblance that the few scattered adobe houses had to an Indian pueblo was purely coincidental.

On my return to the highway an Indian who had been squatting in front of the first house when I had passed before came to the gate and accosted me. Fearful that I would be accused of trespassing, I explained that I was just out for a ride. It seemed that what he wanted, however, was a lift to the highway, which I gladly supplied. In Santa Fe later that day I mentioned the incident to my friend of the Indian Bureau and at his request described the Indian and the house in which he lived. "That," said my friend, "was the governor."

A picture came to my mind of the annual election in Pojoaque. Surely no elaborate caucus, no lengthy committee meetings in a smoke-filled kiva would be necessary to select a candidate from among the heads of five families. Perhaps they finally draw lots, like the Indians of Ácoma and Laguna. Whatever their method, the choice certainly is not made without due deliberation.

Some of the pueblos have complicated systems of internal organization to deal with religious and tribal problems, but the governor, elected annually, is their agent in civil affairs—which concern property and equities in material things—and is their representative in dealings with the United States Government. San Ildefonso is built around two large plazas. It has long been the custom to take turns in supplying the governor—one year he is chosen from the South Plaza, the next year from the North Plaza. Last year it was the turn of the North Plaza. But the people of the South Plaza decided to elect their own governor anyway. So there were two. The United States Government can recognize only one at a time. What to do? As far as I know, the controversy is not yet settled; and Fray Mariano de Jesus López is dead.

San Ildefonso is due west of Pojoaque and not far from the Rio Grande. It is almost reached on Highway 4, a good paved road which carries the traffic from modern Los Alamos to the Santa Fe highway. A dirt road leads a short distance to the north into the village. Though one of the smallest of the pueblos it is one of the most interesting, not for its church—a modern boxlike structure with a tin roof— but for its site, its plazas, its kiva, its people, and its pottery. The pueblo once had one of the finest of the Rio Grande churches, with a monastery adjacent; but it belongs to the past.

The plazas are large and open, especially the one on the north which is partially shaded by a giant cottonwood. Adobe houses of one and two stories surround the plazas, many of them shaded by porches the flat roofs of which are supported by wooden posts and long, carved postcaps. In the south plaza is a circular kiva which is probably the most photographed of all Indian kivas. The pueblo is noted for its fine black pottery which has become a source of prosperity, a prosperity which is reflected in the appearance and the attitude of the friendly, courteous, and progressive people. A receipt is even given for the photography fee! And it is fifty cents rather than the usual dollar.

On the west side of the Rio Grande, a little beyond San Ildefonso, Highway 30 leads north to Santa Clara. Two miles north of San Ildefonso can be seen the Black Mesa, a basaltic butte rich in Indian mythology and legend and often in the past their place of refuge. The Indians of Santa Clara claim to have come from the cliff dwellings of Puyé, which lies within their present reservation, after which they occupied several different sites near by before establishing their present pueblo about 1700. Like San Ildefonso, Santa Clara is noted for its black pottery.

When the eighteenth-century church of Santa Clara was in the process of being remodeled in 1909, the roof timbers having been removed, a storm arose and caused the walls to fall. In the present structure, built in 1918 but following faithfully the original design, only the old paneled doors remain from the earlier church. A new choir loft was built as recently as a year ago.

Nambé, on a side road north of Pojoaque, is almost as moribund and scattered as its neighboring settlement; but San Juan, five miles north of the Rio Grande bridge at Española, has been well known ever since Oñate appropriated the original village of the Indians and named the pueblo which the latter were forced to build on the east bank San Juan de los Caballeros. The pueblo, so close to present-day life and traffic, has lost much of its Indian character. Its eighteenth-century church has been replaced by an uninteresting brick structure and by a small stone chapel across the road.

The Indians of San Juan were the first to come in constant contact with the Spaniards and the first to be introduced by the Franciscan friars to the mysteries of Christianity. They were told the story of the Saviour and were taught to pray to the images of the Virgin Mary and Jesus for help in time of need. The need soon arose, it is said, for their growing corn turned yellow and dry and the water in the river was too low to be led to the irrigation ditches on their high side of the river, the Spaniards having taken the land on the side where the banks were low.

Accustomed to appealing to their gods to bring rain, the chiefs of the pueblo went to the little church which the friar had had them build and asked if they might borrow the blessed image of the child Jesus to carry around the fields, that he might see how dry they were and have pity on them and send rain. The friar agreed, and after they had paraded up and down among the rows of parched corn with the little figure they returned to their homes to await results. Soon a great cloudburst rose over the Jemez Mountains and swept up the Rio Grande Valley. It deluged the fields, beat the corn to the ground, and, what was worse, it was followed by hail which completely destroyed the crops.

After holding a council the Indians went again to the friar and asked for the loan of the Virgin Mary. When asked why they hesitated; but when the friar said he would let them take the figure only if they gave a good reason, they said; "Padre, we wish to carry the Mother Mary around so that she can see for herself what a mess her naughty little boy has made of our cornfields."

17

The High Road to Taos

THE DRIVE from San Juan to Taos on Highway 64, part of it along the Rio Grande Canyon, is a very pretty one. The road winds between the high walls of the narrowing canyon and then leaves the river to enter the wide valley of Taos, with that old Spanish town in the distance and the high mountains to the north as a backdrop for the scene. The drive is not at all difficult for the road is paved all the way.

But there is another road. It is longer and much poorer—unpaved, narrow, steep, winding, and slippery when there is snow—but infinitely more interesting scenically, historically, socially, and architecturally. This is the High Road (name unofficial—the maps and guidebooks call it 76, 75, and 3). It begins a few miles south of San Juan and leads almost immediately from New Mexico into Old. There are no cities; there are no towns of more than a few hundred people. There are no haciendas, no long, rambling houses of *ricos*, no peons—some of them are there, though they are no longer peons but independent property owners and *Penitentes*.

After winding through some ten miles of farming country the road leaves the valley of the Rio Grande and climbs up the mountain ridges, up and over them into high valleys a hundred years or more away from the world. In each of the valleys is a village, with a muddy plaza and an old church facing it, with horses roaming around at will and clusters of small adobe houses, some of them with exterior mural decorations. Each house has a beehive-shaped adobe oven outside the door and in the fall scarlet strings of drying chile adorn the walls.

Spreading out from the houses to fill the small valley are the fields where the *paisanos* harvest their crops by hand, goats or horses stamping out the grain as they did a hundred years ago. Streams, cold and clear, rush down from the mountains to water the valley and keep the village alive, and an aqueduct carved out of huge logs rests on timbered trestles to cross narrow gorges and bring water to a pool where the people come and get it. The villages have names as musical as the clear, cold streams which rush down into them: Córdova, Truchas, Trampas, Penasco.

Each valley—and its village—is a little world in itself, entirely surrounded by a wilderness unbroken except for the tortuous dirt road, dusty or muddy depending on whether or not it has snowed. If it has not, the surroundings are a mounting sea of deep-green waves; when it has, the wooded wilderness becomes, as far as the eye can see in any direction, a rising and falling tier upon tier of Christmas trees brilliantly decorated in the sparkling sunlight.

When the Spaniards settled New Mexico the *ricos*, with extensive grants of land, brought with them a following of humbler folk. Some of them were Indians from Mexico, Tlaxcalans and Aztecs; some were mestizos, of mixed Indian and Spanish blood; and they included soldiers, artisans, and peasants. Many of them, after arrival, doubtless intermarried with Navahos and Apaches, to produce a varied mixture. Some of them took small homesteads in the less desirable locations which had not been gobbled up by the *ricos;* others came as servants and remained bound in peonage for generations. Some of the latter group, who could pay their debts and thus buy their freedom, took up land of their own, worked it, and achieved a degree of independence.

The rich lands of the valley near Albuquerque were largely in the hands of "the right people"; Santa Fe was the military and social center; and north of the capital and along the upper part of the river the Pueblo Indians had their grants of land. So these people of mixed blood, small homesteaders gradually joined by peons who had become free, took to the lands to the north farther away from the Rio Grande and in the high valleys among the foothills of the Sangre de Cristo Mountains. There they gained a foothold and still live— close to the soil. The mighty *ricos* have fallen but the meek have clung to the earth. In the high valleys they live on it, till it, water it, harvest the crops that grow on it, plant crosses in it, and eventually are buried in it. New Spain in New Mexico has all but vanished but Old Mexico remains—on the High Road to Taos.

These men of mixed blood took with them, into their high valleys, their own interpretation of religion—not an entirely new one, for its practices are ages old, but a curious folk-survival in a land quite foreign to anything like it. The High Road is the heart of the Penitente country. The tiny chapel of the Penitent Brothers dots the countryside throughout; the *calvario* can be seen outlined against the sky on the crest of a hill; and in each village there is a *morada* which, like the kiva of the Pueblo Indians, is the headquarters of the brothers and their secret meeting place. The cross and the whip are still used as instruments of penance though the severity of the imposition has been greatly modified, at least in so far as the eyes of outsiders are concerned. But what goes on inside the secret chamber of the morada no outsider knows.

During those dark days after the Franciscan pioneers had left, and before the reforms of Bishop Lamy, the priesthood had become corrupt. For baptisms, weddings, and funerals the poor man was taxed all that he had. The government took a heavy toll, the trader who brought him goods took a heavy profit, and if there was anything left the Church took the rest. He could not dispense with the government, but in things material he stayed close to his land, requiring little from the trader, and in matters spiritual he dispensed with the priest. The land was his refuge from material masters and the society of the Penitent Brothers became his refuge from spiritual persecution. Still a devout Catholic in his own mind, he developed an earthly interpretation of the Christian religion, brutally realistic in its expression. The Cross was his symbol and became the object of fanatical rites.

There was precedent for his expression of devotion to the Saviour and His sufferings. The flagellant sect, stemming from the Third Order of Franciscans, had been brought into New Mexico with Oñate from New Spain, where it never amounted to much; but in the isolated wilderness of the north, out of touch with the world and lonely, its practices were seized upon and carried to extremes. Nowhere else in the New World was actual crucifixion ever practiced.

Public penance had long been banned by papal bulls, and when New Mexico became a bishopric under Bishop Lamy the Roman

Catholic Church attempted to suppress the Penitentes; but in the remote communities they still cling to their rites—a primitive worship of death in the sacrifice of blood. Though they are said to have secret rites on saints' days, it is during Lent that they are chiefly active as penitents, and during Holy Week they march, to the weird, shrill screech of the flute, dragging heavy crosses to their Calvary, chanting in unison and flogging their bare backs with whips of braided yucca fibre as they march.

Most of the rest of the time the only reminder of this fanaticism will be a little woman swathed in black *rebozo* kneeling at the foot of a great wooden cross planted among the stones at the top of a barren hill.

Only about a mile from Highway 64 is the old Spanish town of Santa Cruz. For more than three hundred years it was on the main road between Santa Fe and Taos, but the new paved highway bypassed it and left it to sleep in the country. Spanish colonists who came with Oñate established a settlement there but it was not until 1695, after the Pueblo Revolt, when sixty families of colonists from Zacatecas were given grants and settled there, that it was made a *villa*, the second in New Mexico. Long outgrown by Santa Fe and Albuquerque, its official name was larger than the city ever became. It was *La Villa Nueva de Santa Cruz de los Españoles Mexicanos del Rey Nuestro Señor Don Carlos Segundo.*

A large cruciform church was begun in 1733 and it now dominates the plaza of the sleepy Spanish-Mexican town. The church formerly had a flat dirt roof, but because of damage done by heavy rains the present steep, gabled roof was superimposed about 1900. The simple front is flanked by square towers with buttressed bases and plain belfries with pyramidal roofs. The interior, with a flat ceiling of vigas and carved corbels, contains many old paintings, religious ornaments and vestments, and a particularly fine wood carving of Saint Francis. On either side of the altar there is a chapel, one dedicated to Our Lady of Carmel and the other to Saint Francis. Interestingly enough, a morada of the Penitentes is near by.

The road to the east (now paved for about ten miles) follows the Santa Cruz Valley and its rocky stream through cornfields and orchards, gardens of beans and melons, and villages of a dozen little adobe houses drowsing under rustling cottonwoods. Onions and corn lie drying on the flat roofs and strips of jerked meat hang from lines stretched across the *placitas*. Tiny chapels dot the roadside and here and there a cross rises out of a heap of stones to mark the place where a funeral procession has stopped to rest.

Eight miles from Santa Cruz is the town of Chimayo, built on the site of an Indian pueblo and long famous for its weaving. A bumpy, narrow road crosses ditches and winds among the scattered adobe houses, lined with hedges and shaded by cottonwoods, to the tiny *Santuario de Chimayo*, so well hidden behind two giant cottonwoods that it is almost sure to be passed by at first.

The sanctuary was built as a private chapel in 1816 by a pious *paisano*, Bernardo Abeyta, who had prospered, and who took that means of offering thanks for his good fortune. It remained in possession of his family until 1929, when it was purchased by the Roman Catholic Diocese of New Mexico. The sand on which it is built, some of it available through a hole in the pavement of a side room, is thought to have miraculous curative powers and pilgrims come from afar to worship at this New Mexican Lourdes.

Quite unprepossessing on the exterior, the little church has one of the loveliest settings in New Mexico and the interior has a great deal of primitive charm. Behind the towering cottonwoods an adobe-walled churchyard with a large cross in the center is entered through a wooden-grilled gate. The formerly flat-roofed façade and twin towers have now been protected by peaked roofs and between the towers is a shallow gallery with wooden posts supporting the roof. Dazzling with rich colors, the interior is a museum of primitive iconographic art. Beneath the round vigas of the ceiling, supported at the ends by carved corbels, beskirted, doll-like figures of saints in polychrome, wearing tin crowns and baby shoes—one of them holding an enormous flower—stand amidst curtained surroundings of similar richness of color and interest to form side altars. The reredos is richly decorated with painted conventional designs and religious symbols and in front of the altar is a rail with carved and painted balusters. Many flickering candles in pierced candelabra illuminate the interior.

On leaving Chimayo and the pavement the road begins to climb, and after about four miles a precipitous and narrow rocky trail leads past a large cross and morada of the Penitentes down to the right into Córdova. The one rough and twisting street is lined with adobe houses with doorways of pink and blue and yellow, some of them perched on the very edge of the steep hill which slopes down to the mountain stream. Several sharp turns lead to the Church of San Antonio de Padua, a small square structure with an arched doorway and a cubical belfry above. The bier is kept conveniently near the door, for there is no room in Córdova for a hearse.

The side road climbs as steeply back to 76, past wooden crosses planted among the rocks and bearing framed photographs of the departed ones. Once regained, the main road balances delicately on a hogback trying its unlevel best to keep from spilling over the sides. From the narrow ridge can be seen the whole panorama of the upper Rio Grande and, beyond, the Jemez Mountains and farther to the south the Sandías—almost lost on the sky line—all belonging to a world that is being left behind. Closer, on the right, the jagged Truchas peaks rise above a dense fringe of trees a full mile higher than our road only to drop into a bottomless sea of green or white. After many dips and climbs along the ridge the road reaches the village of Truchas, so sudden and startling as to be almost unbelievable.

Truchas is on the maps of New Mexico and on New Mexico Route 76, but it belongs in Norway, Finland, or perhaps Siberia. Its one street twists along the top of a narrow ridge which spills into a forested wilderness on either side. Steep-roofed log houses line the road, huge piles of wood banked up at their sides like bulwarks built to protect them.

In most Mexican villages the church faces the plaza in the center and the morada stands apart and apparently deserted, but in Truchas, with its sometimes arcticlike isolation, the morada is almost as large as the church and has a bell tower.

Across mountain ridges and high valleys the sky-line drive (described by the guidebook as being "safer as a pack trip") continues to Las Trampas, meaning "the traps" but known as the "Place of the Early Settlers." The village with its cluster of flat-roofed mud houses surrounding a plaza and an old church, completely hemmed in by high wooded mountains, seems quite out of this world. Yet there is a Spanish church there almost two hundred years old, in character much like the churches in the Keres pueblos of the Rio Grande.

Built of adobe, the Church of Santo Tomás Del Rio de las Trampas has walls four feet thick and thirty-four feet high. A gallery crosses the recessed front and from it, in days gone by, the choir sang while the procession moved outside around the plaza. At one time the church had bell towers, presumably much like those of the church at San Felipe. An old photograph shows a small wooden belfry on the remains of one while the stump of the other projects only a little above the roof; but today they have been cut down to approximately the level of the flat roof.

The church once had two bells, both said to have contained gold and silver. One, because of its soft tone, was called Gracia and was rung for Mass and for the deaths of infants; the other, Refugio, with a lower tone, was rung for the deaths of adults and for Masses for the Dead. Refugio was stolen a few years ago, so now Gracia is used for all occasions. Due to the deletion of the bell towers, Gracia hangs in front of the church from a beam supporting the gallery.

The interior has the typical flat ceiling supported by wooden vigas and corbels, old paintings adorn the reredos and side walls, and a wooden lattice railing serves as an altar rail. Of particular note are the fine wood carvings of the reredos and the pulpit.

For some unaccountable reason the tradition grew up that the church, first known as The Church of the Twelve Apostles and later as San José, is more than three hundred and fifty years old, thus antedating the settlement of New Mexico by Oñate, a tradition even copied on modern maps though some of them have toned it down to three hundred years. It was probably built about the middle of the eighteenth century; the Historic Building Survey gives its date as 1760.

Unlike the situation at Truchas, the Penitentes of Las Trampas have no morada competing with the church; they have simply absorbed the church. Their secret chambers are built onto the rear of the building itself and in the sacristy, just to the right of the entrance door, stands the death cart which is trundled in the Holy Week processions. In the crude two-wheeled cart, its three-foot wheels hewn from solid logs, sits a carved skeleton draped in black, a bow and arrow poised in her bony fingers. Doña Sebastiana, as the figure is called, is said to have once discharged the arrow and pierced the heart of an unrepentant sinner.

In a high valley of its own, reached by a branch road from Penasco, Picurís is the only remaining Indian pueblo in a mountainous land of little Mexicos. Once one of the most powerful and hostile of the Indian pueblos, it is now the smallest of all except Pojoaque. First visited by members of the Coronado expedition, it was assigned as a mission by Oñate in 1598 to Fray Francisco de Zamora. Some time after 1620 a church was begun there by Fray Martín de Arvide, who was later murdered on his way to Zuñi as a missionary. Father Benavides wrote in 1630 that there were about two thousand Indian converts at Picurís, the people of which pueblo he describes as being the most savage in the province.

At the time of the Pueblo Revolt, which had its beginning in the northern pueblos, Picurís was particularly active and its governor, Luís Tupatu, succeeded Popé as leader. But when in 1692 de Vargas reached northern New Mexico, Tupatu, mounted on a fine horse and in full Spanish costume, appeared at the governor's palace in Santa Fe and offered his allegiance to the conqueror.

Shortly afterward the Church of San Lorenzo de Picurís was begun. It has a walled forecourt with a stepped gateway surmounted by a cross. On the front of the church, at the center line, is a simple, square opening for a bell; but the former stepped gable, which was the pierced belfry, and the flat roof have given way to a pitched roof with a small wooden cupola above.

This forlorn and barren church and a few scattered, small square houses of puddled adobe, which the Indians occupy when they are not tending their goats, are all that remain of the once populous and powerful pueblo. In its setting, though not its architecture, the tiny hamlet is reminiscent of a Swiss mountain village.

Through Penasco, a string of several surviving eighteenth-century settlements with a church belfry crowned by a bulbous dome such as one might expect to see in Russia, the High Road continues, joining Route 3 to climb up through the woods onto Government Hill. After winding up and over it follows the heavily-wooded curves of the Rito Grande del Rancho and then the Rio Chiquito for some twelve miles and finally comes down to earth at Ranchos de Taos.

Taos (it rhymes with house, not chaos) is divided into three parts, or rather one might better say that there are three Taoses: Ranchos de Taos, an old Indian farming center; Don Fernando de Taos, the Spanish town and modern art center, usually called simply Taos; and San Gerónimo de Taos, the Indian pueblo.

Ranchos de Taos is the first, approaching from the south. It is a peaceful, quiet village with a fine view of the broad valley and its background of rugged peaks. There is a large dirt plaza, with one-story adobe houses facing it, and a small Penitente chapel; but of greatest interest is the fat, buttressed Church of Saint Francis of Assisi. Facing the plaza, this church turns its rear to the highway, a view that is probably photographed more than the hindside of any church except L'Abside de Notre Dame de Paris. With a wide buttress against the apse and beehive-curved buttresses at the corners of the transepts, it is a fascinating study in planes and in lights and shadows.

The church was built at some time in the early eighteenth century but, falling into disuse, it was rebuilt about 1772. The white-stuccoed adobe building, one hundred and twenty feet long, has exceptionally massive walls and a front enclosed by a forecourt with almost equally thick adobe walls, rounded on top. Two wide buttresses on the front rise the full width of the twin bell towers and flank an arched entrance portal with surface tracery and double paneled doors. On the interior the vigas of the ceiling are unusually close together and rest on elaborate double corbels. The choir loft still has the original dirt floor but the main floor of the church, to make the upkeep easier for the venerable sexton-guide, has new flooring of wood. The large carved reredos, partitioned into panels, contains several old paintings.

In its rugged simplicity, its irregular yet soft contours, and its play of light and shadow the Ranchos de Taos church is one of the finest examples of the Spanish-Pueblo style.

Four miles to the north, over the sage-covered plain, lies the historic little city and popular artists' center of Don Fernando de Taos. The town's harassed postmaster in the 1880's requested that the prefix be omitted and it has been since, but the longer name—now little used—remains officially on the books.

Long a market center, Taos is still the meeting place of the three distinct cultures of the Southwest. During all of the Spanish regime its annual fair attracted Indians from the pueblos and from the plains, traders from Mexico, and *hacendados* and villagers from all the surrounding territory. The plaza is still the center of life in the little town. Now well filled with trees, it is lined on three sides with flat-roofed stores, a nondescript collection from various periods; yet the *portales*, though recent, give the square the appearance of New or Old Spain. Indians wrapped in cotton blankets, farmers in broad-brimmed black hats, bewhiskered artists carrying easels, and visitors from the East affecting the dress of the West, pass by under the *portales*, each thinking the other a little queer.

To the north rows of huge cottonwoods line the road as it leaves the town, headed for the Indian pueblo of Taos two and a half miles distant. Past gardens and fields where buffaloes graze the road leads directly to the gate, for Taos is still a walled town. Just inside the gate, to the left, are the ruins of the old mission built in 1704 and destroyed during the Mexican War in 1847, when it was used as a fortress by the Mexicans and their Indian allies. Remains of twin towers still stand and the low ruins of thick adobe walls, which once enclosed the nave, now contain a cemetery. A freshly-painted little white cross with the date 1949 shows that it is still in use.

Not far away is the small adobe mission which was built about 1848, supposedly on the site of the original church built by Fray Pedro Miranda in 1617 and destroyed at the time of the Pueblo Revolt. Of whitewashed adobe, the church has a stepped gateway to the forecourt and a similarly-stepped false gable on the façade above a square opening for a bell. A row of projecting vigas decorates the side walls. Visitors are not invited inside.

Scattered single houses now extend around part of the plaza on both sides of the entrance, *tapestes* (platforms) supported by poles alongside them for the storage of corn, alfalfa, and firewood. Beehive ovens are clustered about near the houses and the ends of tall ladders, projecting up from bound circles of poles, betray the presence of underground kivas.

But the most distinctive features of the pueblo are the two large, multistoried, terraced community houses facing each other across the creek which flows through the middle of the large central plaza, the finest examples in the Southwest of a survival of the ancient community-house builders. At either end of the plaza a bridge of hand-hewn pine logs connects the two parts of the village.

The people of Taos are quite conscious of their unique standing among the pueblos and jealously guard against innovations. It is only within the last comparatively few years that any single-family dwellings have been permitted. Their houses now have doors and windows but the old ladders are still used since the great community houses have no inside stairways. Though prosperous and in some ways progressive, the people cling to their old customs, to ancient ways and thoughts, to old ceremonies, and to old beliefs. Recently the chief men of the pueblo came to the conclusion that the road leading there should be paved and took the question up with the United States

Government authorities. Agreed; but the road was too narrow; it would have to be widened first. Could not be done; that would interfere with the sacred plums.

From Isleta on the Rio Grande north to Taos is one hundred and fifty miles. There is probably no single stretch of country anywhere, of similar length or even much greater length, that is more thoroughly steeped in history, more diversified in its people, its thought, and its religion, more fascinating in its villages, more progressive in its commercial capital, or quainter in its political capital, the oldest in the United States.

The green valley made by that river, with its tributaries, is very abruptly bounded on either side by arid stretches; but within the limits of that valley three very different kinds of people have lived and built and are still doing so. The three kinds refer only to races or nationalities; blends and developments make the number much greater.

Penitentes rub elbows (when they cannot avoid it) with wealthy ranchers; artists paint Indians who live in the same kind of houses they lived in five hundred years ago; and atomic-age scientists discuss modern politics with businessmen in houses copied from those Indians, modified some by the Spaniards who in turn had been influenced by the Moors.

The Spaniards brought their art by way of Mexico and in a perfectly natural way it merged into the style of the Pueblo Indians, who carried out the feeling of their own art under Spanish direction and produced a blend that did credit to both. There is not a similar situation anywhere else in the country.

For more than three hundred years the Rain Dance and High Mass have been celebrated side by side with neither supplanting the other, and yet they are no nearer a blend than the practice of self-flagellation and the study of nuclear physics which go on in the same mountains.

But in artistic expression and especially in architecture the white people have had to lean on the Indians. Small wonder the Pueblos look upon the world with complacence. The Zuñis thought their villages the center of it. Those Pueblos Indians who lived between Isleta and Taos, especially those of the latter pueblo who dwell in five-story community houses beneath the high mountains, had an even better right to think the upper Rio Grande the center—until some of them, especially those of the former pueblo, driven out by their linguistic cousins of Taos, were forced to find another place along the same river, far to the south.

PART FOUR: *TEJAS*

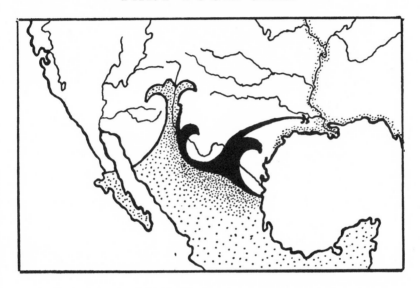

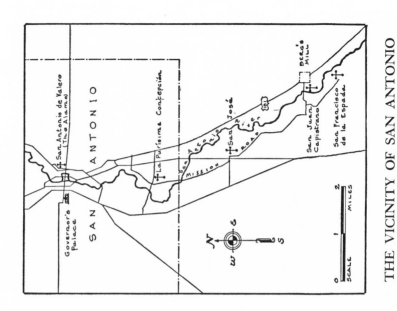

THE VICINITY OF SAN ANTONIO

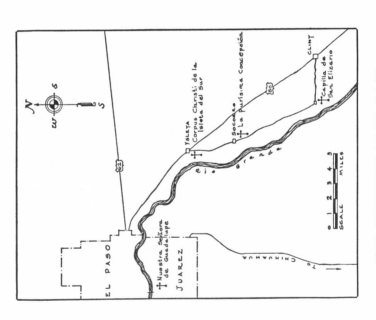

THE VICINITY OF EL PASO

PART FOUR

18

The Pass of the North

EL PASO DEL NORTE the Spaniards called it, because it was the lowest natural pass in that land of deserts and mountains through which to reach the new northern valley extending narrowly along the river in the midst of arid wastes. Ahead lay the dread Jornada del Muerto, before the fertile valley could be reached, and behind—far behind—lay civilization.

Through the Pass went the mission supply train en route from Mexico City to Santa Fe by way of Chihuahua. The caravan must have stopped there to camp and to rest on its long journey, every third year, to the north. There is no record, however, of any permanent settlement before 1659, at which time Fray García de Zuñiga established a mission there in an attempt to convert the native Mansos of the vicinity. The church was completed in 1668 and dedicated by Fray Juan Talaban to Nuestra Señora de Guadalupe.

In the present city of Juarez, on the Mexican side of the river, the church still stands, half hidden now by a new, larger church under construction. Streets lead from the International Bridge past souvenir shops, bars, cabarets, night clubs, and restaurants to the main plaza of the city, which the church faces. Surrounded by a stone wall on three sides, the entrance to the church is reached by a flight of steps leading directly up to a small forecourt which formerly served as a cemetery.

The walls are thick, of adobe bricks plastered inside and out. The one square bell tower, on the left, is in two arched stories with a small octagonal lantern and dome on top crowned by a large cross.

Three high, recessed arches occupy the façade, with a single arched entrance and circular window above on the center and a niche containing a statue in the recessed space on either side. A false pediment above supports a small, square cupola and clock, probably a later addition. The flat roof, recently repaired with modern materials, was formerly covered with more than three feet of earth.

The black wooden vigas of the ceiling are intricately carved and are supported at the ends by corbels, also carved. Resting on the beams are small, round, polished saplings placed in a herringbone pattern. The interior shows its age, especially since it has been opened up at one side to connect with the new church, the only innovation being pews which now take the place of serapes, cushions, and small stools which each worshiper formerly furnished for his own comfort.

On Sundays the plaza, the churches, both the old and the new, and the little churchyard are crowded with people. Although part of the same mission movement, and formerly part of Nuevo México, the little old church, with its environs teeming with Mexicans in the border city of today, is a far cry from the deserted and locked Indian missions of far-off New Mexico.

In 1680 El Paso del Norte had its first boom, but it was a boom resulting from the misfortunes of others. In September of that year a thousand or more Spaniards came straggling down to the river at the Pass, half starved and ragged and many of them wounded. They were the remnants of the Spanish colony at Santa Fe, driven out of the northern country by the revolt of the Indians.

Father Ayeta's caravan of supplies, arriving at the Pass about the same time, was a godsend to the refugees. From the procurador's stores they were fed corn and beef which had been intended for the friars in the northern missions, and they managed to subsist until Ayeta could return from another trip to Mexico City with additional supplies and reinforcements. Shortly after that time a presidio was established near the Guadalupe Mission to serve also as a supply station for the reconquest and protection of New Mexico.

With Governor Otermín and his refugees from the north came many friendly Indians escaping from the conspirators. Among them were a large number of Indians from the pueblo of Isleta who had refused to join the revolt. Some of them, who were too old or too ill to continue the journey to El Paso, were left behind—it is said—at a spot near Las Cruces, where they founded the little village of Tortugas. Others continued to the Pass and were established in a number of pueblos along the Rio Grande to the southeast.

Among these pueblos was Isleta del Sur, named by the Tiwa Indians for their pueblo on the upper Rio Grande. The Mission of Corpus Christi de la Isleta del Sur was built, of adobe, the first mission in what is now the state of Texas, and stood until it was destroyed by a fire in 1907. The church has been rebuilt just as it originally stood, it is said, and is known locally as the Church of Our Lady of Carmel.

The façade has a single arched entrance with a circular window above and is crowned with a curved, pedimented gable in character somewhat like that of the later and larger church of the Mission San Luís Rey in California. A niche in the gable contains a carved statue. Its single tower, on the right, terminates in a tall and rather overpowering aluminum-covered dome surmounted by a large cross. The interior, with a flat ceiling of beams supported by corbels, is richly colored.

On the feast days of saints the missionyard is still the scene of ceremonies which date back to the time of the Tiwa pueblos. Here the Pueblo Indians still perform the pagan dances in the costumes of their forefathers. Among the dancers are descendants of the people of Quarai, who were forced by the Apaches to abandon their village and its beautiful stone mission even before the Pueblo Revolt. The town of Ysleta (usually spelled with a y; the mission with an i), twelve miles southeast of the modern city of El Paso on U.S. 80, is the oldest in the state and still has squat, flat-roofed, whitewashed, old adobe houses among more modern buildings.

A farm road between the highway and the Rio Grande continues to the south among gardens and cottonfields made possible by irrigation from the river. In their midst, three miles south of Ysleta, is the scattered little village of Socorro with its wide and squatty mission church of La Purísima Concepción. The present building is the fourth to be erected since the founding of the mission in 1683. The first was abandoned because of trouble with the native Indians and the second was destroyed by a flood. The present church was built from the ruins of an earlier one built in the early part of the nineteenth century and contains the same carved beams.

The white façade is wide and low, stepped up to a high and square pierced belfry. Proudest possession of the church is an old wood-carved, polychromed statue of Saint Michael. According to tradition the figure was intended for a New Mexico mission but the cart in which it was being transported became stuck in the mud in Socorro. When three yoke of oxen were unable to move it, the people of Socorro bought it and made Saint Michael their patron saint.

The road continues south to San Elizario, which can also be reached directly from Highway 80 by taking a side road at Clint and driving three miles through cottonfields. This sleepy village, originally a presidio town with a chapel rather than a mission settlement, was established soon after 1680. The site has been changed several times because of floods, the first site having been on the Mexican side of the Rio Grande.

The present Capilla de San Elizario is the fourth to be erected, in about 1877, and it much more closely resembles the California mission churches than those of New Mexico. Facing the old plaza and a few squat adobe houses, it is the largest church of the El Paso group. A gracefully curved, pierced belfry containing two bells, one of them said to be from the original chapel, rises above a white-walled façade divided into three bays by buttresses built against it. The three-aisled interior is divided longitudinally into four bays, with square wooden columns supporting round arches and a flat ceiling painted in pastel colors.

This section of the middle Rio Grande is still a bit of old Mexico augmented by descendants of the Tiwa Indians from the pueblos of New Mexico. Except for the Guadalupe church in old El Paso del Norte (the name of which was changed in the last century to honor the Mexican patriot Benito Juárez) the churches are recent replacements, but much of the old character of the sleepy villages has been retained. A little woman in black-lace mantilla may be sweeping rice from the steps of the San Elizario Chapel after a wedding and the quaint low church at Socorro may be filled to overflowing with Mexicans in white pajama suits and Indians in blue jeans kneeling in the doorway and in the dust outside.

The quiet stretch of fertile farmlands and old villages is a striking contrast to modern, industrial El Paso (a mere upstart, founded in the latter half of the nineteenth century) with its tall office buildings and smelters. On approaching from the east the contrast is even greater and is a double one. After mile upon mile of arid plateau suddenly, almost unbelievably, the gardens and farms of the irrigated valley appear—great fields of cotton and of alfalfa and orchards and vineyards—large rambling ranch houses rising among them. And then—for a few miles along the Rio Grande—a little world of two hundred and fifty years ago.

El Paso del Norte grew only slowly during the Spanish regime. It was principally a presidio, with a mission; a string of Indian settlements to the south along the river, each with its mission; and a brief stopping place on the journey to Albuquerque and Santa Fe. Chihuahua remained the metropolis of the north. Far to the northwest from Mexico City a look at the road map will show that it is much more closely linked to El Paso and the north than it is to any of the rest of Mexico. Today it is an easy drive from El Paso; a long and difficult one from anywhere else in Mexico. All during the Spanish period it was the northern receiving station for all goods shipped from abroad and from the Mexican capital. Furnishings and objects of art for the northern missions were shipped from Spain to Vera Cruz and were joined at Mexico City with other riches and with commodities landed at Acapulco from the Orient, thence to be carried by mule trains and oxcarts to Chihuahua.

Every year there was a fair: traders came from New Mexico with buffalo hides, furs, buckskin, blankets, salt, turquoise, and piñon nuts and returned with imported furniture, paintings, silks, gold-framed mirrors, jewelry, and trappings for their horses. As a trading center Chihuahua thrived. It was for many years the richest city in northern Mexico. As such it was fitting that it should have the finest church in the north. So Chihuahua built it; and it was. It still is.

The parochial church (raised to the rank of cathedral in 1891) was begun in 1717 and completed in 1789. It was dedicated to San Francisco, the patron saint of the city—and fittingly enough too, for Saint Francis was also the patron saint of most of the Southwest, with which Chihuahua did business.

Of light-brown stone, the Cathedral has a richly-ornamented façade with statues placed in niches between the highly-decorated baroque columns. A wealth of carving fills the spaces around the single arched opening and the octagonal window above. Tall twin towers rise above plain bases in three stories of columns and arches. An octagonal lantern with twisted columns crowns the dome. The side entrances are even more richly carved than the front.

Representative of the height of baroque wealth in Mexico, it is an edifice of which any American city would be proud. Isolated as

Chihuahua is from the rest of Mexico and tied in through commerce and transportation with El Paso, it belongs physically, even though not politically or spiritually, with the Southwest rather than with its mother country. The cathedral is a beautiful building. Let's claim it for the Southwest.

19

San Antonio de Valero

TEXAS STARTED in the extreme west, an accident of fate for which the Pueblo Indians were responsible. Its next move was in the extreme east, a planned fate which can be laid at the feet of the French.

By the time of the Pueblo Revolt and the subsequent occupation of the middle Rio Grande (then a part of New Mexico) both England and France had become established in North America. England had planted colonies along the Atlantic seaboard from New England to Florida; and with the West Indies as a base English buccaneers were marauding the Spanish towns along the coast of Mexico. The French were an even more immediate menace. In addition to competing with their English rivals for Spanish plunder along the Gulf, they were pushing farther and farther west from the North Atlantic. By way of the Saint Lawrence and the Ottawa Rivers they had penetrated the northern lakes; and in 1673 Joliet and Marquette had descended the Mississippi as far as the Arkansas. When the news spread there was renewed hope of controlling that river and the trade routes to China, still believed to be reached from the north and west.

Among those whose imagination was stirred was Robert Cavalier, Sieur de La Salle, a wealthy and ambitious Frenchman who had recently arrived in Canada. Several years later, with a patent from the French king, La Salle reached the mouth of the Mississippi and claimed the territory along its course for France. After returning to France La Salle sailed once more, headed this time directly for the mouth of the Mississippi to establish a colony. His little fleet missed the mouth of the river, one of the ships was captured by Spaniards, and another was wrecked on trying to land in Matagorda Bay on the Texas coast. This was early in 1685. A fort was built of ship's planks and called Fort Saint Louis, a half-dozen huts clustering about it within a rude stockade. Within two years La Salle had been slain by some of his own men and, except for two or three men and some children taken by the Indians, the whole colony had perished.

News of La Salle's expedition was viewed with alarm not only in Spain but all along the Spanish frontier from Cuba to Chihuahua. Accordingly Alonso de León was sent out from Monterrey to find and destroy the French colony which threatened the borders of New Spain. It was not until his third such expedition, in 1689, that de León learned the fate of the colony. His report, together with the information that the Indians in Texas were friendly, the soil fertile, and the climate excellent, roused the officials of New Spain to action. The following year de León set out again with a hundred soldiers, accompanied by Father Damien Massanet and two other Franciscan friars. Pausing long enough on the way to set fire to La Salle's fort, they continued to a village of the Asinai, or Texas, Indians near the Neches River in eastern Texas. There on May 25, 1690, before the eyes of the astonished natives, they raised the Spanish flag and founded the Mission of San Francisco de los Tejas. De León and his company then departed, leaving the three Franciscans and three soldiers to hold the first Spanish outpost in east Texas.

The following year the little garrison was increased to nine, in spite of protests on the part of Massanet, who did not want a presidio established. But that small force could not combat the increasing hostility of the Indians, and on October 25, 1693, Massanet set fire to that first Spanish mission and fled. For three months the little band marched until finally, weary and hungry, it reached the Rio Grande. For almost a generation Texas remained unoccupied.

In the meantime a Bourbon king on the Spanish throne permitted the occupation of Louisiana by the French, and Spain's colonies on the Gulf Coast were split in two. One who looked with anxiety at the French encroachments was Father Francisco Hidalgo, who had been with Massanet in Texas. Anxious to return to the scene of his endeavors there but not permitted by his superior to do so, he conceived a scheme to open up the field again. Writing to the French priests in Louisiana, he begged them to pacify the hostile tribes in that country. His letter finally came into the hands of the French governor Cadillac who, anxious to open trade with Mexico, forthwith dispatched an envoy to establish a post at Natchitoches on the Red River and then to continue to Hidalgo's mission at San Juan on the Rio Grande, forty miles below Eagle Pass, to consult with the friar.

Father Hidalgo's scheme worked. With this new menace the viceroy of Mexico lost no time in ordering new missions to be founded in Texas, protected this time by strong garrisons. In April of 1716 a colony crossed the Rio Grande, including soldiers, a thousand head of cattle, sheep, and goats, and equipment for missions, farms, and a garrison. Accompanying the group were nine friars including Father Hidalgo.

A garrison was erected near the Neches River and four missions were built in the vicinity, among them the Mission of Nuestra Señora de Guadalupe where the town of Nacogdoches now stands. Shortly afterward a mission was built at Los Adaes in what is now Louisiana (near Robeline), only fifteen miles from the French outpost of Natchitoches.

There followed a turbulent period during which the garrisons and the missions in east Texas were abandoned and then reoccupied until the Spaniards finally settled down to a brief period of reasonably amicable relations with the French, when they were not kept busy battling Apaches and Comanches. But the missions of east Texas were never a success. The Indians refused to be gathered into compact communities and would not tolerate the rigid discipline of the friars. As for the Apaches and Comanches, they never found time to be converted.

The missions that were built were of wood, for lack of suitable stone, and nothing remains in the way of monuments to the work of those early friars. Nacogdoches was the center and still boasts of being the second-oldest town in Texas. It is a most attractive little city but any physical reminders of its part in history as a Spanish outpost have disappeared. It is a city of the South.

In the meantime the need of a base on the route between the settlements on the Rio Grande and the eastern outposts inspired the Spaniards to establish a colony some hundred and twenty miles west and north of the ruins of La Salle's Fort Saint Louis. They chose a spot where a little spring-fed river with grassy banks meandered along in irregular bends and where huge cottonwood trees gave shade.

Cabeza de Vaca must have crossed that stream on his way to the Rio Grande. More than a hundred and fifty years later, in 1691, Father Massanet with an escort of fifty soldiers set up a cross there and erected an arbor of cottonwood bows under which he said Mass and christened the place San Antonio in honor of the Franciscan friar Saint Anthony of Padua.

In March of 1718 Don Martín de Alarcón, captain-general and governor of the province of Texas, and Fray Antonio de San Buenaventura Olivares, after marching through the wilderness from the Rio Grande, reached the "site called San Antonio." With them came seventy-two settlers, soldiers, and friars, driving before them two hundred cows, two hundred oxen, more than five hundred horses, and one thousand sheep.

On the first day of May, Father Olivares founded the Mission of San Antonio de Valero, building a hut to serve as a temporary mission structure. A few days later Governor Alarcón founded the Villa de Bejar (later spelled Bexar and pronounced "bear"), a little less than half a mile to the west, and left a guard of soldiers.

Almost from its founding San Antonio was a combination or aggregation of mission, presidio, and villa. Calls went out for settlers and in 1731 a number of families of colonists from the Canary Islands were landed at Vera Cruz, from where they made the long and wearisome march overland. The settlement (or villa) of San Fernando was established for them, adjacent to the presidio (of Bejar) and across the stream from the Mission San Antonio de Valero. Almost immediately the settlers began to dig *acequias* to water their fields.

Although the mission was convenient to the new settlement, the colonists demanded a parish church of their own and soon afterward it was begun, with the laying of the cornerstone in 1738. Part of it still remains, in the Cathedral of San Fernando, built in the latter part of the nineteenth century and facing the Main Plaza, known in the early days as the Plaza de las Islas for the island settlers.

The Military Plaza, then known as the Plaza de Armas, was the center of the presidio, with the barracks of the soldiers facing it on the north side. It served also as a center of protection for the settlers who lived around the near-by Main Plaza in flat-roofed adobe buildings which could be used as forts in case of attack by Indians. The parish church occupied part of the space between the two plazas.

On the opposite side of the Military Plaza stands the Governor's Palace, with the Hapsburg coat of arms carved in the keystone over the main entrance. It bears the date 1749. The exact date when the palace was built, however, is not known nor has its actual use been determined except that it was a place of residence for the commander of the presidio. Later, supposedly, Spanish governors of the province of Texas made it their home, office, and place for entertainment.

The earliest-known document regarding the building is dated 1804. At that time its owner, Joseph Menchaca, a captain of the presidio, sold it to Ygnacio Perez for the sum of eight hundred dollars. Lieutenant Zebulon Pike speaks of being wined and dined there in 1807 and describes the palace as being candlelit and hung with brocades. In later years it suffered a pitiful decline, becoming in turn a secondhand clothing store, a restaurant, and a barroom called "The Hole in the Wall."

Little remained of the old structure in 1929 when it was purchased by the city from the heirs of the Perez family for fifty-five thousand dollars. It was then restored by Harvey P. Smith, architect, and furnished in the manner of the Spanish Colonial period.

The long, low, white building has a large pair of carved doors, iron-grilled windows, and *canales* projecting from the parapet. At the right of the entrance hall is a small chapel, the Room of the Blessed Virgin. At the left are a ballroom, reception hall, office, and bedrooms while directly behind the entrance hall is a dining room which in addition to a large fireplace has a built-in stone *lavabo* for washing the hands before dinner. Behind that are the kitchen and a corridor with stairway leading to a loft where food supplies were stored. In the patio, filled with flowers and shrubs, its paths paved with colored pebbles, are a central fountain and a "wishing well."

With its furnishings and its fittings giving so well the feeling of Spanish Colonial days, the effect is much more satisfactory than the Governor's Palace in Santa Fe, with its ill-assorted museum collection. It is a superb job of restoration.

Quite in contrast to the elegance of the Governor's Palace were the little adobe houses of *La Villita* (the little town), settled by soldiers and their families after the founding of the mission. Shunned as an undesirable location, the little town survived much of the change that has transformed the modern city and it has now been restored to represent a cross section of San Antonio's early architectural growth.

The most famous monument of old San Antonio, however, is the Mission San Antonio de Valero, more commonly known—from the grove of cottonwood (alamo) trees that surrounded the building— as the Alamo and destined to become the shrine of Texas liberty. In the heart of the modern city, the little church of the former mission is dwarfed by the tall buildings which face Alamo Plaza, although fortunately the immediate surroundings have been purchased by the state and made into a park.

When at the height of its early use the Mission San Antonio de Valero covered an extensive area which included all the northern half of the present plaza and reached well into the site of the present post office and the buildings on the west side of the plaza. Most of the space was occupied by a large patio, with living quarters and service buildings along the west and monastery buildings on the east. The existing walls extending from the church to the west and north are part of the original walls of the mission and enclosed a secondary patio. An *acequia* running from the river along the west wall of the large enclosure brought water to the mission while another, to the east, was the water supply of La Villita.

With the exception of the vine-covered walls already mentioned, all that remains of the mission is the little gray church. The wide and low arched entrance, with carved stonework above, is flanked on either side by a pair of columns, half fluted, half twisted, which enclose a shell-arched niche from which the statues have long since disappeared. Above the entrance is a square window on either side of which is another niche with frame also richly carved—all combining to make a charming example of baroque architecture.

The present curved gable is a restoration made in 1849 by Major E. B. Babbitt of the United States Army when the building was being repaired and fitted for use as a quartermaster depot. At that time the walls were repaired and a new roof was put on the building. Just what form the upper part of the façade originally took is not known. The mission ceased to function as such in 1793 and, although used part of the time thereafter as a fort, it gradually deteriorated and by the time of the siege in February and March of 1836 it was a roofless ruin. Only the façade and part of the walls remained intact.

The building is cruciform in plan, with buttressed side walls, shallow transepts, and square sanctuary. The scale of the façade is such that the size of the interior comes as a surprise; it is much larger than anticipated. On the right, immediately inside the entrance, is the baptistry; opposite it on the left is the confessional, behind which are the friars' burial room and a sacristy.

There is a great deal of confusion regarding the original purpose and use of the Alamo, owing to the fact that in Texas history subsequent events eclipsed any known results of its first use. Even guide- and travelbooks, written with pardonable Texan pride and reverence, add to the confusion by referring to the mission church as a *chapel* and the near-by area now occupied by the Alamo Plaza as a *fortress*. A fortress it came to be, but it was built as a mission for the conversion of Indians. The original presidio was half a mile away across the river. The one building which remains of the Alamo was a *church*. A chapel is a subsidiary building or room—subsidiary to something, whether a church, a private home, or a presidio, the *chief* purpose of which is defense. A mission church was subsidiary to nothing; it was the most important part of the mission, the chief purpose of which was the worship of God and the teaching of the Christian religion and Christian habits. With due recognition of the heroes of the siege of the Alamo who died rather than submit to tyranny, the facts regarding the early history and purpose of the place should be clarified for the benefit of visitors coming from some state other than Texas who should, but may not, appreciate the full significance of it. The heroism of its defenders, forced to be quartered for a last stand in the partially-ruined church of the Mission San Antonio de Valero, roofless and ill equipped for defense, should thus be appreciated even more.

Behind the Alamo the little park is planted with flowering bushes among which winding walks provide a retreat that is as quiet and peaceful as the mission may have been—but probably was not most of the time—in the days when Indian neophytes tended the fruit trees growing beside the little canal skirted with willows in the large, walled enclosure. In front of the Alamo are busy boulevards with a rush of traffic, but they lead in a short distance to other spots more peaceful; for the mission of San Antonio de Valero was only one of five missions established in the vicinity in the early part of the eighteenth century. The other four, but a short distance to the south of the city and all still standing in various states of preservation, merit a chapter of their own.

20

Mission Road

SOUTHWARD the San Antonio River meanders slowly along bounded on either side by a busy highway. Another equally busy highway between the two crosses the river at one point, joins one of the two, and hurries to the south. But a fourth road, not as busy and consequently not in as great a hurry as the others, follows more peacefully the course of the stream, with not quite as many bends but evidently much more in sympathy with the river, jogging along at a slow pace to take in the sights on the way. The sights are principally four missions an average of only two miles apart each from the next; and the road is called, aptly enough, Mission Road.

There is nothing unusual about the road as far as scenery is concerned, but in the sights that form the particular objective for taking it, it is unique. Nowhere else in the country are there four old Spanish missions within such a short distance of each other; in fact, nowhere else in the country, within such a small radius, is there so much of architectural interest dating back more than two hundred years and of historical interest dating back even further.

There are more missions in California, but they are spread out at intervals of what was considered a day's journey. The five missions of San Antonio, including San Antonio de Valero which is in the center of what has become a large city, are built along the course of the river within a stretch only eight miles long from that mission to the one farthest from the city. They were so built for defense: that they might all be close to the presidio and to protection and close to each other for mutual aid in case of attack by hostile Apaches and Comanches, a requirement which did not obtain in California with its more docile and sedentary natives.

Each of the four missions away from the central settlement had at first been established somewhere else, three of them fairly close together in east Texas and all three of them re-established within the same year near San Antonio; the fourth, largest and finest, came from farther afield. Each was an establishment complete in itself, with church, monastery, living and working quarters for the Indians, water supply, granary, gardens, and many head of stock. While in these missions the friars were teaching the Indians the rudiments of the Christian religion and the basic studies of reading, writing, and singing, the lay brothers instructed them in the arts of agriculture, in the weaving of blankets and *rebozos*, and in the building crafts. In spite of the friars' complaints of "want of culture, little talent, and great sloth" on the part of the Indians, the results of their labors with the natives are manifested in those monuments which endure to this day.

The first to be reached on driving south is the Mission Nuestra Señora de la Purísima Concepción de Acuna, only three miles from Alamo Plaza and within the city limits. It had been established in 1716 between the Angelina River and the present city of Nacogdoches, one of that group of east Texas missions resulting from Father Hidalgo's ruse to waken the Spaniards from their lethargy. When on the recommendation of the *visitador* the garrison was withdrawn, the mission was abandoned along with others of that vicinity and in the same year that the Canary Islanders arrived to found their villa of San Fernando it was re-established on the site it now occupies. The cornerstone of the new mission building was laid on March 5, 1731, by Father Bargarro and Captain Perez of the garrison at Bejar.

The Mission Concepción is the best preserved of the Texas missions. Cruciform in plan, with large twin towers at the front, it has heavily-buttressed side walls almost four feet thick. At the main entrance fluted and decorated engaged columns support a steep pediment in which reposes a projecting carved niche with a cross above. A small opening on either side of the pediment, a circular opening immediately above, and two small openings in each of the towers, one above the other, puncture the massive façade of stone covered with plaster. Each of the square towers has arched openings on the four sides, is capped with a pyramidal roof and small lantern, and has a stone merlon at each of the four corners. A low dome, also crowned by a lantern, rises above the crossing.

It is probable that the church of the Mission San Antonio de Valero (Alamo) originally had towers similar to those of the Mission Concepción, or that they were intended, since the plan of the church is very much the same in both. The church of the Mission Concepción has a barrel-vaulted ceiling and on some of the walls the original frescoes may be seen. On the right of the church wide, low arches open onto an arcade which leads into some of the rooms of the mission which remain partially intact.

Among the pioneer Franciscans in Texas was Fray Antonio Margil de Jesus. Born in Valencia, Spain, on August 18, 1657, he entered the Franciscan order in his home city in 1673 and sailed ten years later for Vera Cruz to enter upon a long life of missionary work in the wilds. Working at first in the south, in Yucatán, Costa Rica, Nicaragua, and Guatemala, he came to be known as the Apostle of Guatemala. In 1706 he was appointed the first guardian of the newly-erected missionary College of Guadalupe at Zacatecas and ten years later, in 1716, he led the band of nine friars to east Texas where he helped to found several missions. It was said of him that he always walked barefoot, without sandals, that he seemed to require little sleep and was often found at prayer in the middle of the night. After pioneering among the Indians in the deep pine woods of east Texas, in 1720 he gained permission to leave the missions of the Angelina River in the hands of others and to found a new mission on the San Antonio River. So on February 23, 1720, the mission of San José y San Miguel de Aguayo, originally founded in Coahuila on the right bank of the Rio Grande, was begun on its new site.

The result of Fray Antonio's efforts stands beside Mission Road about two miles farther to the south, the finest of the Texas missions and unsurpassed by any in the Southwest. For its intricate carving of the façade and of the south window of the baptistry it stands alone in this country. Even in the days of the Spaniards it was spoken of as the "queen of the missions." Recently restored, the whole group presents an excellent picture of what an eighteenth-century mission was like and of the life that went on in such a place.

Although begun at the time of the founding by Fray Antonio and dedicated to Saint Joseph and the Marquis of San Miguel de Aguayo, governor of Texas at the time, the mission was a long time under construction. The cornerstone of the present church was not laid until May 19, 1768, thus making it almost contemporaneous with the earlier mission churches of California; and the building which later served as a granary and is now restored to its former appearance served in the meantime as a church.

The granary is the first building on the left on entering the immense and completely-enclosed quadrangle. In addition to its use as a church, it served not only as a granary but as blacksmith, carpenter, and tailor shops and contained looms for the weaving of cotton and woolen cloth. The building is of stone with a high, barrel-vaulted interior supported in part by great flying buttresses at the sides. The vaulted roof is a restoration but some of the walls and flying buttresses are original. The building has the distinction of being the oldest structure standing in the state of Texas.

Extending along the west, south, and east sides of the quadrangle were the Indian quarters. There were eighty-four apartments built of stone, each—according to Governor Barrios, reporting in 1758—"with flat roofs, parapets, and loopholes. Each apartment consists of a room and a kitchen with its *metate* (stone for grinding corn), a pot, a *comal* (iron griddle), water jar, closet, pantry, bed, and dresser." The apartments extended in a continuous row, forming part of the outer wall, and were from fifteen to eighteen feet in length and twelve feet in width.

There was a gate in each of the four corners, over each of which was a bastion for defense, and at the side of each gate loopholes were made through the walls of the adjoining rooms. In those rooms the most trusted Indians lived, in order that they might fire upon the enemy in the event the gates were stormed. On the west side of the enclosure in front of the church there was a fifth gate, the only one to be opened every day. Trees and brush for some distance in front of it were cut down to give a wide view and to prevent a surprise attack.

To the left of the granary was the prefecture (in its restored state used as the home of the custodian) and beyond that were the soldiers' quarters, each mission having its own garrison assigned from the presidio. Outside the enclosure, behind the soldiers' quarters and down a small but steep hill, is the old mill, fed by water from an irrigation ditch. Part of it discovered in 1933 when debris was being cleaned from the old ditch, it has been completely restored and is as fascinating as any part of the mission. A vaulted chamber contained a horizontal water wheel fed from the bottom of an adjacent reservoir with water from the ditch. The vertical axis of the wheel extended up into a room above and on it the millstones were mounted directly, thus doing away with the need for any gears. This may well have been the first gristmill in Texas.

But most notable of all, of course, is the church, extending along part of the north side of the quadrangle with the monastery rooms and cloister behind. Planned for two towers on the front, only one of which stands, the façade of the church, of tufa, is severe and plain except around the entrance portal which is, in contrast (and typical of Spanish Renaissance architecture), elaborately carved in limestone; indeed it is without question the richest entrance portal north of Mexico.

In the early part of the eighteenth century the florid Spanish baroque developed into an unrestrained elaboration of ornament which is credited to—or blamed on, depending upon the viewpoint—José de Churriguera, of a family of architects in Spain. Although the style reached its greatest extravagances after his death, it was named for him Churrigueresque. Quite unconventional in its exuberance, the style nevertheless maintained symmetry. With increasing wealth, Mexico, always some years behind the mother country in point of time but not in extravagances in architecture, adopted the style with fervor and employed it throughout the country during the middle part of that century. San Antonio, then part of a province of New Spain, was the recipient of one of the finest examples of this sculptured exuberance in the portal of San José—or one might better say two of the finest examples, for the baptistry window too is a gem of carved-stone ornament.

There are many legends of Pedro Huizar, the sculptor sent from Spain to execute this work. The one most repeated is as follows: Young Pedro had left behind him a sweetheart, who was to follow him when he had made his fortune. Receiving the commission to carve the façade of the Church of San José, he poured his heart into his work. Losing all sense of time, his carving became more and more intricate and thirteen years passed before it was completed, so he could return to Spain to claim his bride.

But alas! she had lost hope and married another.

Heartbroken, Pedro returned to San Antonio and, determined to forget his lost love, devoted all his talent to the carving of the baptistry window. For five years the cool stone soothed his skillful fingers and assuaged his grief, but when the carving had reached perfection the talented but forlorn sculptor died of a broken heart.

The one tower of the church, rising seventy-five feet above the ground, somewhat more slender and graceful than those on the church of the Mission Concepción, has, like the other church, four arched openings and a pyramidal roof. A hemispherical dome rises from an octagonal base over the crossing. The roof and the dome stood for exactly one hundred years, but one stormy night in December, 1868, the heavy mass fell in.

Of curious interest is the spiral stairway leading to the tower. Built into the angle between the tower and the wall of the nave, it is composed of steps hewn from live-oak logs, each step set fanwise on the preceding one without nailing in such a way that the pivot end resembles a column rising up through the center of the spiral.

The baptistry, adjacent to the church on the right, with low, triple hemispherical-domed ceiling and richly-carved doorways and oak doors, is a most interesting study in itself; while the cloister, to the rear, though in a semi-ruined state gives a good picture of the life of the friars. It must have been used as an open-air dining room, for a kitchen with separate oven room and a serving room with adjacent storerooms open into it. Behind the cloister are the friars' quarters and in the farthest corner of the building is the prison.

Mission Road continues to the south and after a couple of jogs turns east to cross first the old *acequia* and then the San Antonio River. A short turn to the right (south) leads into the quadrangle of the Mission San Juan Capistrano. It may also be reached directly from Highway 181 by turning at the sleepy old village of Berg's Mill and following the shady side road a short distance west.

Founded in 1716 at a site about twenty miles northwest of Nacogdoches, the mission was moved, like the Mission Concepción, to its present location near the San Antonio River in 1731. Originally founded as the Mission San José de los Nazones, its name was changed to honor the fifteenth-century Italian Franciscan theologian and inquisitor Giovanni de Capistrano.

Although some of the buildings of the original quadrangle still stand in various degrees of repair—enough to give a picture of the mission plan—little is left complete except the restored chapel, which is still used by the Roman Catholic Church. And this *is* a chapel, the larger church of the mission across the quadrangle being in a state of semi-ruin. Small and simple as compared with the churches of Mission Concepción and San José, the chapel is a long, narrow building with recessed segmental arches along the front and above, at the right, its most distinctive feature: a pierced *campanario*.

Farthest to the south in the San Antonio group is San Francisco de la Espada. It is the successor to the first mission, San Francisco de los Tejas, founded in 1690 by General Alonso de León and Father Damian Massanet just west of the Neches River in east Texas and burned and abandoned three years later. It was re-established in 1716 a few miles away and again maintained for only three years, when the Spaniards were driven out by the French, an echo in the wilderness of war between the mother countries over European problems. In 1721, with France and Spain again at peace, the mission was established once more as San Francisco de los Neches. This time it lasted for ten years, but in 1731 it was moved to the San Antonio River under its present name. So peaceful and quiet is it now that it is difficult to imagine its turbulent beginnings.

Espada Road, leading south a short distance to the mission, winds among small farms which have been occupied by the same families since the latter part of the eighteenth century, when churchlands were given to them. Their ancestors were taught by the early friars two hundred years ago and their children are now instructed by the successors of those friars. The Roman Catholic Church, which owns the mission, conducts services in the church and the children of the neighborhood attend classes in restored buildings once used as barracks.

As at San Juan Capistrano, some of the old buildings of the original quadrangle remain. One of the most interesting is a *baluarte*, or fortified tower, which has a round bastion with thick stone walls, vaulted roof, and loopholes for rifles. There was once a church larger than the present one, of which only the foundation walls remain, across the road that now winds through the old quadrangle. The existing church is a charming little structure. Above the Moorish doorway, outlined in cut stone, the rough stone and brick walls rise to a triple-arched campanario surmounted by a wrought-iron cross said to have been fashioned by the early friars. The place seems many miles away from a busy city; indeed in spirit it is a delightful surviving trace of a simple and peaceful past.

In addition to the San Antonio mission group, but on the same river, there is one other building dating from Spanish days that is deserving of mention. It stands at some distance to the southeast. When Governor Aguayo, who shared in the official name of the Mission San José, returned with his army after re-establishing the missions of east Texas in 1721, he stopped at San Antonio (Bejar) to take steps to strengthen the post. He then proceeded to the site of La Salle's ruined fort near Matagorda Bay to superintend the erection of a presidio there and to found a new mission under its protection. This was in the early spring of 1722. The presidio was named Nuestra Señora de Loreto de la Bahia (Our Lady of Loreto of the Bay) and the mission Nuestra Señora del Espíritu Santo de Zuñiga. Ninety men were stationed at the new presidio. The Indians of the bay almost immediately began to give trouble and within four years they had deserted the mission and killed the captain of the presidio.

In 1726 the friar in charge of the mission moved farther inland to a site on the Guadalupe River near Victoria, and the new captain soon followed with his force. Again in 1749 both presidio and mission were moved to a new location, on the San Antonio River, and there they remained, near the present town of Goliad ninety miles southeast of San Antonio. During the remainder of the Spanish period it was the only stronghold other than San Antonio de Bexar between the Sabine and the Rio Grande. Nacogdoches was a rather feeble eastern outpost. Goliad, like the Alamo, was destined to play a heroic part in the Texas Revolution.

The mission fell into disuse and became a ruin, which has now been restored; but the chapel of the presidio still stands, on a commanding site at the top of a hill. Two miles from the present town, in Goliad State Park, a steep road leads from the highway directly up to the side of the presidio chapel. Of rubblework, with a monumental arched entrance and a massive, squat bell tower with a pyramidal top, it is one of the most delightful of the historic buildings of the Southwest.

Above the entrance an octagonal window lights the choir loft and above it a semicircular pediment, crowned with a cross, frames a rough, stone arched niche containing a statue. In the groin-vaulted interior a shell-formed doorway leads on the right into a side chapel and on the left, adjacent to the sanctuary, is the sacristy, projecting from the outer wall.

From its deserted hilltop the old chapel looks out over cultivated fields much more peaceful now than during most of its two-hundred-year history. Much less visited than the mission churches of San Antonio, it ranks with the best of them as an architectural monument of an earlier era.

After a hundred years of Spanish occupation Texas boasted fewer than three thousand people. There were only three centers of population: San Antonio, Nacogdoches, and Goliad (El Paso del Norte was still New Mexico). The artificial society which occupied these centers was not of the stuff from which empires are built. The viceregal court in Mexico City was their example. They drank good wine, dressed fastidiously, and entertained lavishly; but they did not grow. The Spaniards and the Spanish creoles would not farm and mines to be developed could not be found; so the few settlers hung around the vicinity of the military posts and danced.

Only in the missions was there any real earnestness of purpose. Great efforts were made on the part of the friars to convert the Indians to Christianity and to make useful people of them. It was difficult, for the Indians could not be made to till the ground except under duress. As a result the Texas missions were given up even before the seeds of discord in New Spain began to sprout into revolution. The one remaining legacy of that era is the architecture. The friars should at least be praised for leaving us the missions.

It was to be left to another people to develop the other great possibilities of the province.

21

Desert Interlude: San Xavier Del Bac

U NTIL 1853 it appeared that what has since become the state of Arizona was not going to be able to boast any old Spanish missions. But in that year, by the grace of Gadsden, two were automatically placed within its borders: one of the very finest and most complete of all Spanish missions, and the picturesque ruins of another. The annexation of a thick slice of Sonora, covering some forty-five thousand square miles along the border between the Rio Grande and the Colorado, for which the United States paid Mexico ten million dollars, was for the purpose of laying out a route for a railroad to the Pacific along the thirty-second parallel. James Gadsden, then minister to Mexico, conducted the negotiations. Had he had his way, the acquisition would have included half a dozen more fine missions and the ruins of still others, which would probably now be accessible; but just as he had to be satisfied with a compromise so Arizona will have to be content with the two. Together they make up an inheritance from the early Spanish friars well worth the price.

In the extreme northwestern corner of the mainland of Mexico, bounded on the west by the Gulf of California and on the north by Arizona, lies the state of Sonora. Until the Gadsden purchase the province extended north to the Gila River. Only one paved highway traverses it, stretching down from Tucson and on from Nogales on the border, headed for Hermosillo, the state capital, and Guaymas on the Gulf, which Mr. Gadsden wanted for an Arizona seaport.

East of that highway rise almost impenetrable mountains into the foothills of which there is scarcely a passable road; while to the west, where the best road is but a series of slow, painful bumps over dry washes, the Sonoran Desert stretches all the way to the Gulf and on up to the north to include part of Arizona. It is not a desert in the sense that the Sahara is a desert—with vast, rolling stretches of bare sand—but is cut up into pieces by jagged mountains and is green with such vegetation as mesquite, sage, and cacti of various kinds. The cholla with its dense masses of fuzzy, sharp spines and the prickly pear with its flat, paddlelike joints add color to the land while the sinister giant saguaro raises its unruly arms and fingers high above the other plants. The misty-green paloverde with its feathery leaves is found scattered over the sand and the clustered ocotillo projects its colorful slim branches into the desert air.

Out on these vast stretches of green-and-yellow desert the twilight is short and night falls suddenly. Darkness wraps up the desert plants in its folds and the mountains form a jagged outline to contain a sky full of stars. When the moon comes up it announces its impending arrival with a pale glow to the east and then places thin, silvery outlines on the cactus plants before it shows its brilliant self beyond the distant mountains.

Dawn is as quietly spectacular. A faint white light appears first and then follow in series pastel pinks, yellows, and pale greens to spread gradually over the sky. Both dusk and dawn prove that this desert, though lonely, is not lifeless. Large white rabbits with long pink ears bound over the sand seeking both food and shelter, chipmunks scurry for cover under low-growing bushes, and an occasional coyote skulks across the road. Before the sun appears the scattered songs of birds in one direction are taken up in another and then another until the surrounding desert is filled with a medley for all the world like a rendition of the appropriate part of the *William Tell Overture*. Then suddenly the desert world is lit up as rapidly as the darkness had fallen.

Into this land in 1536 came Cabeza de Vaca to make his way back to the south and civilization. Through it three years later Estebanico marched to his death, and among the giant saguaros Fray Marcos hurried over the sands to spread the wild tales that set off the Coronado expedition.

Its penetration after that was made more slowly. In the vanguard were the Jesuits, moving northward among the Indians to convert and to civilize them and to heal the wounds made by such ruthless conquerors as Nuño de Guzmán. Valley by valley and tribe by tribe they moved forward and with kindness and patience gained the confidence of the Indians. They persuaded the natives to gather in villages about the missions which they founded; there they taught them to pray and to farm. Settlers followed, driving cattle and sheep and goats before them, and settled down to establish homes beside the streams.

By 1687, the year La Salle met his death after founding his ill-fated colony in Texas, the Jesuits had reached the upper Sonora Valley. The northern outpost was Cucurpe on the San Miguel River, about a hundred and fifty miles south of Tucson. In that year there arrived the man who was to carry the work on to the north, one of the greatest figures not only in missionary endeavor but in exploration of the Southwest: Eusebio Francisco Kino.

Born in the village of Segno in the province of Trent, Italy, in 1645, Kino entered the Society of Jesus at the age of twenty on November 20, 1665. Having distinguished himself as a student at Freiburg, he was offered a professorship of mathematics at the royal university of Bavaria; but he had made a vow during a serious illness that if he recovered he would devote his life to missionary service, so he declined the offer. It was not until thirteen years later that he was to turn his face to the New World. He had hoped to be sent to China, but when a call came for missionaries in New Spain he accepted the opportunity with eagerness. He boarded ship at Genoa on June 12, 1678, to sail to Cádiz but, detained in Spain, he did not arrive in Mexico until the late spring of 1681.

After two years of exploratory work in Baja California, Kino was sent to Sonora as rector of the missions of Pimería Alta, the land of the upper Pima Indians. From Cucurpe, the frontier mission station at the time, Kino marched fifteen miles to the north to a site where a mesa juts out into a wild and beautiful valley. There he founded the mission of Nuestra Señora de los Dolores—Our Lady of Sorrows—which was to be the mother of all the missions of northern Sonora and what is now southern Arizona. And there for twenty-four years Kino made his headquarters.

From the little mission of Dolores during those twenty-four years Kino made more than fifty journeys varying in length from a hundred to a thousand miles. Often alone or accompanied only by Indian guides, he crossed and recrossed the desert in various directions from the Magdalena to the Gila and from the San Pedro to the Colorado. Everywhere he went, not satisfied with mere preaching, he gathered the Indians into missions. For their support he brought stock with him and started stock ranches and grain farms. The missions he founded dot the Pimería Alta to this day and the ranches he established were the foundation for the later settlement of California.

Father Kino had never been satisfied with the accepted belief that Lower California was an island. By 1702 he had explored the Colorado from the mouth of the Gila to the Gulf and had proved that the land was, as he had at first believed, a peninsula. The map which he made was not improved upon for more than a century. Several years earlier in his travels he had visited the ruins of Casa Grande on the Gila River, the first white man definitely known to have seen the Great House.

Great as a missionary and as an explorer, the intrepid padre was as great as a general. The Apaches were constantly conducting raids against the little settlements which he established. Kino would send out his Pima charges to war against the Apaches and when the Spanish officials questioned the number of scalps to be paid for Kino himself rode out to count them and to see that his children were not cheated.

It was in 1691 that Kino began his explorations in what is now Arizona, going as far north as Tumacácori, a Pima village on the Santa Cruz River. He was accompanied by Father Juan María Salvatierra, who had been made visitor. There, under an arbor which the Indians erected for them, Father Kino said Mass, the first Christian service to be held in southern Arizona. The following year he reached the *ranchería* at Bac, which he named for San Francisco Xavier, his patron saint, to whose intercession he attributed his recovery from illness and whose picture he always carried with him. In 1700 he began the foundations of a church and house at San Xavier del Bac. Three thousand Indians beseeched him to remain with them; he was willing, but his request to move his headquarters to that strategic point in his plans for advance was denied and he returned to his mission at Dolores.

Kino's last years seemed to be a period of frustration. The Pima and Papago Indians were friendly enough and begged for more missionaries. At the *rancherías* they built rude churches, planted fields, and tended livestock, patiently waiting for missionaries who in most cases never came. The rector never had more than four assistants at any one time in the whole of the Pimería Alta. No one else seemed to believe in the docility and good faith of the Indians, who were accused of being treacherous and in league with the Apaches. Kino alone had faith in his children.

While Kino was working in Sonora, Texas had become the danger point because of the French menace. Funds were needed there and the establishment of missions in the Pimería Alta served no political purpose. So help was not forthcoming, and there is no record that any of the missions which Kino founded in Arizona were ever finished. In 1711 Kino died at Magdalena, one of the missions which he had founded across the mountains west of Dolores and the only one on the present highway south of Arizona. The church which stands there today is a modern structure built on the foundations of a church of the Franciscans which was erected some years after the death of Kino.

Of the founder of these missions a companion said: "He died, as he had lived, in the greatest humility and poverty. . . . And having for his bed—as he had always had—two sheepskins for a mattress, two small blankets of the sort that the Indians use for cover, and for his pillow a pack-saddle. . . . He was merciful to others but cruel to himself."

For twenty years after Kino's death no Spaniard is known to have entered Arizona. In 1732 there was an awakening and a new band of Jesuits took up the work which the founder had left; but in 1751 the Pima and Papago Indians joined in an uprising throughout the Pimería Alta and the priests who did not escape to southern Sonora were killed. In the following year a presidio was established at Tubac in the Santa Cruz Valley, the priests went back to their posts, and for fifteen years more the Jesuits carried on. In 1767, for political reasons of his own which he never saw fit to explain, Charles III banished the Jesuits from his dominions.

The mission churches that now stand in northern Sonora and in Arizona are the work of Franciscans of a later date; but Father Kino had paved the way.

On the expulsion of the Jesuits in 1767 all of their mission property was confiscated by the Spanish government and its care entrusted temporarily to royal *comisarios*. The missions in southern Sonora were secularized, but those in the Pimería Alta were put in charge of fourteen Franciscans of the College of Santa Cruz in Querétaro, Mexico. Among these assigned to the missions in what is now Arizona was Padre Francisco Tomás Garcés, a worthy successor to Kino both in missionary zeal and in exploration. He was given charge of San Xavier del Bac, where he served as resident friar for eight or ten years. During part of that time he made a remarkable journey to the Pacific, accompanying Captain Juan Bautista de Anza of whom we shall hear more in California. Returning alone, he made his way up to the Hopi mesas as already related.

In 1780 Garcés founded two missions on the Yuma River which were protected by a few soldiers and a handful of colonists who had appropriated all the best land belonging to the Indians. The following year the lieutenant-governor of Lower California arrived with a company of soldiers bound for the California mission settlements. They pastured their horses in the fields of mesquite beans on which the Indians depended for food. Indian hatred, long stifled, burst into flame. That night—July 17, 1781—they struck, led by one who had been a convert and protégé of Father Garcés. All the soldiers and colonists were killed and Father Garcés was clubbed to death while celebrating Mass. Thus ended the work of the friars along the Colorado River.

But to return to San Xavier del Bac. When Garcés took charge of it in 1768 the mission was in bad condition. The neophytes were scattered and had forgotten what they had been taught, at least so they said; but they consented to return if not compelled to work. In that same year the mission was destroyed by the Apaches. By 1772 Garcés had rebuilt the church which, like the others of the vicinity, was a simple structure of adobe covered with wood, grass, and earth and described as being moderately capacious but poorly supplied with furniture and vestments. The official report also showed a population at Bac of two hundred and seventy.

At that time San José de Tucson was a *ranchería* and *visita* (with no resident friar, but visited only occasionally by a missionary) of San Xavier del Bac. There were about two hundred families congregated there but there was neither church nor padre's house. In 1776 the presidio was transferred thither from Tubac. The oldest Spanish town in the state of Arizona, Tubac began to settle down to its present status as a quiet and picturesque village of adobe houses and stores clustered about a small white-plastered church, just off the highway to Nogales; Tucson was to grow into a thriving city.

Farther to the south on the Santa Cruz River, Guevavi had eighty-six inhabitants and a church, the crumbling ruins of which now mark the site. The near-by *visita* of Calabasas had neither church nor house for the missionary, though both were built a few years later. It, like Guevavi, is now marked by a few scattered ruins. Quiburi, on the San Pedro River to the east, is in a similar state.

Tumacácori, which Kino visited as early as 1691, though only a *visita* from Jesuit times, was chiefly important as a cattle ranch. There was a small adobe church there when the Franciscans took charge but it was destroyed the following year in an Apache raid. The church was rebuilt and in 1784 San José de Tumacácori became a mission instead of a *visita*. Again it had to be abandoned, owing to another Apache raid, but toward the end of the eighteenth century a new and larger mission was begun. Finally completed and dedicated in 1822, this is the one the ruins of which are seen today.

After Mexico had won her independence from Spain in 1821 the missions were secularized and the friars were forced to leave their newly-completed church and monastery buildings at Tumacácori to the depredations of the Apaches and the later vandalism of treasure hunters. In 1908 Tumacácori was made a national monument, the only area in the National Park System—with the exception of Gran Quivira in New Mexico—which deals chiefly with Spanish mission history. Forty-eight miles south of Tucson on U.S. Highway 89, and only two miles south of the side road into Tubac, the monument has parking facilities, an excellent museum, an attractive patio and garden, and a resident ranger guide.

Although partially in ruins, the church of the mission is a most interesting study. The church and monastery (the latter long since fallen into ruin) were built facing a plaza in the center of a large walled enclosure. The church, about a hundred feet long by fifty feet wide on the front, was built of sun-dried adobe bricks and burned bricks laid in clay mortar and plastered on the surface. The walls are five to six feet thick at the base and are nearly ten feet thick under the massive tower at the right. The arched entrance portal is framed by coupled columns with a niche between, with similar but smaller coupled columns and broken pediment above, over which rises an arched gable.

The small room within the thick walls of the tower was used as a baptistry, and a similar though larger room projecting from the sanctuary was the sacristy. A dome with a lantern rises above the sanctuary at the north end of the aisleless nave. To the north of the church was the cemetery in which an unroofed, circular mortuary

25. (*Top*) RESTORED CHURCH OF ISLETA DEL SUR, near El Paso. (*Bottom*) MISSION CHURCH AT SOCORRO, near El Paso

26. THE CATHEDRAL OF CHIHUAHUA, Mexico

27.　SIDE ENTRANCE, Cathedral of Chihuahua

28. (*Top*) THE ALAMO, San Antonio. (*Bottom*) MISSION CONCEPCIÓN, San Antonio

29. (*Top*) MISSION SAN JUAN CAPISTRANO, near San Antonio. (*Bottom*) MISSION SAN JOSÉ, near San Antonio

30. WINDOW IN BAPTISTRY, Mission San José, San Antonio

31. ENTRANCE PORTAL, Mission San José, San Antonio

32. (*Top*) THE GOVERNOR'S PALACE, San Antonio. (*Bottom*) THE AR-
CADE, Governor's Palace

33. (*Top*) RECEPTION ROOM, Governor's Palace. (*Bottom*) KITCHEN, Governor's Palace

34. DINING ROOM, Governor's Palace

35. THE PRESIDIO CHAPEL, Goliad, Texas

36. CLOISTER ARCHES, Mission San José, San Antonio

37. (*Top*) GENERAL VIEW OF SAN XAVIER DEL BAC. (*Bottom*) MISSION
SAN XAVIER DEL BAC, near Tucson, Arizona

38. ENTRANCE PORTAL, Mission San Xavier del Bac, Arizona

© *Frashers Photos. Pomona, Calif.*
Courtesy of Franciscan Fathers, San Xavier Mission

39. ALTAR AND REREDOS, Mission San Xavier del Bac

40. (*Top*) RUINS OF MISSION SAN JOSÉ DE TUMACÁCORI, Arizona. (*Bottom*) THE MORTUARY CHAPEL, Tumacácori Mission

chapel still stands. Since the *campo santo* was often used in later days as a corral during roundup times, the graves of hundreds of Christian Indians have been obliterated by milling cattle.

When after secularization the devout Indians were forced to flee sorrowfully from Tumacácori, they left their buried dead to be trampled upon and took the statues of saints, the sacred vessels, and other precious objects with them to San Xavier del Bac for safekeeping. There many of these objects may be seen today and once more the Indians gather in the church to pray and to listen to the teachings of the Franciscan fathers.

The church which Garcés rebuilt in 1772 was considered as only a temporary structure, for just about that time the present large building was begun. Succeeding Garcés were Friars Baltasar Carillo and Narisco Gutiérrez, who had as assistants Friars Mariano Bordoy, Ramon López, and Alonso de Prado. It was that group which was responsible for the mission that we see today. For years they labored with the Indians at the tremendous undertaking, the work being done under the direction of two architects, the Gaona brothers.

Out on the desert nine miles southwest of Tucson the mission of San Xavier del Bac appears silhouetted against the mountains so white and gleaming as to seem a mirage of the Orient. Its curved parapets, its white towers and whiter dome against a dark blue sky add to the oriental effect. Only one of the towers—the one on the left—was ever completed, and its high buttressed walls are crowned with a dome and lantern; the other stops short of the dome—it is said, to avoid paying a tax to the Crown, required only of a completed church.

In front of the church a narrow enclosed plaza, or atrium, extends to the left to a tiny, white mortuary chapel and on the right along the front of the monastery buildings which are built around a patio to the rear. In keeping with the Spanish tradition, the façade of burned brick covered with lime plaster is divided into three parts—the outer thirds being relatively plain, each broken by a balconied window—above which rises the tower supported by flying buttresses. The central portion is richly decorated with swirling volutes, shells, canopied figures, and arabesques weathered to a soft red which affords a striking contrast to the gleaming white plaster walls on either side.

In plan the church is cruciform, with low domes carried on pendentives and with a high dome over the crossing raised on a drum.

The interior is the richest and most ornate in the Southwest, literally filled with carved, gilded, and polychromed Churrigueresque *retablos* supplemented by paintings and carved figures. Carried out by Indians under the patient direction of Spanish artists and friars working together in the desert, it is reminiscent of the most elaborate work in Mexico.

I have, I hope, given a fair though all too brief picture of the work of Father Kino in the Pimería Alta. The value of his pioneering cannot be overestimated. Writers, however, in describing the mission church of San Xavier del Bac, almost invariably attach Kino's name to it. There seems to be little doubt that he was instrumental in establishing a *ranchería* at Bac and that he visited the place and said Mass there. He also mentions starting the foundations of a church, but whether his church ever got beyond the start of foundations is not recorded. When Father Kino left the place it was still a *ranchería*. From an architectural standpoint, therefore, and in fairness to its builders, it should be pointed out that Father Kino had nothing whatever to do with the church which today is often described as "The White Dove of the Desert." It was built by the Franciscans in the closing years of the eighteenth century.

Building great church edifices was not Padre Kino's role in life. He was an explorer, a pioneer, a great missionary; somebody always has to pave the way and Kino was one of the greatest of those who had a right to say: "Anybody might have found it, but—His Whisper came to Me!" He was not, as has been claimed, greatest as a builder, to use the word in its more limited sense. He did not have time. He had too much territory to cover. God's Whisper came to Kino for something else that had to be done first. And he did it well, amazingly well. Riding thirty miles a day for long periods, making valuable maps of exploration, baptizing and spreading the gospel as he went, his endurance in the saddle is still a marvel to seasoned cowboys. But one cannot build churches on horseback.

An inscription over the doorway to the sacristy in the church of San Xavier del Bac bears the date 1791. Presumably that was the year when the Franciscans who built it completed the church, or at least that portion of it. It was consecrated in 1797. By that time other Franciscans were building a chain of missions up the coast of California.

PART FIVE: *ALTA CALIFORNIA*

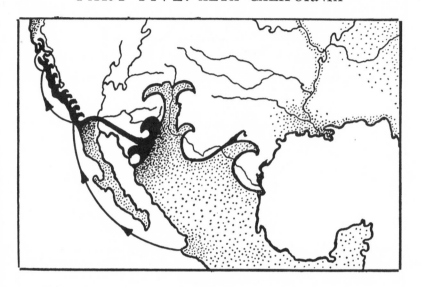

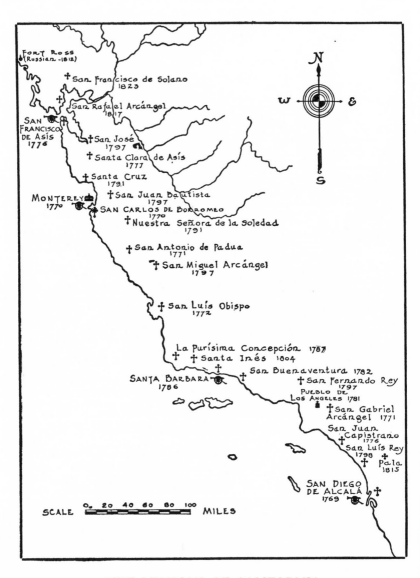

FORT ROSS
(Russian -1812)

✝ San Francisco de Solano
1823

San Rafael Arcángel
1817

SAN
FRANCISCO
DE Asís
1776

✝ San José
1797

✝ Santa Clara de Asís
1777

✝ Santa Cruz
1791

MONTEREY
1770

✝ San Juan Bautista
1797

SAN CARLOS DE BORROMEO
1770

✝ Nuestra Señora de la Soledad
1791

✝ San Antonio de Padua
1771

✝ San Miguel Arcángel
1797

✝ San Luís Obispo
1772

La Purísima Concepción 1787
✝ ✝ Santa Inés 1804

San Buenaventura 1782

SANTA BARBARA
1786

✝ San Fernando Rey
1797

PUEBLO DE
LOS ANGELES 1781

✝ San Gabriel
Arcángel 1771

San Juan
Capistrano
1776

San Luís Rey
1798

✝ Pala
1815

SAN DIEGO
DE ALCALÁ
1769

SCALE 0 20 40 60 80 100 MILES

N
W — E
S

THE MISSIONS OF CALIFORNIA

22

The Founding of the Missions

I N ALL OF his explorations and missionary travels Father Kino never gave up his early interest in the possibility of founding missions in Baja California. More than a century and a half had elapsed since the first unsuccessful attempt to establish a colony there was made by Cortés. Expeditions beginning in 1683, one of which Kino accompanied as royal cosmographer, also resulted in failure, but the padre's interest in the country had been aroused. As things turned out it was not to be his field of endeavor as a missionary, but he was influential in persuading an equally-worthy substitute to take over the work on the peninsula.

Father Juan María Salvatierra had been sent out by the Jesuit order as *visitador* of missions and it was in that capacity that he met Kino and traveled with him into Arizona. Kino imbued Salvatierra with his own enthusiasm and the latter decided to take charge himself of the Jesuit occupation of Baja California. There were obstacles to overcome, for both the government and the Jesuit Order were opposed to the plan; but in 1697 permission was granted with the proviso that the Jesuits raise the funds for the occupation. For this purpose Salvatierra found an able assistant in the person of Father Juan de Ugarte, a professor in the Jesuit College of Mexico City, a giant of a man who was not only a genius at raising money but a zealous missionary fully able to cope with recalcitrant Indians. Thus began the Pious Fund which was to become the principal support of the Spanish missions in both the Californias.

On October 10, 1697, Father Salvatierra with only six men crossed the Gulf in a single day and two weeks later established the first permanent European settlement in the Californias and the first mission there, which was named in honor of Our Lady of Loreto. The first few years were times of great hardship, what with Indian revolts and uncertainty of supplies, but with the aid of the Pious Fund more missions were established and the hold of the Jesuits on the peninsula became secure—for seventy years.

Salvatierra served as president of the missions for twenty years until his death in 1717, when he was succeeded by Father Ugarte who served until he died in 1730. Together with their successors they erected fourteen missions which extended from Cape San Lucas on the south to Santa María, not far from the mouth of the Colorado River, on the north. They had converted the Indians, sustained them, taught them arts and crafts, charted the whole coast line, made scientific reports, and cultivated and irrigated hundreds of acres of arid land. Then in 1767 came the order for the expulsion of all Jesuits. Those who were arrested in Mexico were sent to the remote island of Corsica in the Mediterranean. Each man on landing was handed a letter saying that as long as he stayed there, refrained from criticizing the act which had banished him or trying to communicate with anybody, even with relatives in Spain or Mexico, he would receive a yearly allowance of one hundred dollars. Further, if any one of them violated any of the conditions the allowance would be withdrawn from all.

In September of 1767 Captain Gaspar de Portolá, a native of Catalonia, arrived in Baja California as governor. On February 3, 1768, he gathered the Jesuit missionaries together at their mother church in Loreto "with no effects other than their clothing, breviaries, and one theological and one historical book" and from there they were escorted to the port of embarkation, accompanied by the Indians "all wailing and crying aloud."

Whatever may have been in the mind of Charles III in banishing the Jesuits, he made a good choice in the selection of a man to send to New Spain to reorganize the administration, largely for the purpose of increasing the revenues of the Crown. José de Gálvez, *visitador-general* (or royal inspector), arrived in the peninsula in 1768 and immediately set to work upon the reforms which were to make possible the occupation of Alta California. The military commissioners to whom the missions had been turned over cared little about Indians and devoted their energies to a search for the treasure that the Jesuits were thought to have accumulated. Not only was the government removed from mission control but the mission properties were left in the hands of the commissioners. The result was the complete demoralization of the Indians and the near ruin of the missions. Only the church buildings and spiritual interests were left to the Franciscans who had arrived from the College of San Fernando in Mexico City to take over the missionary work. One of the first acts of Gálvez was to give back the temporalities—flocks, crops, and economic resources in general—to missionary control. In the meantime, as president of the missions on the peninsula the College had selected Fray Junípero Serra.

Miguel José Serra was born on November 24, 1713, in the village of Petra on the island of Majorca in the Mediterranean Sea off the coast of Spain. At the age of sixteen he was admitted to the Franciscan monastery at Palma, and it was while there that he took the name of Junípero out of love for that companion of Saint Francis of whom the saint once said: "Oh that I had a forest of such Junipers!" Among his close friends was Francisco Palóu, who was to accompany him to California and through whose biography of his hero Serra's name was to become justly famous. Although he distinguished himself as a student and was made a professor of philosophy while still very young, it was foreign missionary service that interested Serra and August 28, 1749, found him at Cádiz about to embark for New Spain.

Although a conveyance was waiting for him at Vera Cruz he, like Saint Francis, preferred to walk; so with only one companion he set out for Mexico City on foot. That long and difficult march through swamps and over mountains brought on a leg infection from which he never fully recovered. After serving for nine years among the Indians of the Sierra Gorda in northeastern Mexico he was ordered to a new and more dangerous post among the Indians of northern Texas. Before he had a chance to enter this new field there occurred the massacre of San Saba in 1758 which wiped out the post. The plan to re-establish the mission there was given up and Serra was saved for California. So close did he come to being proclaimed an early hero of Texas!

The next eight years he spent at the College in Mexico City and in 1768, when he was sent as father-president of the missions of Baja California, he was already in his fifty-fifth year.

In Gálvez as *visitador-general*, the Marqués de Croix as viceroy, Portolá as governor, and Serra as president of the missions, Baja California had an almost unbeatable team for further advances. Francisco Palóu and Fray Juan Crespi, the latter another college classmate of Serra, gave able assistance.

Gálvez and Serra were an especially fortunate combination. The former had discussed with the viceroy the advisability of occupying Alta California, largely as a defensive measure to ward off further encroachments of the Russians, who had established fur-trading posts in the north and whose vessels were cruising the waters of the Pacific along the coast. Plans were made by Gálvez for an expedition in which soldiers and missionaries, according to established custom, were to go forth side by side. In this project the energetic *visitador* had an enthusiastic supporter in the new father-president of the missions. Gálvez was himself a devout Catholic and he took Serra into his confidence. Together they discussed the plans, using as a guide a map based on Vizcaíno's explorations one hundred and sixty-six years earlier. Gálvez proposed that three missions should be founded at once; one was to be located at San Diego, another at Monterey, and a third mission halfway between the two in honor of San Buenaventura.

"But," asked Serra, "what about a mission in honor of our founder, Saint Francis?"

"Brother Junípero," replied Gálvez, "San Diego and San Buenaventura, and the Count of Monterey as well, each provided a harbor. If there is to be a mission for Saint Francis, let him too show us a harbor."

Serra bided his time.

Plans were made for two expeditions by land and two by sea. Gálvez took over and repaired two old transports, the *San Antonio* and the *San Carlos*, while as a precautionary measure a third ship, the *San José*, was rushed to completion. Laden with supplies, the auxiliary ship set sail the following year and was never heard of again. Down with her went ten thousand pounds of dried meat, eight casks of wine, two casks of brandy, twelve hundred pounds of figs, quantities of dried fish, beans, raisins, clothing, vestments, church bells, and articles to trade with the Indians.

In the meantime Father Serra had busied himself visiting missions up and down the peninsula, collecting the needed equipment for his new establishments. On January 9, 1769, the *San Carlos* set sail with sixty-two men, including Lieutenant Pedro Fages, later to be one of California's governors. A month later the *San Antonio* followed.

The land expeditions started out about the same time. With the first, under the command of Captain Rivera, went Fray Juan Crespi. With the second went Father Serra, limping badly because of his ulcerated leg. In command was Gaspar de Portolá.

On the first day of July Serra's party came in sight of the beautiful harbor of San Diego. Two vessels with folded sails rode at anchor and on the shore they could see the tents of their comrades. Portolá's soldiers fired their muskets in salute and were answered by a salute from the camp of Rivera. But it was a sad sight that greeted Father Serra when he reached the camp. Captain Rivera and Don Pedro Prat, surgeon of the *San Carlos*, were busy with the sick and dying. The *San Antonio* had made the voyage in fifty-five days but the *San Carlos*, having been blown south by storms, was twice as long on the way. Her crew had been almost wiped out by scurvy and those who were left were so ill they could not launch a shoreboat. By the time Serra had arrived with the second land party one fourth of the three hundred men who had started with the four expeditions had died and many of the Indians had deserted. Undaunted in spite of this terrible handicap, Serra two weeks later raised and blessed the Cross and said Mass; so on July 16, 1769, was founded the mission of San Diego de Alcalá, first of the missions of Alta California.

At the same time, sending the *San Antonio* back to San Blas on the west coast of Mexico for additional supplies and men, Portolá started the long and terrible march north to Monterey. Sixty-three men, "or rather say skeletons, who had been spared by scurvy, hunger, and thirst," as the captain put it, made up the party. The *San Carlos* was to sail for Monterey as soon as the crew was ready and the depleted camp at San Diego was left in charge of Rivera, Serra remaining with him to start work on the mission. That was not easy. The Indians, who had at first been merely curious, began to steal everything that was movable, including clothing and the sails from the *San Carlos*. This they followed with an attack on the camp. A small handful of soldiers left as a guard managed to put them to flight, but only after one soldier had been killed and three others wounded. When on January 24, 1770, Portolá and his party staggered back into the camp at San Diego, only half the original small force left there remained alive.

Portolá's expedition had not fared much better. They had reached the Bay of Monterey but, failing to recognize it, they had marched on until they were stopped by the Golden Gate, seen for the first time by Europeans. Discouraged and exhausted by hunger they turned back to San Diego, "smelling frightfully of mules," which they had been forced to eat to keep alive. Half the men had to be carried on litters strapped to the backs of the remaining mules.

When Portolá discovered that the little group at San Diego had fared even worse, he decided that unless relief came they would have to return to Mexico despite Fray Junípero's determination not to give up. The date was set for March 19, the day of the Feast of Saint Joseph. On that day a sail was sighted. Fray Junípero's prayers had been answered. Not until four days later did the *San Antonio* sail into the harbor, the captain having been given orders to continue to Monterey to support Portolá and his settlement. Natives along the Santa Barbara Channel, where the ship had put in for water, told the crew of Portolá's return south and the abandonment of San Diego and California was thus prevented.

There was nothing to interfere now with the return to Monterey. Portolá, with Lieutenant Fages and Padre Crespi, again marched by land; Serra sailed with Captain Perez on the *San Antonio*. On the shore was found the cross which Portolá had planted when he had reached the spot before without knowing where he was and near by were small heaps of seeds and shells, offerings of the Indians. On June 3, 1770, a shelter of branches was erected on the beach, a cross was raised near an old oak, bells were hung and blessed, the ground was consecrated with holy water, and thus the second of the California missions was founded and dedicated to San Carlos Borromeo.

Portolá's work was now done. He had been ordered to return to New Spain upon the founding of the two settlements and to turn over the command to Fages. The following month he sailed with the *San Antonio* and, upon arriving at San Blas, sent dispatches to Mexico City telling of the success of the enterprise. In the capital bells were rung, banners were raised, and a special High Mass was celebrated. Alta California had been occupied!

The following year brought ten new Franciscans to aid Serra and and with them came bells, sacred vessels, and other religious objects for the missions as yet unfounded. Five more missions had been authorized. Sending two of the friars to San Diego to relieve the padres there, two to found a mission at San Gabriel, and two others to San Buenaventura, Serra started inland to a location southeast of San Carlos. In a beautiful oak-filled valley which he found he established the mission of San Antonio de Padua.

Friars Somera and Cambón arrived in the south from Monterey shortly afterward and on September 8, 1771, founded the mission of San Gabriel Arcangel.

In the summer of 1772 the *padre-presidente* was called to Mexico to make an accounting of mission affairs. Stopping on the way to establish the mission of San Luís Obispo de Tolosa, Serra continued to San Diego and thence to the capital, on the way almost succumbing twice to illness. In Mexico City Serra presented to the viceroy a carefully-prepared report which included a long list of recommendations. Fortunately for the future of California, the man who had been appointed to succeed Croix as viceroy was a leader of great ability with a keen interest in the problems of New Spain—indeed, probably the greatest viceroy that country ever had: Antonio Bucareli. Serra's pleas did not fall on deaf ears.

Among the recommendations which Serra made was the opening of a land route into California. Thus far supplies had been sent by ship from San Blas on the west coast of the mainland of Mexico to Loreto on the peninsula and thence northward by pack train, a difficult march of seven hundred and fifty miles through arid country. As it happened, Bucareli had already received a letter requesting permission to make such an expedition of discovery. It was from Juan Bautista de Anza, captain of the presidio at Tubac in Sonora (now Arizona). Receiving the enthusiastic support of Fray Francisco Garcés, who had already crossed the Colorado Desert in his travels, and of Serra, who knew nothing of that country but was exceedingly earnest in his desire to open up a trail, the request was approved.

On January 8, 1774, Anza set out from Tubac with thirty-four men, including Father Garcés and another Franciscan, thirty-five mules laden with provisions, sixty-five head of cattle, and a hundred and forty horses. Descending the Altar River through the Pima missions to Caborca, the last Spanish settlement between Sonora and Serra's San Gabriel Mission, they reached the juncture of the Gila and Colorado Rivers with little difficulty. But on reaching the Colorado Desert they lost their way in the shifting sand dunes, where they wandered helplessly for two weeks. Finally, turning to the south, they found water and good pasturage. Within a few days they had crossed the Sierras, the first white men to do so, and then across the wide green valley at sundown on March 22 they reached San Gabriel Mission, seven hundred miles from Tubac.

After continuing to Monterey Anza returned over the trail he had blazed to Tubac. Toward the end of the following year he led the first colony destined for San Francisco, arriving with four more colonists than had started on the long journey. They pitched camp on the peninsula between the Pacific and the Bay of Saint Francis just three weeks after the Declaration of Independence was signed on the other side of the continent. On September 17 the presidio was formally dedicated and on October 9 was founded the mission of San Francisco de Asís, with Padres Francisco Palóu and Benito Cambón installed as resident priests. Saint Francis had provided a harbor!

The mission at San Juan Capistrano was at last established on November 1, the father-president himself conducting the dedicatory Mass. An attempt a year earlier had been diverted by news of an Indian uprising at San Diego, accompanied by the destruction of the buildings and the murder of Friar Luís Jayme. The following winter Serra established the mission of Santa Clara de Asís, the last for five years.

Almost immediately after its founding, however, newly-arrived Governor Neve established the first pueblo, or civilian city, San José de Guadalupe, about midway between the presidios of Monterey and San Francisco. Four years later the same governor established the pueblo of Nuestra Señora, Reina de los Angeles on September 4, 1781.

With the founding of San Buenaventura on March 31, 1782, the first on the Santa Barbara Channel, so long proposed and so long delayed, Serra's work was done. The equipment, which had been so carefully packed by Gálvez thirteen years earlier for the mission which he had said was to be his own, was at last unpacked and Serra preached the dedicatory sermon. It was the father-president's ninth mission in Alta California. Two years later, after a lingering illness, he prepared himself for death and when, on August 28, 1784, the bells of San Carlos were tolled the grief-stricken Indians came from far and near to cover his coffin with native wild flowers. Near the remains of his companion Crespi he was buried in the chapel of the Mission San Carlos Borromeo in the beautiful valley he loved so well.

Pending the appointment of a successor to Serra, Father Palóu served as president. He had remained in Baja California when Serra started north to organize missions, but when the care of the missions in the peninsula was turned over to the Dominican Order he joined his superior and worked with him until the latter's death. Palóu had wanted for some time to retire because of his advanced age, and this he was permitted to do a year later when he was elected guardian of the monastery of San Fernando in Mexico City. There he completed his biography of Serra, which for almost a century remained the only history of Alta California of the period.

Father Fermín Francisco de Lasuén was a worthy successor to the first president. A native of Vitoria, Spain, he had come to Baja California in 1768, where he served for five years until he went to Alta California to make the mission of San Gabriel the most prosperous in the new chain. Serving then successively at San Juan Capistrano and at San Diego, he was well qualified by experience as well as by natural ability to fill Serra's shoes. He lacked only a devoted biographer to make him as justly famous as the first president. Like his predecessor he founded nine missions during his eighteen years of service as president.

The first was Santa Barbara, which has become perhaps the most noted of the California missions and is the only one which has been continuously under Franciscan supervision. It was founded December 4, 1786. The following year Lasuén established the mission of La Purísima Concepción, not far to the north and west. Almost four years passed before the Mission Santa Cruz was established, in 1791, but it was followed almost immediately by the founding of the Mission Nuestra Señora de la Soledad, so named because of the solitary, dreary spot in which it was located.

Again almost six years intervened, but in 1797 five missions were established in little more than a year: San José, San Juan Bautista, San Miguel Arcángel, San Fernando Rey de España, and San Luís Rey de Francia. The president was in his seventy-seventh year at that time. Even greater as an administrator than as a founder, Lasuén lived to see the missions enter their most prosperous era both materially and spiritually. In his eighty-third year, on June 26, 1803, he died and was buried beside Serra in front of the altar in the chapel of the Mission San Carlos.

Only one mission was established during the term of Father Estévan Tapis who succeeded to the office. The founding of Santa

Inés on September 17, 1804, completed the chain of missions up the coast. For reasons in the first case of health of the Indians and in the second case of security, two more missions were established north of the Golden Gate at a much later date: San Rafael Arcángel in 1817 and San Francisco Solano at Sonoma in 1823. The Indians at the former staged a remarkable recovery and at the latter the Russians surprised the Spaniards by appearing with gifts of useful and ornamental articles for the new mission.

This, very briefly, is the story of the founding of the missions of California and of the men who founded them. It was one of the most remarkable social experiments in history, resulting in an architectural heritage of which California is justly proud. The missions these men established have so far been merely mentioned, in the order of their founding. In the pages that follow each mission is described in some detail, though still briefly. For the sake of convenience they are taken up in geographical order from south to north rather than in the order of their founding.

Four presidios were established for the military guardianship of the missions and civil settlements, each presidio being responsible for the missions and settlements under its jurisdiction. Those four districts of responsibility were, from south to north: San Diego, Santa Barbara, Monterey, and San Francisco. To simplify the arrangement further, the following four-chapter tour has been divided into chapters which coincide with the four jurisdictions.

23

San Diego to Los Angeles

ALTHOUGH THE first to be founded, the mission of San Diego de Alcalá never became one of the largest or most important of the California missions. Nor was it ever as prosperous as some of the other missions. Named in honor of Saint James of Alcalá, a Franciscan who had lived and worked in southern Spain in the fifteenth century and was canonized in 1558, the first mission was built upon an eminence back of "Old Town," not far from the harbor and the open sea.

To obtain a better water supply and to get away from too close contact with the soldiers, the mission was moved in 1774 to a new site in a valley some six miles inland. In that year a small wooden church was built and decorated with a simple altar and a set of the Stations of the Cross. A padre's house was built close by and other buildings included a granary, blacksmithshop, corrals, and fourteen Indian houses.

Troubles with the Indians, which had begun almost immediately upon arrival in San Diego, did not cease with the move to the new location. On the night of November 4, 1775, eight hundred Indians swept down on the little mission and, after intimidating the neophytes, sacked the church of its vestments and sacred vessels and set fire to the buildings. In the onslaught the carpenter and the blacksmith of the mission were killed. Father Luís Jayme walked boldly out to the Indians but before he could say more than "Love God, my children!" he was seized and clubbed to death. The few soldiers stationed on guard at the mission put up a brave battle but it was not until daybreak that the Indians retired with their dead and wounded. The soldiers at the presidio, six miles away, had slept quietly through the whole assault on the mission.

In January Captain Rivera arrived on the scene with Juan Bautista de Anza, who was on his way to San Francisco with his party of colonists; but it was not until Padre Serra came to San Diego the following summer that work was begun on new buildings for the mission. A church, very little larger than the first, was built of adobe and roofed with thatch; other buildings included a monastery of two rooms, refectory, kitchen, storerooms, a harness room, and a dormitory for the neophytes. In 1780 the church was enlarged and, together with additional appurtenant buildings added from time to time, served the needs of the mission until 1808 when the present church was begun. The latter was completed and dedicated November 12, 1813.

Owing to neglect the mission began to deteriorate about the middle of the nineteenth century and by 1930 little was left of the church except part of the crumbling façade and some of the side walls. It was restored, however, in 1931, so that today it is possible to picture it as it was in the days of the Franciscan fathers. Its most interesting feature is the whitewashed-brick façade with its graceful, curved pediment and restored pierced belfry on the left. The latter is in three stories with two arches in each of the first two supporting a third story with a single arch. The building, on the brow of a hill overlooking the broad valley, is now maintained as a museum.

Northward from San Diego the highway (101) follows the shore of the Pacific to Oceanside, where a paved side road turns inland to San Luís Rey, the "King of the Missions." It well deserves its popular title. Although nearest to the Mother of the Missions, it was one of the last to be established. For almost thirty years the friars at San Diego had borne the brunt of the work in the extreme south of California, but when San Luís Rey finally was established in June, 1798, it soon outstripped the first mission both in prosperity and in the size and beauty of its church. This was due very largely to the talent and energy of the man who for almost thirty-four years was padre-in-charge.

Antonio Peyri was born in Catalonia in 1765 and sailed to Mexico in 1795, arriving in California the following year. After serving at San Luís Obispo for two years he was assigned to the new mission to be established at San Luís Rey by Father Lasuén, then in his seventy-eighth year. The aged but still efficient father-president stayed for six weeks to supervise the start of the work, made possible by donations received from the older missions near by. When the new resident friar took over he went to work with a zeal quite equal to that of his superior.

Within a year Peyri had supervised the construction of a temporary chapel, padre's quarters, guardhouse, soldiers' quarters, and a storeroom, all of adobe and roofed with thatch. Within the next three years a larger church, quarters for girls and for boys enclosed around patios, and additional granaries and corrals all had been built, tile replacing thatch and earth as roofing materials.

In 1811 Peyri launched a building program more ambitious than any yet undertaken in the whole mission chain. Plans were made and the foundations laid for the present large church. It was dedicated four years later but work on it and the adjacent mission buildings continued for another fifteen years. In 1829 the dome at the crossing was reported as finished and the church was completely decorated.

That year the energetic friar asked to be relieved of his duties on
the ground that he was an old man and no longer able to fulfill the
arduous tasks required of him. It was three years, however, before affairs at the mission made it possible for him to depart. The story is told
that he decided to leave the mission secretly during the night to
avoid any demonstration on the part of his beloved Indians. When
they discovered his absence in the morning many of them mounted
their ponies and rode to San Diego to try to persuade him to stay.
His ship, however, had already weighed anchor, with Father Peyri
standing on deck, his arms outstretched, blessing his charges amid
their tears and cries. Many of them, it is said, even swam after the
ship, begging their father to come back; and for years afterward they
would place candles and flowers before the picture of Padre Peyri
at San Luís Rey and plead with him to return. Even after his death
they continued to pray to him rather than to a saint they did not
know.

For sixty years the Mission San Luís Rey suffered neglect, pillage,
and even destruction. Finally in 1893 Father Joseph O'Keefe came
down from Santa Barbara to restore the property for use as a Franciscan missionary college. For almost twenty years he stayed there
supervising the work on the mission; patiently and carefully and
with adobe bricks made by descendants of the first Indian workmen,
he gradually brought back some of the glory wrought by Padre
Peyri. He was succeeded by an equally careful and devoted Franciscan, Father Peter Wallischeck, so that today we may see why
San Luís Rey, named for King Louis IX of France, came to be called
the King of the Missions.

With the exception of San Juan Capistrano when its stone church
was in its short but very real glory, San Luís Rey is the finest of all
the California missions. It is also the largest. In the cruciform plan
of the church it resembles the former great church of San Juan Capistrano, the only other California mission to adopt that plan. The
nave is a hundred and sixty-three feet long by twenty-seven feet
wide with transept arms each about twenty-seven feet by fifteen
feet. The thick side walls of the nave are relieved by large pilasters,
decorated in imitation of black marble, which divide them into five
bays. The large ceiling beams have now been returned to their places.
An elaborate doorway leads on the left into the patio and another on
the right leads into the mortuary chapel, one of the finest rooms in
any of the missions. Octagonal in plan, it contains an altar composed

of coupled engaged columns supporting a curved, broken pediment, all elaborately executed in brick and plaster.

On the façade of the church the main portal is enclosed by simple pilasters and moldings flanked by niches containing statues, one of Saint Francis of Assisi and the other of Saint Francis of Solano. Above is a circular window which lights the choir and crowning the façade is a curved and pedimented gable. Two towers were doubtless intended but only one, on the right, was ever completed. It rises in two stories, with arches on four sides of the irregular octagon, and is capped with a dome and lantern. Of unusually fine proportions, this tower has been taken as a model for much modern work. Indeed the façade of the church and other features of the mission indicate not only a master hand at design but a unity which points to one man as being responsible for the whole carefully-preconceived plan. That man must have been Padre Peyri.

Not content with a large mission to serve the Indians along his section of *El Camino Real*, Peyri turned his attention also to those Indians farther inland, out of reach of San Luís Rey. For them he built a chapel that they might be visited by a friar from San Luís Rey who could hold services in a place these Indians could conveniently reach. Such a tributary chapel is known as an *asistencia*. Most famous of these is that chapel at Pala built by Peyri. It is also the only one restored, and to its former use! Beautifully situated at the base of Palomar Mountain, some twenty miles east and a little north of San Luís Rey, Pala is one of the most charming places to visit in the whole mission chain. The road winds among the hills to the tiny country-crossroads village in the midst of which stands the "assistant" mission, half hidden in a garden behind a stone wall.

The group was evidently never completed since the patio was never entirely closed. The small church occupies the center of the space while the other mission buildings extend to the left of it. The simple interior of the church (see Plate 43), with its whitewashed walls, exposed wood-trussed roof (happily now reinforced with iron tension members so that intermediate posts could be removed), and its figures, in a niche above the altar and two false niches painted on the wall on either side, has just the character one would expect to find in the quiet little Indian village.

The most charming feature of all is the detached campanario in the garden on the corner. It stands upon a base of granite boulders set in cement and consists of two arches, one above the other, four feet thick, of burned brick plastered with stucco.

After a long period, during which the Indians were scattered and the buildings were falling into disrepair, the descendants of the Indians finally were returned to their former home and the buildings were repaired. Once more the Indians could gather in their simple little church, bury their dead in the cemetery beside it, and listen to the bells in the campanario calling them to prayer.

Then one day in the winter of 1916 a heavy storm arose and swept the valley. Floodwaters from the river poured around the base of the campanario and on the afternoon of January 27 it toppled and fell.

Upon examination it was found that the base was of adobe, only the surface being covered with boulders. It had stood for exactly one hundred years. Funds were raised, the Indians contributed the labor, and the campanario was rebuilt exactly as it had stood. Except for one thing. Hidden behind the granite boulders is solid concrete. Since it cannot be seen, even Padre Peyri himself would probably not be able to tell that his belfry had ever fallen.

Most people on hearing the subject of California missions mentioned think immediately of San Juan Capistrano. The romance and tragedy of its history and the beauty of its site are as much responsible as the grandeur of its ruined church, which served God and the mission for such a short time and which Rexford Newcomb calls "the most glorious attempt at church-building during the Spanish period of California." If San Luís Rey is justly called the "King," San Juan Capistrano certainly deserves the title "Jewel of the Missions." The carefully-preserved, vine-covered ruins in their lovely flower-filled gardens provide the most popular pilgrimage in all of California.

After the first interruption, when Father Lasuén was forced hastily to bury the bells, the mission of San Juan Capistrano was founded November 1, 1776, by Padre Junípero Serra assisted by Padres Pablo Mugártegui and Gregório Amúrrio. It was the seventh link in the chain. The bells were disinterred and under an arbor the father-president celebrated the Mass on the Feast Day of All Saints.

Work was begun immediately on an adobe church one hundred and twenty feet long and seventeen feet wide. Intelligently and faithfully restored by Father John O'Sullivan—who came there in 1910, broken in health, and stayed to work for twenty-three years— it is again in use. Known as Serra's Church, it has the distinction of being the only one remaining in California in which the first father-president actually celebrated Mass and administered the sacraments of baptism and confirmation.

Within twenty years the adobe church was considered too small to accommodate the increasing number of new converts so the priests in charge, Fathers Vicente Fuster and Juan Norberto de Santiago, decided on the building of a great stone church which would surpass anything yet built in California. Isidoro Aguílar, a master stonemason from Culiacán, supervised the construction and took charge of the stonecutting. Sandstone was quarried and transported, with the help of oxen, from a point about six miles northeast of the mission. Women and children joined in the work, bringing small stones, sand, and gravel to the site. For nine years the work continued until finally, on September 7, 1806, the great church was dedicated. In the ceremonies Father-President Tapis was assisted by many visiting padres, and among those present was the governor with his staff and officers and soldiers from the presidios at San Diego and Santa Barbara. It was one of the most noteworthy events in early California history.

The plan of the church was that of a Latin cross, with a total length of a hundred and eighty feet; the nave was thirty feet wide, with the transept arms each projecting about twenty feet. At the south end stood the stone campanario a hundred and twenty feet high, which according to tradition could be seen from a point ten miles to the north and whose bells could be heard even farther. The church was covered with seven low domes of stone, one of which, over the sanctuary, can be seen today.

On December 8, 1812, on the day of the Feast of the Immaculate Conception, an early Mass was being held. High Mass would be celebrated later so there was a small congregation at this sunrise service. Suddenly the kneeling men and women felt the earth rock with great violence. Seeing huge cracks in the domes overhead the worshipers were terrified. Another shock and panic broke out. The padre called to the people to come into the sanctuary but only the neophytes serving at the altar could hear him. They escaped into the sacristy. Just as they did so the great bell tower crashed through the roof, piling masses of stone and mortar up over the doorways. During the next two days forty bodies were taken from the ruins. Only six, including the padre, were saved.

Nine years it took to build; for six years it served to glorify God; in a matter of seconds it was a mass of debris. It was never rebuilt.

San Juan Capistrano is but a short distance from the ocean and north from there one is very conscious of the Pacific. The foaming surf breaks on the rocky shore beside the road, resort hotels spread out over the hills to gain the view, and farther along hundreds of craft from humble fishing boats to luxurious yachts bob at anchor, waiting for a chance to be unleashed. Or, if one prefers oranges to salt water, the inner drive is almost one continuous grove. Through one or the other—and the traveler has his choice—the road, or roads, lead to that suburb of Los Angeles named for the archangel Gabriel.

After Fathers Pedro Benito Cambón and José Angel Fernandez de la Somera had set out from San Diego with an escort of soldiers and pack drivers, following the trail of Portolá, they were stopped en route by a band of hostile Indians. According to Palóu, the unfurling of a banner bearing a painting of the Virgin immediately quieted them and they cast their beaded necklaces at the feet of the Mother Mary. Following the padre to the selected site and helping to build temporary shelters, they witnessed the founding of the Mission San Gabriel Arcángel. The date was September 8, 1771.

Troubles between the soldiers and the Indians began almost immediately and, what with the added misfortune of floods, the site was moved five years later to the location it now occupies. Temporary buildings there were replaced in 1794 by the building of a stone church which was completed in 1806.

Though not prosperous at first, San Gabriel gradually became, under exceptionally competent leadership, one of the wealthiest missions in the chain. The first of her great leaders was Lasuén, who later succeeded Serra to the presidency of the missions and who was responsible for the choice of the present location. He was followed by Padres Antonio Cruzado and Miguel Sánchez, who served at the mission during the period when the stone church was built. The present campanario may have been built by Padre José María de Zalvidea, who was in charge from 1808 until 1826. Those last eighteen years saw the mission reach the height of its prosperity. Owing to Zalvidea's management the mission lands extended from the sea to the mountains and the mission became famous for its vineyards and orchards and particularly for the fine wines and brandy made at the mission distillery.

Both because of its location and its cellar the Mission San Gabriel often served as host to travelers, a role which it began to play even in its early days. One homesick neophyte, who had come from Baja

California with Palóu, escaped to cross the Colorado into Sonora only to fall into the arms of Captain Juan Bautista de Anza. Instead of chastising the Indian, Anza employed him as a guide; and thus Sebastián Tarabal was largely responsible for leading the captain to the gates of San Gabriel, and that homesick Indian could later claim a share in the founding of San Francisco.

At the northeast corner of the present church of the mission there was once a tower, which was ruined by that earthquake which destroyed the great church of San Juan Capistrano. There was also once a vaulted roof, which explains the heavy buttresses along the side, but that roof collapsed before the church was completed and was replaced by a flat roof of heavy crossbeams, now also given way to a modern roof.

With the absence of a tower the front of the church is severely plain, with only a simple arched entrance and square opening above. Much more interesting is the side toward the street, with its massive buttresses capped with pyramidal merlons. Near the front an exterior stone stairway leads up to a doorway opening into the choir loft.

But most striking of all is the campanario which rises from the side wall at the rear of the church. Pierced with six arched openings of varying sizes and surmounted by a beautiful wrought-iron cross, it is not only a unique and lovely feature of the mission but, more than any single feature in any mission, that campanario is the one thing that comes to mind whenever anyone speaks of mission bells.

After the founding of Los Angeles in 1781 the first settlers were forced to attend services at the Mission San Gabriel if they wanted to go to church at all. A small chapel was built for them a few years later but, because of the added attention required of the padres from the mission, approval was granted in 1811 for the erection of a church with a resident priest. The cornerstone was laid in 1815, but because of floodwaters from the Los Angeles River the location was changed to a new site facing the plaza and the public buildings of that day. So it was not until 1818, thirty-four years after the establishment of the village, that Los Angeles was to have its first church.

The citizens contributed five hundred head of cattle to defray the cost, but they were taken over by the governor to feed his starving army. The governor agreed to include construction costs in the territorial budget the following year, but the government that year was bankrupt and the original capital had been eaten up. The appeals of the people were at last answered by the padres of San Gabriel, who donated seven barrels of that mission's famous brandy. A glassful at a time, the brandy was converted into cash and work on the church was begun. It was dedicated on December 8, 1822.

Architecturally the church is not particularly interesting. A simple arched portal is flanked by thin pilasters which support a projecting horizontal band above which two square windows light the choir. A circular window in the gable opens into an attic. A low, square buttressed tower is surmounted by a pierced belfry of the simplest type with three arched openings in which the bells are hung.

The big city has so completely surrounded and all but swallowed the old church that one takes his life in his hands trying to get a view of it.

24

The Santa Barbara Channel

SAN FERNANDO too is now completely surrounded by the city of Los Angeles, but at least it is more peaceful out here than it was around the old plaza. Across the street is a beautiful park and among the trees is an old tile fountain moved from among the ruins of the Mission San Fernando, Rey de Espana. Beside it stands a statue of Fray Junípero Serra with an Indian boy. The most interesting part of the mission, and the only old part remaining intact, is the monastery or mission house which faces the street and the park. More of that later.

San Fernando was one of two California missions dedicated to sainted kings. The other, San Luís Rey, named in honor of Louis IX of France who was canonized in 1297 because of his crusades, has already been described. His cousin Ferdinand III, king of León and

Castile, was similarly honored with a mission less than a year earlier. King Ferdinand, who lived during the first half of the thirteenth century, was canonized by Pope Clement X in 1671 for his religious zeal and his victories over the Moors. He is considered one of the greatest of Spanish kings. The mission named for him was founded September 8, 1797, by Father-President Lasuén to fill the gap between the Missions San Gabriel and San Buenaventura.

The mission never attained the architectural eminence of some of the other missions of the south. The missions of California all followed similar steps in architectural development: first, after a most temporary brush shelter, a building of wooden posts plastered with clay and roofed with twigs and mud, or thatch; second, buildings of adobe roofed with tile; and third, larger buildings of burned brick or of stone. San Fernando never got beyond the adobe stage. An adobe church a hundred and sixty-six feet long by twenty-five feet wide was completed and dedicated in December, 1806. It was damaged in the earthquakes of 1812 and rebuilt six years later. After secularization the building disintegrated rapidly, but it has recently been restored and is again in use.

Much the most interesting building, however, is the monastery facing the street, known variously as the "long building" and the "House of the Fathers." A rhythmic row of wide brick arches opening onto a corridor along the front is its outstanding feature. There are nineteen of these arches supporting a heavy timbered roof covered with tile. This arcaded structure, two hundred and thirty-five feet long by sixty-five feet wide, was once the center of mission activities and was used also as a place for entertaining the many guests who stopped to spend a night or longer at the mission. Its twenty-one rooms include a large reception room, "governor's room" for distinguished visitors, chapel, kitchen and smokehouse, refectory, library, offices, and quarters for the padres. In its presentation of a picture of mission life of the early nineteenth century it is one of the most interesting places among the missions.

The other old buildings connecting the House of the Fathers with the church at the far end are now being faithfully restored with adobe bricks. Upon completion of the restoration the archbishop will take over the mission and the elderly Franciscan friar who for seventeen years has been guiding parties through the fascinating rooms of the monastery will be able to retire, perhaps only to other work. His grim humor will be missed. But he is not sorry; he has been handling the job all that time seven days a week.

Ventura is a sizable little city and the mission there faces a busy street. The church of San Buenaventura—all that is left of the mission—is easily identified by the two tall pine trees which tower above it on the right.

The Mission San Buenaventura, scheduled to be the third in the California chain after San Diego and San Carlos, was several times delayed owing to troubles between soldiers and Indians. Finally on March 31, 1782, at a site selected by Serra near the ocean where the beautiful Ojai Valley begins, the Cross was raised in a brushwood shelter and the father-president dedicated the ninth of the California missions. It was Easter Sunday. Witnessing the ceremony was Governor Neve in full regalia attended by a guard of soldiers from Monterey.

Fray Junípero stayed for three weeks assisting Father Cambón in starting the settlement, even preparing the registers himself. The first buildings erected were destroyed by fire but Captain George Vancouver, visiting there in 1793, reported that a new church was under construction and that other permanent buildings had almost been completed. That hardy traveler was delighted with the orchards and gardens and with the fresh fruits and vegetables that were set before him. When he left, Vancouver was accompanied by a small flock of sheep and twenty pack mules laden with all of the fresh fruits and vegetables they could carry. What a feast his sailors would have!

The stone church under construction at that time was evidently not completed for some years for it was not dedicated until September 9, 1809. Because of the earthquakes of 1812 extensive repairs had to be made, and to avoid further similar damage the large buttresses now to be seen on the front, along the left-hand side, and against the tower were added.

Nothing remains of the original mission buildings except the church. The entrance is reached by a flight of steps, the grade line at the front having been lowered in modern times. A curious steep pediment rises above the arched entrance, pierced by a square window on the center and with a bracketed niche at the apex. The terraced tower is not as graceful as that at San Luís Rey and its arched upper stories do not center on the base; nevertheless it is picturesque withal. But more interesting is the side doorway, where a mixtilinear Moorish arch is flanked by stone pilasters, a decorative design in stone framing a niche above it.

Fortunately or unfortunately the building has long continued in use as a parish church: unfortunately because of the damage done by misguided zeal; fortunately because otherwise the church might not be here at all. The interior does not remotely resemble what it was at one time. The worst of the damage was done in the nineties when the church was "remodeled" by the resident priest, Father Ciprian Rubio. In addition to tearing down all the appurtenant buildings, even including the sacristy to make room for a parish school, he "did over" the interior. A matched and beaded wooden ceiling and a wooden floor, built over a tile floor, had already been installed; and to complete the damage Father Rubio cut large rectangular windows in the wall on either side of the garden doorway (which fortunately he left) and replaced the Indian murals with meaningless stenciled decorations.

Padre-Presidente Junípero Serra wanted so badly to found the Mission Santa Barbara before he died. He did bless the presidio there, established April 21, 1782; but the founding of the mission was to be left to his successor, Father Fermín Lasuén. On December 4, 1786, the Feast of Saint Barbara, the site was blessed and the mission dedicated. The formal founding, however, with Holy Mass, did not take place until the sixteenth, in the presence of Governor Fages.

The name Santa Barbara was given to the islands, the near-by mainland, and the channel between them by a Carmelite friar who accompanied Vizcaíno on his voyage in 1602. Sailing through the channel the expedition landed (whether on mainland or islands is not known) on December 4, the birthday of Saint Barbara. Saint Barbara was a Roman maiden born A.D. 218 in Asia Minor. At the age of seventeen, pleading with her father to spare the Christians in whose relentless persecution he had been participating, she was suspected of having accepted the faith. Failing even by torture to compel his daughter to abjure her religion, he slew her with his own hand. She is venerated as the patroness against thunder, lightning, firearms, and sudden death.

The site selected for the mission, half a league northwest of the presidio, is a beautiful and commanding one high above the channel at the foot of the Santa Inés Mountains. In the spring of 1787 work was begun on the mission structures. They included a small church, a house for the missionaries, a carpentershop, a granary, and houses both for unmarried men and for unmarried women. They were built of adobe and roofed with thatch. Within five years a larger church had been built, also of adobe but roofed with tiles. In addition there were other granaries, toolhouses, a guardhouse, and a missionhouse containing refectory, kitchen, and storerooms.

The water system at Santa Barbara was the most complete of all the missions. The water was obtained by damming Pedregosa Creek some two miles above the mission, from where it was conducted by means of a stone aqueduct to a settling-basin and thence to a stone reservoir a hundred and ten feet square and seven feet deep on the hillside above the mission. Completed in 1806, this reservoir is still used by the city water department. Two years later an ornate fountain was built in front of the mission. With water fed from the reservoir, the overflow from the large octagonal basin flowed through the mouth of a carved stone bear into a stone laundry vat more than seventy feet long by six feet wide and three feet deep. Here the Indians brought their family wash. After dipping the clothes into the water the women pulled them up onto the large, rounded rim of the vat, where they were soaped and beaten with paddles just as is done in Mexico and Spain today. The structures are still in place, the photogenic fountain serving as a popular foreground for the candid shots of tourists.

In the earthquake of December, 1812, the adobe church was so badly damaged that Fray Antonio Ripoll decided the time had come to build a new and still larger stone church. The following two years were devoted to the preparation of the design and the gathering of materials and in 1815 the cornerstone was laid. Work progressed steadily for five years and the church was dedicated September 10, 1820.

Built entirely of native sandstone blocks, the church is a hundred and seventy-five feet long, thirty-nine feet wide, and forty-two feet high. The walls are six feet thick strengthened by solid stone buttresses eight feet square. The towers, each about twenty feet square, rise to a height of seventy-eight feet and are of almost solid stone-masonry up to the belfries. The one at the right *is* solid while the one at the left is cut out only to provide a narrow, spiral stairway leading to the belfry. To reach the belfry on the right it is necessary to cross the roof behind the pediment.

The façade of the church is unique in the mission chain in containing so much of the Classic. Not trained as an architect, Ripoll was nevertheless a student and he was resourceful enough to take good advantage of whatever was available in the way of source material. In the library at Santa Barbara was a copy—and it is still there—of a Spanish translation of the Latin Vitruvius, containing plates of the orders of architecture. Plate X of that volume unquestionably served as the inspiration for the design of the façade of Santa Barbara. The Greek Ionic volutes atop attenuated engaged columns, the interlaced Greek fret motif, the dentils of the pediment are all there. Placed between the massive and thoroughly Spanish-Colonial towers this applied Classic façade combines with other elements to make a mixture which will not bear architectural analysis; but why quibble about analysis when the spirit is so admirably expressed? Padre Ripoll achieved a stateliness that is highly commendable; the incongruity of relationships can be overlooked.

Vitruvius helped with the interior too. The wood-carved and painted designs on the flat ceiling, referred to locally as "thunderbird" ornaments, came from another plate in the old volume already mentioned. The design was seized upon enthusiastically by the Indians who attributed to the wings and barbed-lightning tongues a pagan meaning, and Padre Ripoll had no trouble getting his ceiling decorated.

The high altar is of stone and the reredos behind it is adorned with five wood-carved statues. Santa Barbara stands in the center and on her two sides are the Blessed Virgin, Saint Joseph, Saint Francis, and Saint Dominic. Side altars on either side of the nave are surmounted by large oil paintings which were sent from Spain in the last decade of the eighteenth century. The painting at the left is of the Assumption while that on the right is of the Crucifixion. Near the entrance, on either side, a small chapel is built into the heavy masonry of the nave—one dedicated to Saint Anthony, the other to Saint Francis.

A doorway on the right of the church leads into the cemetery, a beautiful garden of roses and rare plants and trees. A large crucifix stands in the center surrounded by a trimmed hedge of native cypress trees. The monastery rooms in the long wing at the left of the church include a museum with a collection of old records, relics, brocaded vestments, and other ecclesiastical objects. The rest of the building is in use by the Franciscans as living quarters, and to the rear of it is their "Sacred Garden." Santa Barbara is the one mission which has never passed out of Franciscan control, and it now serves as a theological seminary, a parish, and a center for historical studies of the early mission period. It is also the mother house of the Franciscan province, which comprises all the Pacific Coast. Which is quite the proper role for the Queen of the Missions.

On June 29, 1925, the scene of more than a hundred years earlier at San Juan Capistrano was almost re-enacted. Fortunately the shock was not quite so severe and the damage not so sweeping. As in 1812, it was while worshipers were attending early Mass that the church of the Santa Barbara mission shook. Only the presence of mind of the attending priest, urging everyone to remain at prayer in his place, saved all from injury, for masses of stone were falling from the huge towers onto the steps at the entrance.

The damage to the buildings was severe. One of the towers fell, the other was in dangerous condition, the pediment was partially destroyed; almost everything in the church was badly battered and the second story of the monastery was so shattered that it fell through to the floor below.

The restoration was thorough and complete. After very careful surveys the buildings were reinforced with steel beams, tie rods, concrete columns and lintels so that they were stronger than ever before. Half the cost was subscribed by the general public of California.

Two years after the disaster, on the day of the opening of the annual fiesta, August 10, 1927, a solemn thanksgiving procession moved along the restored arcade and into the church. A small casket containing a list of all the donors to the restoration fund was placed in the base of the west tower, where a memorial tablet marks it. Santa Barbara was still Queen of the Missions.

Saint Agnes, like Saint Barbara, was a Roman maiden who suffered martyrdom. An outstanding beauty, she was sought by many nobles all of whom she refused, saying she was espoused to a heavenly bridegroom. Accused of being a Christian, she was condemned to death. She is the patron saint of young girls, who formerly on the Eve of Saint Agnes turned to magic to discover whom they were to marry. The California mission founded in her honor is the youngest of the missions south of the Golden Gate. It lies some thirty-five miles northwest of Santa Barbara. The approach is a beautiful one winding through a forest of gnarled and twisted oaks over San Marcos Pass and on through the little town of Santa Ynez, for the mission lies three miles beyond at the edge of the charming and spick-and-span little Danish community of Solvang. Or it can be reached by the Coast Highway, which skirts the ocean most of the way and then leads into the scenic Gaviota Pass.

The Mission Santa Inés was founded September 17, 1804, by Fray Estévan Tapis, the only one founded during his presidency. During its brief history it had more than its share of troubles, Indian and others. The mission shared in the earthquake of 1812 which destroyed the first adobe church; but another church was begun in 1815 and completed and dedicated July 4, 1817.

The church is of adobe faced with brick and the adjacent monastery, to which a second story has recently been added, has a long arcaded corridor on the front, of brick, and a roof of tile. The façade of the church is plain, consisting of a simple low-gabled wall with an arched doorway and arched window above flanked with flat pilasters. At the right-hand side of the front of the church once stood a heavy campanario of brick and adobe, pierced with three arches, two of them widely spaced with a third arch centered between them above. It collapsed in 1910 but it has been replaced by a new belfry of reinforced concrete. It is an unfortunate restoration, or reconstruction rather. Instead of two arches in the lower story there are now three, the middle one larger than the ones at either side, and it does not look like a mission campanario, in keeping with the heavy buttresses and deep revealed windows on the side of the church; it looks like what it is: a thin, hollow shell of concrete.

The interior is happier, retaining much of its ancient splendor, including a ceiling of heavy beams, old tile pavement, many original pieces of furniture, and Indian decorations.

The mission of La Purisíma Concepción never did amount to very much nor did it ever have any claim to architectural distinction. Northernmost of the channel group, its history was as turbulent as any of the missions, even necessitating a move from the original site where it was founded on December 8, 1787, by Father-President Lasuén to a new location where earthquakes and floods might spare it.

The adobe buildings did not withstand secularization, time, and weather and there was little left but ruins when in 1934 the mission property was made a state historical monument and the Civilian Conservation Corps undertook the reconstruction of the buildings. They have done an admirable job and today the long, low group looks much as it must have when the padres so bravely withstood frustrations one after the other.

The group of buildings lies in a valley not far from the town of Lompoc and about twenty miles west of the Mission Santa Inés. It is a lovely, peaceful spot made most attractive by the extensive, well-kept gardens which have recently been laid out and planted.

A placard in the reconstructed church of the mission reads:

DEC. 7, 1941, 1200 PERSONS GATHERED IN THIS CHURCH TO COMMEMORATE THE 154TH ANNIVERSARY OF THE FOUNDING OF LA PURÍSIMA MISSION. AT THE CLOSE OF THE SERVICES, THE FIRST IN 105 YEARS, NEWS OF THE BOMBING OF PEARL HARBOR WAS ANNOUNCED.

25

North to Monterey

AS THERE were two missions named for sainted kings, Saint Ferdinand and Saint Louis, so too were there two missions named for a Saint Louis: one for Louis IX, king of France, whose mission has already been described, and the other in honor of Saint Louis, bishop of Toulouse. To distinguish the missions they are spoken of as San Luís *Rey* and San Luís *Obispo*. The latter is in the heart of the small city of the same name, some fifty miles north of the Mission La Purísima Concepción, and consequently a longer day's journey than most of the intervals.

In 1772 the unpopular Governor Pedro Fages redeemed himself to some extent by staging the most celebrated bear hunt in the history of California. When the early friars were facing starvation while awaiting ships and supplies, the governor with some of his men went on a hunting expedition and sent back to the missions on pack mules nine thousand pounds of bear meat, to the great delight of the friars and Indians alike. The scene of the hunt had already been traversed by Portolá on his first expedition to Monterey, and because of the great number of the ferocious animals they encountered they named the place the Valley of the Bears. At a spot in that valley where two streams meet, Serra, on September 1 of the year of the hunt, established the Mission San Luís, Obispo de Tolosa. After the ceremonies in a chapel of boughs Fray Junípero continued south, leaving Padre José Cavaller, with a guard of five soldiers and two Indians, to start work on the mission.

Attacks by wild Indians, whose burning arrows repeatedly destroyed the thatched roofs, were responsible for the first roofing tiles made in California. Their manufacture began at San Luís Obispo in 1790 and their use spread rapidly to the other establishments. The architectural history of the mission after that date was typical. Lasuén in 1793 mentions a "new church of adobes with a tile roof" and says that "a portico was added to its front." That is probably the church which, after suffering a painful remodeling, can be seen today, again restored. After the mission became a parish church the colonnaded portico in front of the monastery to the left was torn down, the triple-arched narthex with belfry above—cracked by an earthquake—was removed, the three bells were hung in a spindly, open steeple on the roof, and the whole group was covered with siding and painted. Even the historic roof tiles were replaced with wooden shingles. The result looked like a turn-of-the-century midwestern interpretation of a New England meetinghouse.

Fortunately all that has been changed. Recently, under more intelligent direction, the colonnaded portico and the arched narthex have been rebuilt, the buildings have been roofed with tiles, and once more the bells hang where they belong—in the three small arches above.

There had long been need to fill the gap between San Luís Obispo and San Antonio de Padua to the north. That need was supplied on July 25, 1797, by the founding of the mission named for the Most

41. (*Top*) MISSION SAN DIEGO DE ALCALÁ. (*Bottom*) MISSION SAN LUÍS
REY DE FRANCIA

42. INTERIOR OF CHURCH, San Luís Rey

43. (*Top*) ASISTENCIA OF SAN ANTONIO DE PALA. (*Bottom*) INTERIOR
OF CHURCH, Pala

44. (*Top*) CAMPANARIO, Mission San Juan Capistrano. (*Bottom*)
SANCTUARY OF RUINED CHURCH, San Juan Capistrano

© *Photo. Bob Plunkett*

45. CLOISTER ARCHES, San Juan Capistrano

46. (*Top*) MISSION SAN BUENAVENTURA. (*Bottom*) PLAZA CHURCH, Los Angeles

47. CAMPANARIO, Mission San Gabriel

48. (*Top*) MISSION SANTA BARBARA. (*Bottom*) INTERIOR OF CHURCH, Santa Barbara

© *Frashers Photos. Pomona, Calif.*

49. (*Top*) MISSION SANTA INÉS. (*Bottom*) GARDEN, Mission San Miguel Arcángel

© *Frashers Photos. Pomona, Calif.*

50. (*Top*) MISSION SAN MIGUEL ARCÁNGEL. (*Bottom*) PRESIDIO CHAPEL, Monterey

51. (*Top*) MISSION SAN CARLOS BORROMEO. (*Bottom*) INTERIOR OF
CHURCH, San Carlos Borromeo

52. INTERIOR OF CHURCH, San Miguel Arcángel

53. INTERIOR OF CHURCH, San Francisco de Asís

54. (*Top*) MISSION SAN JUAN BAUTISTA. (*Middle*) MISSION SAN AN-
TONIO DE PADUA. (*Bottom*) RUINS OF MISSION, La Soledad

55. (*Top*) RUSSIAN CHAPEL, Fort Ross. (*Middle*) MISSION SAN FRAN-
CISCO DE SOLANO, Sonoma. (*Bottom*) MISSION SAN LUÍS OBISPO

56. (*Top, Middle, and Bottom*) THE KING, THE QUEEN, AND THE GEM
OF THE MISSIONS

Glorious Prince of the Celestial Militia, Archangel Saint Michael. Friendly Indians appeared with fifteen children for baptism the first day.

A small adobe church soon replaced the original temporary structure, only to be badly damaged by fire in 1806. It was not until 1816, however, that the foundations were laid for the present church which was completed two years later, except on the interior. In 1821 Estéban Munras, a Spanish artist, came down from Monterey to supervise the interior decorations which, applied with the aid of Indians, are the most distinctive feature of the mission today.

The artist, or the friars stationed at the mission like Ripoll at Santa Barbara, must have had a book of the orders of architecture which included color plates of the Egyptian temples, as the brilliant red-and-blue capitals atop the thin, marbleized columns of the reredos testify. Occupying the space above the altar stands a wood-carved Saint Michael with sword and scales; in front of panels at either side are other wood-carved, gilded, and polychromed statues, one of Saint Francis and the other of Saint Anthony. The space within the panels, above the entablature which the Egyptian columns support, and the entablature itself are all decorated with geometric and floral designs. Mounted on the entablature at the center is an All-seeing Eye with radiating beams in white and gold, giving the whole group the character of an oriental throne.

A polychromed, simple pulpit with domical canopy above hangs from the wall at one side; along the side walls a series of bays is formed by painted Greek Doric columns supporting a painted entablature with triglyphs (all properly supplied from the book at hand) which in turn supports a painted balustraded balcony. These painted bays form a background for the Stations of the Cross which, neatly framed, center in them. The whole decorative scheme is absurd but charming.

Over the sanctuary the heavy, squared beams of the ceiling, resting on carved corbels, are painted; throughout the length of the nave, however, the sturdy beams remain undecorated except for water stains. The simplicity of the beamed ceiling, contrasted with the quaint and unrestrained decorations, makes the interior of San Miguel the most delightful in the mission chain.

The exterior is simplicity itself, frankly expressing the long single nave, with an unadorned façade and a simple pitched roof covered with tiles. It is relieved by the walled monastery at the left, the arcaded buildings of which are set behind a well-kept garden with a fountain in the center. This fascinating mission today faces directly on Highway 101 just as it used to face El Camino Real.

San Miguel Arcángel is spoken of as "The Mission on the Highway." Although the low wall in front of its gardens affords a degree of seclusion, a steady stream of traffic passes in front of the door of the church. The next mission, forty miles to the northwest, affords the opposite extreme. It lies miles away from everything, about halfway between Highway 101 and the Coast Highway, Number 1, overlooking heavily wooded, rolling hills. An excellent new paved road leads to it, however, and it is now easily accessible, its seclusion only adding to the charm of the beautiful drive.

After founding the missions of San Diego and San Carlos Borromeo, Fray Junípero Serra's enthusiasm could not be held in check. The founding of the Mission San Antonio de Padua was the result of that zeal and the site was his choice. When the bells were hung on a live oak tree, Serra grasped the cords and rang them loudly, shouting: "Hear, oh Gentiles! Come! Oh come to the holy Church of God! Come, oh come and receive the Faith of Christ!" Chided by his confrere, the father-president was delighted to see a lone Indian cautiously approaching. Encouraged by colored glass beads, he soon brought others; and so the mission had its beginning on July 14, 1771.

By the end of 1773 a church and dwellings for the padres and for the neophytes had been built of adobe and roofed with thatch and the next year an irrigation ditch was dug and fields planted. In 1780 a large church was erected, considered to be one of the best yet built in California. When tiles came to be used it was reroofed. It too was replaced by a new church, completed in 1813 and still standing today. Its façade is one of the most interesting in California. The church proper, a simple structure with pitched roof like that of San Miguel, is preceded by a narthex constructed of brick which forms the actual façade. In the lower story is a triple-arched entrance and above it is a unique and beautiful curved gable pierced by a central arch with a balcony and flanked by two low towers, each pierced with an arch. In these arches were hung the bells; and soon they will hang there again, for the whole mission is now being carefully restored for use as a training school for lay brothers. The peaceful valley now hums with activity as workmen clamber over the roof and soon the old mission, so long headed toward ruin, will again thrive and the bells can ring out in *La Cañada de los Robles*, as they did for Father Serra a hundred and eighty years ago.

"This place is constituted a Mission dedicated in honor of the Most Sorrowful Mystery of the Solitude of Most Holy Mary, Our Lady." So wrote Padre-Presidente Lasuén in recording the founding of the thirteenth mission in the chain. Our Lady of Solitude was well named.

On the brown and bleak plains of the Salinas Valley, a place so dreary and so lonely that Padre Crespi had named it "La Soledad" the first time he saw it, Lasuén, with two priests and a small guard, solemnly proceeded with the ceremonies of founding the Mission Nuestra Señora de la Soledad. The date was October 9, 1791. They must have been the only occupants of the thousands of bare acres that stretched away on every side in silence. But a mission was needed to fill the gap between San Antonio de Padua and San Carlos Borromeo and the wide vacant fields gave promise of good pasturage.

Scarcely a dozen Indians appeared during the first year. The two friars assigned to the post, men of poor records and therefore an especially unfortunate choice, hated the country and grumbled at planting beans. The soil did not prove as fertile as had been hoped and constant irrigation was necessary. Ten years after the founding an epidemic carried off several natives every week and the converts ran away in fear. Few friars would stay more than a year or two and assignment there was dreaded by all. In later years Fray Sarría, *comisario prefecto* for many years and later president, had to take the post himself because no one else would; and during the Mexican regime, when the missions were secularized and their decline began, the faithful padre refused to leave his poverty-stricken Indians. One Sunday morning while saying Mass in the little adobe church he fell before the altar, dead of starvation. No one succeeded him.

The church in which Sarría died may have been the last. Or the last one may have been built later. No one seems to know for certain. Early photographs show only a long, low group of tile-roofed adobe buildings surely and not too slowly succumbing to the elements. When toward the end of the nineteenth century sentiment was aroused for the preservation and restoration of missions, Soledad was considered beyond hope. "Weep! Weep!" wrote George Wharton James, "for the church of Our Lady of Solitude. It is entirely in ruins. . . . The winds howl around it, the rains beat upon it, the fierce sun shines upon it, and all do their part to aid in its more speedy dissolution."

The ruins stand today, hardly more than a few heaps of crumbling adobe marked by a plain wooden cross in a flat, grassy field surrounded by acres and acres of lettuce and carrots. It is not *entirely* lonely today. Here and there in the distance a crouching figure can be seen pulling carrots from the ground, and in the field adjacent to the scattered adobe piles a farmer drives his tractor back and forth, back and forth, plowing his field for another crop.

The Lord must have decided, after making that part of the earth which was eventually to become the United States, to add just a little bit onto the bulge that became the California coast and there try out some experiments in beauty which He hitherto had not dared. Whether at the time it was given a name is not recorded, but after the explorations of the Spaniards it came to be known as the Monterey Peninsula. Both geography and history have been unkind to the place chosen in memory of the sorrowful and solitary Mother of Christ, so perhaps compensation was intended in the predestined location of the next mission north, even though it was founded at an earlier date, which means nothing in predestination.

A lovelier location could not have been found as a place to establish the headquarters of the missions. From the Bay of Monterey the rocky shore twists irregularly around the peninsula far out beyond a dark background of tall pines, which huddle closely together but away from the water, leaving the rocks and the roaring surf to the barking seals and to the twisted and tortured cypresses which the Maker had reserved exclusively for that spot where He was conducting His experiment—for they are to be found nowhere else. Farther to the south a great, white, curving sweep of sand outlines the shore of Carmel Bay and through a wide valley a little beyond the steep wooded hills that rise abruptly from the sand the Rio Carmelo finds its way to the ocean. There, beside the little river, Serra built the mission that was to be his "Cathedral of California."

The padre-presidente not only had good taste and unquestionably a love of beauty but he was a wise administrator who solved his problems with discretion. He soon recognized that soldiers and Indians do not mix. Very shortly after arriving at Monterey, therefore, he decided to move the mission far enough away from the presidio to be relieved of the nuisances, yet near enough for protection. In May of 1771 official permission to make the move was granted and in the Valley of the Carmelo, four miles south of the Bay of Monterey and the presidio, Serra began construction of the mission which was to be his ecclesiastical seat and his home for the rest of his life.

The buildings comprised a temporary church, padre's dwelling, storehouses, a guardhouse, and corrals, all surrounded by a stockade. In December he led Fray Juan Crespi and a band of converts through the pine woods to the new mission which he rechristened San Carlos Borromeo del Carmelo. There in their humble quarters Serra and his devoted lieutenant, when not traveling to found other missions, were to spend the rest of their days.

Three years later the first structures had been replaced by buildings of adobe, which was to remain the material used, except for the later church which was to be built of stone. By that time more baptisms had been performed at San Carlos than at the other four missions added together. Serra often talked of the proposed stone church, and before he died he said to Palóu: "I wish you to bury me in the church next to Fray Juan Crespi, for the present, and when the stone church is built, you may place me where you will." He was buried in the sanctuary of the church, on the Gospel side of the altar, beside his beloved colleague whom he had buried two years earlier.

Quite evidently the new stone church was erected on the same site, for the graves were never moved. It was begun in 1793, nine years after the death of Serra, and was completed and dedicated in September, 1797, Padre-Presidente Lasuén conducting the ceremonies.

Under Mexican civil government rule San Carlos suffered the fate shared by nearly all the missions, and in 1852 the tiled roof of the church, having fallen into disrepair, collapsed and grass and weeds began to cover the floor. When Father Angelo Casanova undertook the restoration of the old mission he had the debris cleared away, and on July 3, 1882, in the presence of four hundred people, he had the tombs of Serra, Crespi, and Lasuén opened to quiet rumors that the bodies had been removed. At that time a new roof was put on the church which, with its steep pitch and wood-shingle covering, saved the structure but marred its beauty. That has in turn been replaced (in 1936) by a low-pitched tile roof; and the monastery buildings at the left, which had entirely disintegrated, have since been rebuilt so that today the mission of San Carlos Borromeo, usually called simply

Carmel, presents much the appearance it did one hundred and fifty years ago.

The mission nestles in the valley below the pine-covered hills of the beautiful village of Carmel-by-the-Sea. Entrance to the church takes the visitor through a lovely garden adorned with fountain, statues, and a cross. The monastery buildings are to the left, completely surrounding a large plaza. The church is not impressive for its size, owing to the low walls, but how much more satisfactory than when the steep roof rose high above the arched façade, competing with the larger tower and dwarfing the smaller, can soon be realized by comparing it today with photographs taken before 1936.

The tower at the right, with its tall single arch, contains a spiral staircase leading to the choir loft; the larger tower at the left, with two smaller arches, is built over the baptistry. A stone stairway leads up at the side of the church to the belfry in the larger tower, which is without question one of the finest bell towers in the whole mission chain. Above the arches the tower transforms to a low, octagonal drum on which is built an egg-shaped dome, surmounted by a finial supporting a wrought-iron cross.

The circular pediment is pierced by a star-shaped window in the center directly above the weak and characterless arched and framed entrance. That entrance, lacking the rugged individuality that characterizes the rest of the church, must have been an omen of what was to be done to a much greater degree in the presidio chapel at Monterey, quite probably by the same master mason, Manuel Estévan Ruíz. The soft sandstone used, which became hardened upon exposure to the air, was easily worked—perhaps too easily worked.

On entering the church one is immediately struck with the unique form of the interior. The long, narrow nave is divided into four approximately equal bays by Doric pilasters which, with the walls, curve in near the top to form the transition to a parabolic vaulted ceiling. The ceiling as it stands is a restoration and for a time, when the steep, high roof was in place, a flat, semielliptical ceiling of wood covered the interior; but photographs of the earlier ruins clearly show the original form, which has now been revived. Those photographs should be enough to dispel forever the myth of the anthill method of construction so often attributed to the Spaniards. That subject is discussed at greater length in Chapter 27.

In the sanctuary, reached by the original stone steps, marble slabs mark the graves of the founder and his confreres. In the adjacent sacristy is a curiously-carved stone *lavabo* with two basins, one above the other. On the opposite side an elaborately-carved stone doorway, a curious combination of Classic and Gothic forms, leads into a side chapel which was added to the church about 1817. The doorway, however, harmonizing perfectly with the pilasters, must have been done at the time the church was built and therefore was carved by Ruíz.

A door in the corner of the nave, at the front, leads into the baptistry under the larger bell tower. It is unique in the mission chain. About ten feet square, the corners are cut to form an irregular octagon and against them are built quarter-engaged Doric columns from the capitals of which spring the ribs of a Gothic vault of stone. Although a mixture of styles, it is utterly charming.

I did not have the privilege, or pain, of seeing the church when it was unroofed, a near ruin; or of seeing it with its overpowering roof of the late nineteenth century. When I first visited there it had been restored as it is today, and on entering the church for the first time the organist, practicing in the choir loft, happened to be playing Schubert's *Ave Maria*. Without realizing it, my steps led me to the baptistry, at the left of the entrance. It may have been the influence of the musical accompaniment, but after visiting there again later and trying to view that little room objectively I still think that baptistry, with its rib-vaulted ceiling, is the finest little bit of interior architecture in the whole Southwest. It is as if the sixteenth-century Franciscan friars of Mexico, who built Gothic churches there, had saved one little piece to hand down to their successors to produce in California. Unlike modern revivals, it stems from medieval religious fervor and is therefore, as far as I know, the last Gothic interior ever built.

With its setting, its towers, its quaint exterior stairway, its unique interior, and its baptistry, the first Cathedral of California ranks high among the missions. Several of them have their popular names—the "King," the "Queen," and the "Jewel." I herewith nominate San Carlos Borromeo del Carmelo the "Gem of the Missions."

When the mission was moved to Carmel, to become the most important of the California churches from the ecclesiastical standpoint, the presidio chapel at Monterey became the most important church in a political sense when Monterey became the capital of the province. As the place of worship of the royal governors, representatives of the king of Spain, the chapel became "La Capilla Real" or Royal Chapel. It is the only extant presidio chapel in California. When the original chapel was so badly damaged by fire in 1789 that it had to be abandoned, a new structure was begun and was completed about the same time as the church of the mission at Carmel, and probably under the same direction. Additions were made to the building from time to time through the middle part of the nineteenth century, after it had come to be used as a parish church, but the façade remains almost as it was originally built.

The Royal Chapel in Monterey was a victim of that second Classic Revival which followed the establishment of the Royal Academy in Spain, and subsequently in Mexico, when Classic studies were made and the results of those studies were dictated to such an extent that regimentation took the place of imagination. It is doubtful that Ruíz (if he was responsible for the design) was forced into it, but the time was exactly right to follow that fashion of the day and the sterile Classic Revival was all the "rage." The craftsmanship in the hands of a master stonemason, and with the aid of a workable yet durable stone, is good; but the cold, academic design with arched doorway surrounded by Doric pilasters and entablature, surmounted by a segmental window with more pilasters climbing almost to the stilted curved, pedimented gable, is relieved only by the Virgin of Guadalupe in a shell-headed niche too high up to see. The steep tile pyramid atop the tower, added in the nineties, does not help the appearance of the façade; and the crosses, both on the tower and on the segmental top of the façade, are much too large and too close together.

Largest of all the Spanish mission churches of California is that at San Juan Bautista. Its builders, not content with the long, single nave typical of the mission churches, built high and wide side aisles opening through round arches into the sides of the nave, thus making the church the nearest approach to a three-aisled basilica in the whole mission chain. These side aisles either proved to be not needed after they were built, and were cut off, or else the arches that connected them with the nave were filled in at a later date as a safety measure. In either event five of these arches along the nave have been filled in with adobe bricks to form shallow recesses in the wall, and on the exterior the gaunt, adobe-filled arches of the nave stand exposed to the sun and wind. This filling in was probably what saved the church at the time of the earthquake in 1906, when the outer walls caved in and part of the roof over them fell. The last two bays, on either side in front of the sanctuary, were left open to be used as side chapels, resulting in a church cruciform in plan.

On either side of the sanctuary is a sacristy, and at the front a mortuary chapel on one side and a baptistry opposite it complete the huge rectangle. Projecting in front of the baptistry is the tower, the first floor of which is a severely-plain room covered with matched and beaded boards painted gray. For some time following the middle of the nineteenth century, when the old bell tower collapsed, an ugly and flimsy balustraded wood tower marred the beauty of the old church. It was built there, so they say, to save paying bell ringers, the priest—who slept in the upper room—pulling the bell ropes himself. This belfry has now been replaced by a suitable one, with walls too thin as at Santa Inés, but Spanish-Mission in character, with a single wide arch on each of the four sides and a low domical roof surmounted by a cross.

The old red-tile floor remains, bears, coyotes, mountain lions, and oak leaves all having left impressions in the tiles while they were drying in the open before being fired. The original beams of the ceiling, however, are hidden by a later covering of boards. Semicircular arches spanning almost the full height and width of the church separate both narthex and sanctuary from the nave.

Three steps lead up to the sanctuary, separated from the nave by a wooden balustrade. The gilded reredos rising behind the main altar contains six niches with backgrounds in red, each niche containing a figure. The reredos and altar are unique in that they were painted by the first American settler in California. It seems that the Mexican painter hired to do the work demanded six reals (about seventy-five cents) per day for his services, whereupon Fray Felipe Arroyo de la Cuesta, in charge of the mission at the time, shook his head sadly and decided that the reredos would have to remain unadorned. About that time along came Thomas Doak, recently arrived (in 1816) on a sailing vessel from Boston. Glad to be on solid ground again and equally happy to be assured of board and room, he took the job. That Tom mixed good paints is proved by the colors which can still be seen; that he was not an artist the designs give equal assurance.

The simple front of the church, with large, round-arched entrance with square window above, is heavily planted with cedars and the colorful, overgrown cloister garden at the left is an equally lovely and peaceful place. The round brick arches of the monastery corridor, interrupted by two wide, square openings for the benefit of processions, extend the full length of the plaza. Two hundred and seventy feet long, that arcaded structure even exceeds in length the famous "long building" of San Fernando.

Founded on June 24, 1797, San Juan Bautista was one of those five missions established within such a short time by Lasuén. Not without Indian troubles at the start, the mission soon became prosperous and on June 3, 1803, the cornerstone of the present church was laid. Completed in 1812, the church was dedicated on June 23, several Franciscans from the neighboring missions assisting Father de la Cuesta in the rites. When in 1815 Father Estévan Tapis had served nine years as Lasuén's successor in the presidency, he joined de la Cuesta at San Juan Bautista and there, after another ten years' service, to make a total of thirty-five years in California, he died on November 2, 1825. He is the only Franciscan to be buried in the San Juan church. So noted was he for his musical talent and his musical direction that for years after his death the chorus of Indian boys of San Juan Bautista was famous throughout the province. And so devoted were the boys to their music that even their children, when distribution of the white man's whiskey became widespread, would go to the American priest on Saturday and ask to be locked in the guardhouse so there could be no temptation that would interfere with their presence in the choir the next day.

Although other missions have been more completely restored and thus present a more finished appearance, San Juan Bautista, in spite of the great gaping holes in its side aisles (the filling of the arches of which, however, saved the church), remains the best preserved of all the missions. It has an atmosphere quite unlike any of the other missions of California, imparting a feeling of dignified serenity belonging to another age; not so much the remote period of the earliest Franciscans but more that of the period after the American flag had been raised, closer to us and therefore more keenly felt. It appears as if suddenly deserted within our possible memory. Those of us who can remember horse-and-buggy days have only to think on them and the whole place comes alive. This may be partly due to the large grassy square which the old mission faces and to the buildings on that square which look more like pioneering America than like Mexico or Spain. One expects at almost any moment to see a stagecoach arrive at the old Plaza Hotel, or a lady with hoopskirts and parasol emerge from the Castro House next door, or perhaps to hear a violin tuning up for a gay ball to take place in the great second-story room of the Zanetta House across the wide dusty plaza lined with locust trees with hitching rings still projecting from them.

A steep hill drops down from the open edge of the plaza to a wide valley stretching away into the distance. Where a rodeo arena now stands was once the mission orchard and the entire valley was once part of mission land. The business street of the village is a block away, behind the old houses, and the sunny, sleepy plaza dreams on undisturbed. El Camino Real had to go a bit out of its way to reach San Juan. The modern highway does not even do that. A side road, well paved, leads over and back. Which is fortunate. Modern highways and San Juan Bautista do not belong together. One really should drive there in a surrey with a fringe on top.

26

Around San Francisco Bay

OF THE missions north of the Bay of Monterey little remains. Only the oldest of these, that of San Francisco de Asís, founded in the year of American independence, contains more than fragments of the mission period.

The attractive little city of Santa Cruz lies across the wide-sweeping Bay of Monterey. Extending along the northern shore it is a busy place and a popular summer resort. Salt is in the air, in the summertime visitors throng the promenade, terraces above provide pleasant places to sit in the sun, and at night, as at Monterey, seals can be heard barking on the rocks off the coast.

There is little to suggest that it was once a mission center. The establishment of the village of Branciforte across the river was largely responsible for the fact that the mission never progressed very far. It never had a chance. It was founded September 25, 1791, by Lasuén and within two years the cornerstone of the mission church was laid.

What with the murder of one of its padres by the Indians, the inter-ference of the civil settlement encroaching upon Indian lands, and the fear of raids by pirates, the mission was almost abandoned several times until finally, in 1857, a violent earthquake completed the havoc that a similar quake and tidal wave in 1840 had begun; and the Mis-sion of Santa Cruz was no more.

Built upon a hill away from the bay a modern church occupies the site, marked by a standard planted at the curb, and on an adjacent side of the square a few hundred feet away a tiny church recalls to mem-ory that there was once a mission there. This church, built in 1931 from old paintings of the mission church, was the donation of a local resident. It is not a replica, as it is often called; it is a half-size model.

Little more is left of the Mission Santa Clara de Asís established on January 12, 1777, the next to the last of the missions founded during the presidency of Fray Junípero Serra. Floods were its great problem, necessitating a move to a new site where a church, said to be the finest structure in California up to that time, was completed and dedicated on May 15, 1784. It was designed by Father Murguía. Four days be-fore the dedication the padre-architect died and was buried in the church by Palóu.

Destroyed by the earthquake of 1812, the original church was re-placed in 1817 by a new structure only a remnant of which remains today. Behind the chapel of the University of Santa Clara is a piece of old adobe wall, forming a porch with wooden posts and tile roof with a gnarled old olive tree beside it; it is a lovely spot—and all that is left of the old mission. After Santa Clara College was founded in 1855, later to become the University of Santa Clara, the church of the mission was repaired and used as a chapel of the new college. In the course of time earthquakes, then fires completed the destruction of the building and today the fine new chapel of the university is patterned after the church of the mission. It is, however, just a fine, new university chapel. To feel anything of the impact of the old mission it is necessary to walk around to the attractive garden in the rear and to dream.

The drive from Santa Cruz, by the sea, to Santa Clara takes one over a beautiful pass with far-reaching vistas of valley after valley with high mountains in the background. Thence orchards of fruit line the road leading to the university town. From Santa Clara the *alameda* of old still continues to San José, the first *pueblo*, now grown so large that the two towns appear to be one. The Mission San José de Guadalupe, however, lies fifteen miles to the north of the pueblo near the southern tip of San Francisco Bay.

One of those established by Lasuén in rapid succession to fill the gaps, the Mission San José was founded June 11, 1797. A new church of chalkstone was completed in 1809, replacing an older wooden structure. It stood until an earthquake in 1868 completed the ruination begun by secularization and neglect. A modern church now occupies the site. Beside it stands a remnant of an old monastery corridor, with square wooden posts supporting a wood-beamed roof covered with tiles and with doors leading through adobe walls into the rooms of a pathetic little museum. A typical mission-bell signpost marks the location of the remnant which is so well hidden that attempts to photograph it result only in an excellent detailed view of a row of spreading palms.

A visit to the mission of San Francisco de Asís will make up for the lack of existing remains of other missions in the vicinity of the Bay. Actually, of course, a visit to the city of San Francisco will make up for the lack of almost anything. But we cannot go into a discussion of the city here.

Missions at San Francisco and at Santa Clara had been proposed within a year after the first entrance into Alta California, but it was not until Juan Bautista de Anza arrived in 1776 that final surveys were made and the sites of the presidio and the mission were located. The former was to be established at the entrance of the port and the latter in the valley of a stream which was named Arroyo de los Dolores because it was discovered on the Friday of Sorrows (the Friday before Holy Week). That name has been attached to the mission ever since. Dedicated to San Francisco de Asís, founder of the Franciscan Order, who had shown his followers his harbor— and such a harbor—it is commonly called simply Mission Dolores.

As was almost invariably the case, the first buildings were of wood and thatch. The construction of a permanent church was begun on April 25, 1782, the cornerstone being laid by Padre Palóu, who was to make San Francisco his home up to the time of his retirement to Mexico. Lack of building records during part of that period

makes it impossible to state with certainty whether that church was
the one which remains today or whether the present church, mentioned by Vancouver in 1792, was a somewhat later replacement.
The present church seems to have been completed and decorated by
1810, at which time two side altars of carved and gilded wood were
reported as having been installed.

Having suddenly arrived on the inside, it is well worth while
staying there for some time. Much smaller and with none of the
naïveté of the church of San Miguel Arcángel, the interior of Dolores
is the richest and most sophisticated of all the mission churches. If the
interior of San Miguel is delightful, the interior of San Francisco is
better described as splendid. Though more finished in appearance
and with much greater sophistication, it is oddly reminiscent of the
interior of the little church of San José in Laguna, New Mexico.

The squared beams of the ceiling are still in place, decorated with
the colors applied by the Indians. A wide arch also richly decorated
separates the sanctuary from the nave. Finest of all is the baroque
retablo with many panels and figure-filled niches decorated in mel-
lowed colors of gold, red, and blue. It is elaborate, of course, but one
has only to compare it with the *retablos* of San Xavier del Bac to
realize that it is far from unrestrained.

A door at the left leads into the little enclosed cemetery, as peaceful a spot as could possibly be found in the heart of a large city. The
façade of the church, facing a wide boulevard, is quite unlike that of
any other mission. A round-arched entrance is flanked on either side
by a pair of heavy Doric engaged columns on a high pedestal. These
support a widely-projecting ornamental band that divides the façade
into two parts vertically. A balcony with a railing originally projected from this band and, although missing for many years, a new
balcony has replaced it. Above, three more columns on either side
of the center, of varying heights, continue almost to the widely-
projecting tile roof (probably not the original). The three spaces at
the center, between columns, are pierced with bell openings in each
of which hangs a bell.

A monastery formerly extended for a considerable distance to the
right, in the space now occupied by a tall-towered modern church
which dwarfs its venerable neighbor. In an elaborate adaptation of
the Churrigueresque style, the façade of the new church and the
upper stories of its towers are richly adorned. The new church would
be attractive any place in any direction—a mile away.

A brief discussion of the two northernmost missions of California can always be undertaken with an advantage. Even those writers who choose to describe the missions in chronological rather than geographical order cannot do anything but place them at the end, for they are as widely separated from the others in point of time as they are by the Golden Gate. The padres had to depend upon Indian canoes to cross the narrow but sometimes-tempestuous opening if they did not want to go the long way around, but today the finest bridge in the world leads to San Rafael and Sonoma. It might have chagrined Padre Serra, who in 1777, while he stood gazing at the waters flowing out to the setting sun, exclaimed with joy: "Thanks be to God that now our father Saint Francis, with the Holy Cross of the Procession of Missions, has reached the last limit of the California continent. To go farther he must have boats."

It took a little time, but by 1817 Saint Francis had boats. The health of the Indians at San Francisco de Asís made them necessary. Once out of the cold and damp San Francisco fogs and in the warm, bright sunshine of San Rafael's combination mission and hospital, the Indians improved remarkably.

Founded December 14, 1817, the Mission San Rafael Arcángel never made any pretense of architectural distinction. The simple, small rectangular church had a square doorway with a star-shaped window above and no belfry, the bells being suspended from a wooden frame out in front. At right angles to the church extended the mission house, with a long, low corridor at the front supported by square wooden posts. The buildings soon decayed until not a vestige remained. A church was built on the site in 1869, burned down later, and a new one, built in 1917, now stands where the little mission once stood. Not far away, property has been cleared and a copy of San Rafael Arcángel is now under construction.

An overzealous friar with the support of the governor, neither of whom liked the San Francisco climate, was responsible for the premature establishment of the mission farthest north. Without proper authority the civil government approved the removal not only of the San Francisco mission but of the comparatively new mission of San Rafael to a new site, and ambitious young Fray José Altimira set to work. For his "New San Francisco" he chose the Valley of the Moon (Sonoma), and there, on July 4, 1823, he blessed the site and celebrated Holy Mass, thus illegally founding the new mission.

After the mission authorities had learned of the impulsive move and had voiced their objections, a compromise was finally reached whereby both of the older missions were to continue and the new one would be recognized as a separate mission under the patronage of San Francisco de Solano, to distinguish it from the other San Francisco. To make the distinction even clearer today, it is usually spoken of by the name of the valley where it is located: Sonoma.

Architecturally the youngest mission was almost a duplicate of San Rafael, except that for a time the front was "adorned" with a small square belfry with wooden louvers and a pseudo-Gothic parapet, said to have been added in 1835 by a Mexican general. Old photographs would seem to point, rather, to the late nineteenth century and to a pioneer Methodist from Iowa. The buildings have now been restored and are used by the state of California as a museum where the visitor may see old newspapers, photographs of army officers, World War souvenirs, antique chairs, bicycles, sewing machines, and other equally-relevant religious relics rescued from boosters' bulging basements.

The Russians were in some measure responsible for the military and civil authorities' anxiety to establish settlements north of the Golden Gate. The Russians had worked their way down the California coast until in 1812 they had established a fort and settlement within seventy miles of the "California continent." But, as later events proved, that was to be the limit.

The drive from Sonoma to Fort Ross is a beautiful one. Through the Valley of the Moon the road leads north to the Russian River, which it then follows at the bottom of a canyon through dense woods, making every twist that the river makes, but with good pavement, to Jenner-by-the-Sea. The road from there on is a different matter.

The restored buildings of Fort Ross are as different from the Spanish missions as Siberia is from Spain. The little Russian Orthodox Chapel (see photograph, Plate 55) established there in 1812, with its domical cupola over the altar and another cupola at the front, both rising from a steep roof above a square wooden building, is quite unlike anything else in the country.

That was the Russians' farthest south. Beyond that was the kind of country to which they were not accustomed. Sonoma was the Spaniards' farthest north. The same reason applies. If Fort Ross was far enough to go, it was a good place to stop. Even today the rough road cut out of the precipitous cliff above the breaking surf of the Pacific winds so tortuously and is so narrow that it is necessary to find a rock pile beneath the beetling cliff above onto which to turn when a lumber truck approaches. It is small wonder the Russians gave it up.

27

The Decline of the Missions

THE HISTORY of California almost up to the time of the American occupation is principally the history of its mission movement. So too is the early history of architecture in California. Of the three colonizing institutions—the mission, the presidio, and the pueblo, or civil village—the missions and the work carried on in them dominated the early development of the province. Though it was never intended that they be permanent as missions, they grew to prosperous proportions, especially during the late years of the administration of Lasuén.

By the turn of the century the missions had grown into wealthy estates and the padres who administered them became not only the preachers and teachers of the province but also the farm managers, merchants, and captains of industry. Stock raising was the principal source of wealth. Sheep and cattle brought in from Mexico grew into great herds and provided not only meat but hides for clothing, tallow for candlemaking, and fats for soapmaking. Great grainfields and orchards followed closely in importance and large gardens of vegetables and flowers were carefully cultivated by the Indian neophytes.

In addition to being orchard, farm, and ranch, each mission was a manufacturing center and included shops where Indians were kept busy at weaving, tanning, shoemaking, blacksmithing, and soap- and candlemaking. They were taught lumbering, carpentry and cabinet-making, wood carving, and furnituremaking and many of them became skilled as bricklayers and stonemasons.

This practical education made possible the building of the great mission structures which remain California's greatest heritage from the early days of the province. As has already been stated, the first structures were always simple and small and equipped by gifts from missions already established; but as the missions became prosperous and as the Indians, increasing in numbers, became skilled the earliest buildings were replaced with larger structures of adobe bricks, which the Indians learned to make, and then, even later, in some cases with still larger structures of stone. Under the direction of the friars the Indians helped to build such churches in stone as that ill-fated masterpiece at San Juan Capistrano and those at San Gabriel, San Buenaventura, Santa Barbara, and San Carlos Borromeo. The last named even had a roof of timbers and tile carried upon stone arches which spanned the nave.

That brings up a point that should be made in fairness to these early builders. There is one vicious bit of slander that continually crops up in connection with the building of the Spanish missions, probably innocently enough and merely stupidly: that is the hackneyed myth that the Spaniards constructed their arches and their vaults by piling up dirt to the desired height and shape, laying bricks or stone upon the pile thus formed and then digging out the dirt somewhat in the manner that children used to make snowhouses. The mission church at San Antonio de Padua is a particularly popular victim of such slander. But I have heard it at Tumacácori in Arizona (not from the guide who firmly, but *too* politely, disputed it) and at other places in the Southwest, all over Mexico, and twenty years ago all over Spain. It is not only absurd; it is an insult to the Spaniards, greatest of builders since the days of the Romans, and to the Franciscan friars who against overwhelming odds reared such beautiful structures in the northern wilderness.

The architectural background of the California missions is of course Spanish, with an admixture of Moorish due to the long occupation of much of Spain by those people who added an oriental tinge to the Spanish art; and with some additional influence from the Flemish and Dutch, long politically connected with Spain, but from a different direction. The changes in fashions that the resulting architecture underwent in the home country were reflected in New

Spain where, instead of merely following the leader as might be expected of a colony, the architects, owing to the growing wealth of the country, often outdid the homeland. All of this was reflected in turn in the Southwest, in varying degrees of elaboration depending upon materials, distance from the source of inspiration, availability and training of workmen, and to no little degree the individual guiding hand. Thus there grew up in each of the northern provinces styles which all came from the same source but which came to show variations among themselves.

The mission churches of California, far from the cultural base in New Spain and remote in the minds of royal officials yet at the same time built in rapid succession, or even simultaneously, could not be expected to show the elaboration of the Mexican churches. The result was simpler structures erected by Indians under the direction of the padres, but with certain characteristics forced by the necessity of simplicity, which gave the mission churches a distinction that makes them unique. Elaborate decoration being decidedly limited, emphasis was given to form and line. Herein lies much of the beauty of the California missions.

Among the most distinctive features that emphasize this simplicity are the curved, pedimented gables as at San Diego, San Luís Rey, and San Antonio de Padua; pierced campanarios as at San Gabriel, San Juan Capistrano, and the charming, free-standing one at Pala; and, not by any means the least effective, the long, arcaded corridors with arches carried upon heavy brick piers because lack of stone and skilled craftsmen made carved columns impossible. Most noteworthy of these are the arcades at San Luís Rey, San Juan Capistrano, San Fernando Rey, Santa Barbara, Santa Inés, San Miguel, San Juan Bautista, and now, happily, again San Antonio de Padua.

The terraced bell towers, simple in outline but sturdy in construction and fine in proportion, as at San Luís Rey and Santa Barbara, are equally characteristic as are also the massive walls, heavy buttresses, and low-pitched, red tile roofs to be found in all the mission structures.

The patio with fountain and garden, introduced into Spain by the Moors, is not by any means peculiar to California but it has been especially successfully adopted there. Particularly fine examples exist at San Luís Rey, San Juan Capistrano, Santa Barbara, and San Juan Bautista.

A question often asked about the Spanish mission churches of the

Southwest is why there should be such differences among those of different sections and seemingly such inconsistent differences. Why, for example, should the churches of Texas be so elaborate while those of New Mexico, next door, are the simplest of all? Why should San Xavier del Bac in Arizona, still farther west, more closely resemble San José in Texas in its elaboration than it does the churches of New Mexico which lie between? And although San Xavier del Bac bears some resemblance to the California churches, why should the latter, *in their simplicity*, seem more closely akin to the churches of New Mexico so far away?

There are two answers to the questions, the one geographical and the other cultural. From the geographical standpoint New Mexico was not only the first province to be settled but it was particularly difficult of access, far from the source of supplies, and reached only after long and arduous marches over deserts. There are not good road connections between Mexico City and Chihuahua even today. North of Chihuahua lie many miles of burning desert and the settlements of New Mexico were yet far away in the northern half of the state.

San Antonio, Texas, lies much closer to Mexico, and by the time the missions there were established Mexico was fairly well settled up to the lower part of the middle Rio Grande. The same applies to Arizona. When the present mission of San Xavier del Bac was built in what was then Sonora, and much farther south than *northern* New Mexico, it was merely at the end of a continuous chain of established settlements. Being in lands more readily accessible to Mexico, both San José and San Xavier del Bac have elaborate Churrigueresque façades; and that the façade of the former is much the more sophisticated is due partly to the materials used but even more to the individual artist engaged to do the work.

California, geographically more closely akin to New Mexico in its remoteness, and without skilled workmen from New Spain, was forced to keep her churches simple. But architecturally they are very different from those of New Mexico, and that is where the cultural reason enters the picture. The missions of Texas, Arizona, and California were built to attract Indians of low culture (the only kind there were in those localities) who came to the missions, lived there, worked there, and were taught there. Although they helped with the construction, they had to be taught everything from the beginning; consequently the buildings, in spite of the distinctive features of the California missions already mentioned which were the result of remoteness, remained essentially Spanish. There was no basic intellectual help from the Indians as was the case in New Mexico, where the churches were built in villages already established by the Indians and were greatly influenced by centuries of Indian building experience. The ancestry of the New Mexican architecture is as much Indian as it is Spanish.

Constant incursions of hostile tribes were largely responsible for the fact that so few of the great New Mexico missions remain. In that respect California was luckier. If she did not have semicivilized tribes to influence her architecture, neither was she as badly bothered by powerful warlike tribes. Built at a much later date, and in spite of local disturbances, the California missions attained a prosperity that the New Mexico missions never knew. All of this prosperity was viewed by officials, soldiers, and settlers with jaundiced eyes. The immense herds of cattle, the waving fields of grain, the orchards of ripening fruit, the vines heavy with grapes, and the handsome and well-kept mission buildings contrasted unfavorably in the minds of the civil authorities with the poverty of presidio and pueblo.

It had never been the intention of the government that the mission system should be administered solely for the benefit of the Indians. The friars were charged with their conversion and with the responsibility of making useful citizens of them, all with the end in view of settling the province and expanding the power of Spain. The friars were familiar with the plan to free the Indians, to let them be established in pueblos, and to turn the mission churches over to the bishop and the secular clergy. They had done their work well; they argued, however, that the Indians were not ready for secularization. That they were right is proved by the results. The question remains: would the Indians ever have been ready?

The question of secularization of the missions, with ensuing results, is a long and complex one which finds no place here except to review very briefly the facts. Secularization was first decreed by the Spanish Cortés in 1813, but it was not carried out. With independence of Mexico from Spain, the question again came up several times and finally, in 1834, secularization was enforced. The Indians were to be permitted to go free, with grants of part of the mission lands; the rest of the lands were to be taken from the padres and given as grants to settlers; and local civil governments were to be established. The results were disastrous: the Indians, unable to take care of themselves, would not work without compulsion; they sold the lands which had been granted to them and spent the proceeds on liquor and gambling; others fled to the hills and reverted to wild habits for which they were unprepared after fifty years of civilization and strict discipline.

The mission buildings fell into disrepair and were plundered. To cap the climax, Pío Pico, the last Mexican governor, in 1845 sold the mission lands, at prices so low as to seem almost grants, to defray the expense of administration. The cattle were slaughtered and not replaced, the waving fields of grain withered and died because there was nobody to take care of them, fruit fell off the trees and rotted on the ground, even the wine presses were stilled, the mission buildings were left to the elements and to thieves, and the Indians were on the way to extinction. The prosperous missions belonged to the past.

Only in comparatively recent years have the old missions come to be truly appreciated; sympathetic Californians have restored many of the buildings to at least a semblance of their former beauty and the Roman Catholic Church and the Franciscan Order have restored and are using others. The life is no longer there, though in some of them Franciscan friars, now in robes of brown, go about their daily duties and yet always welcome visitors. Most of them are but shells, but where in history can be found more fascinating shells?

PART SIX: *AMERICAN SOUTHWEST*

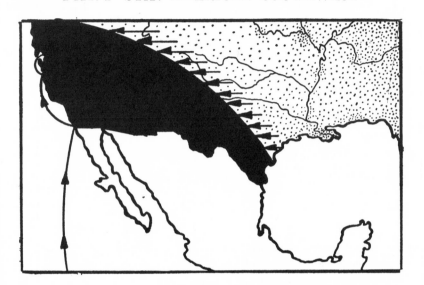

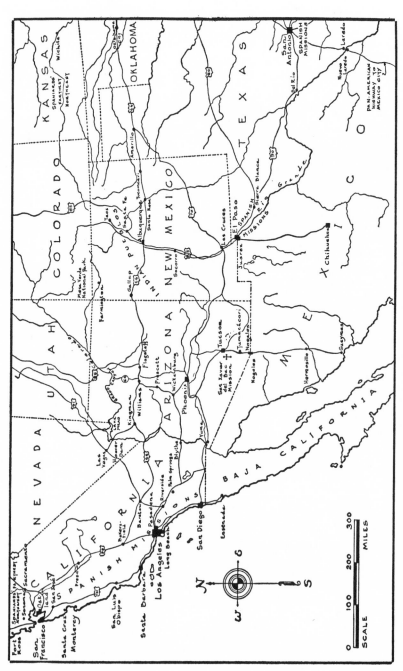

THE AMERICAN SOUTHWEST

28

Pioneers

IN MAY of 1789, during that lull between the founding of the mission of La Purísima Concepción and that of Santa Cruz, the governor of the province of Alta California, acting on advices from New Spain, warned the commander of the presidio at San Francisco of the approach of a vessel called the *Columbia* "which is said to belong to General Washington." Orders were given for its capture. As things turned out the ship from "Boston," which meant the United States in general, did not make port, but a year later it arrived in Boston with a cargo of tea from China, the first ship flying an American flag to sail around the world.

The naval vessel *Otter*, putting in at Monterey in the late fall of 1796 to take on a load of wood and water, was the first American ship to anchor in Alta California. It was soon followed by others; but they were all preceded by the first American to land there, but on a Spanish ship. John Groem was supposed to have come originally from "Boston," but he had shipped from Cádiz as a gunner on a voyage of discovery sent out to determine, once and for all, whether there really was a Strait of Anián. After the expedition had followed the coast south, John was landed at Monterey on September 13, 1791, and was buried the same day.

The first American to come to Alta California and remain in the province *alive* was our friend Tom Doak who, as we have seen, was turned loose on the interior of the church of the Mission San Juan Bautista. Landing in 1816 at the age of twenty-nine, the young man from "Boston" spent the rest of his life in and around Monterey and Santa Cruz.

A more colorful foreign resident of the Spanish period, as well as being a most useful one, was Joseph Chapman, a young man of New England extraction who had escaped from Bouchard's pirate ship. Hippolyte Bouchard was a Frenchman with an American ship said to be in the service of the Mexican insurgents for the purpose of terrorizing the California coast, still loyal to Spain—a feat in which he was successful, destroying the port of Monterey and driving the friars and Indians inland to the desolate mission of Soledad. The American, Chapman, claimed to have shipped from Hawaii ignorant of what he was getting into. Upon landing at Monterey in the fall of 1818 he was immediately arrested since only Spanish citizens were permitted in the colonies; but, proving useful, he was soon freed and ultimately married the daughter of a wealthy Spanish family of Santa Barbara and became the father of five children.

Though making no pretense of being an artist, Joe was more versatile than Tom Doak, particularly in matters mechanical. He built the first successful water-power gristmill in California, for the Mission San Gabriel; with the help of Indian laborers, he prepared the timbers for the construction of the Church of Our Lady of the Angels at Los Angeles; and in his spare time he planted large vineyards, built a schooner, and served as a surgeon.

While Chapman was serving as a handy man at various missions and building gristmills at a number of them, another American came along to contribute a bit of romance to the otherwise rather dull Plaza Church at Los Angeles.

Josefa Carrillo, who lived in Old Town in San Diego, was one of the beauties of California, much besought by suitors, among whom were Pío Pico and the new Governor Echeandía. But one day in 1826 a Yankee ship hove into the harbor and its handsome young mate, Henry Fitch, met the Spanish belle. It was a case of love at first sight.

Her family was outraged; so she confided in Pío Pico that her heart belonged to the Yankee. Brokenhearted as he may have been, Don Pío was at least a good sport and he told Josefa to be ready at her window at a certain hour. On his trusty steed, with Josefa in the saddle behind him, Don Pío galloped to the harbor where the Yankee had a boat waiting. He got there just in time to toss Josefa into her lover's arms before the governor's guard, in hot pursuit, reached the shore.

The ship sailed away to South America and returned a year later with Fitch and his bride prepared to face the wrath of the girl's parents and the Church. There was much fuss and to-do, at the end of which the ecclesiastical court finally ruled the marriage valid; but the scandal called for penance. In addition to a period during which the young couple had to appear daily at the church with lighted candles in their hands, Fitch was commanded "to give a bell of at least fifty pounds weight for the church at Los Angeles, which has a borrowed one." So that is how the Church of Our Lady of the Angels came to have a bell of its own.

Other Americans began to arrive in California more rapidly after that, some of them as settlers, sailing around the Horn from the Atlantic seaboard, usually from Boston, the home of the clipper ships and consequently the port which gave the name by which the new young republic in the East was known in California; others, more transiently, as hunters and trappers coming overland. Monterey, as the capital, was the recipient of most of these early immigrants.

The first towns in the province, entirely apart from the missions, were of two kinds: the presidio towns on the one hand and the pueblos, or civil settlements, on the other. The latter, at first settled by the kind of people who could hardly be expected to make significant advances—as witnessed by the difficulty in getting the plaza church in Los Angeles under way—were slow in growing. Branciforte, built too close to the Mission Santa Cruz to please the friars, became absorbed at a later date by the city which retained the name of the mission. Both San José and Los Angeles were to have their "booms" much later.

Although there were ranches scattered along the province, in the hands of wealthy hacendados who spent most of their time on horseback, the centers of activities apart from the missions, and certainly the centers of social life, were the presidio towns.

Farthest to the south was San Diego, which for a brief period during the Mexican regime served as the capital because Governor Echeandía preferred the "climate" there. "Old Town," where the first mission was built and which became the first "city," retains something of its early character. Away to the northwest from the center of the modern city, it is built around a large plaza now beautifully planted with trees. Around it are several old houses dating from the Mexican period, including the adobe Casa de Carrillo where Henry Fitch first met his bride-to-be. More famous and of equal romantic interest is the house built in 1825 by Don José Antonio Estudillo, better known as "Ramona's Marriage Place," a distinction which, according to some California historians, is shared by as many houses as George Washington is reputed to have slept in.

The one-story adobe structure is built around three sides of a patio filled with flowering shrubs, climbing vines, and roses, into which garden courtyard the numerous rooms of the house enter. At one end of the garden is the old *cocina*, with a large fireplace for cooking, iron and copper utensils, old wooden furniture, and, just outside the door, the characteristic beehive oven.

Nothing remains of the old presidio at Santa Barbara but there are a number of old houses still standing, including the rambling adobe house built in 1819 by José Antonio de la Guerra, commander of the presidio, and formerly the center of many a brilliant social event; the Joaquin Carrillo House, partially restored, which boasts of being the birthplace of the first American child born in California; and the adobe Casa Covarrubias, built about 1817 and still in excellent repair.

If San Diego was the first port of call and long the commercial and social center of the south of California and if Santa Barbara was a favorite place of residence for many old Spanish families, Monterey as the capital was throughout the Spanish and Mexican periods and well into the American period the most important town. It was the social, military, and political center of the province.

Retaining more of its early houses and more of its early atmosphere than any other city in California, it is without question one of the most interesting small cities in the country. This fortunately is well recognized by its citizens and by the Chamber of Commerce which has done a splendid job of sharing the city's history and charm with its visitors. The result is one of the most fascinating outdoor and indoor museums anywhere.

Many of the early houses have disappeared but there are still enough of them left to fill days of fascinating wandering, not to mention filling a book. Only a few of them can be described here.

It was during the Mexican period, especially during the decade of 1830–40, that the houses of Monterey began to give the character to the town that it still retains. Social life at first centered around the residence of the governor at the presidio of which unfortunately only the chapel remains. The inauguration of a new governor always called for elaborate ceremonies and social functions, ending with a grand ball at which the custom obtained of breaking eggshells filled with gold and silver paper, or scented water, over the head of the chosen when requesting the honor of a dance.

Although the locale was to be changed, these affairs continued during the Mexican period and even later; but they did not interfere with business at the increasingly prosperous port. *Rancheros* brought their hides and tallow to the port and trading with the East Coast was brisk. The old customhouse still stands and is said to be the oldest government building in California. The oldest part, that at the north end, was erected by the Spaniards in 1814; the central one-story section was added in 1822 by the Mexicans; and the southern end, duplicating the northern portion, was built in 1846, after the American occupation.

It was in the eighteen-thirties that Americans began to arrive in considerable numbers. In 1832 came Thomas Oliver Larkin from Boston, who was not only to become Alta California's most influential American but who was to have a greater influence on California's residential architecture than any other single individual in that state's history. He opened the first retail and wholesale store, built Monterey's first wharf, founded the first nonmilitary hospital, brought the first American woman to live in Monterey, and became the father of the first Yankee child born in the capital.

When, in 1835, he built himself a house it created such a sensation that a new style of domestic architecture was evolved which to this day is copied all over the country and called by the name of the little city where he built it. Up to that time the Spanish and Mexican adobes had been long and rectangular, of one story, covered with roofs of thatch or tile sloping two ways. Larkin, remembering his native New England, applied Cape Cod to adobe and built a two-story house with a four-way sloping roof and a two-storied balcony at the front and sides. Neighbors who could afford it immediately began building two-story homes with balconies and verandas. The year 1835 was a busy one in Monterey. The hip roof puzzled the neighbors so there arose the companion type, with a simple, long gable—but in many cases with only a second-floor cantilevered balcony along the front supporting an overhanging roof. Thus was born the "Monterey" style, which was to make that city a modified adaptation of a New England town planted on the Pacific Coast.

Less than a block away is the Casa Amesti, built by a wealthy Spanish *ranchero* and judge as a wedding gift for his daughter. With a balcony the length of its front, its vines, and its formal planting, it is one of the finest examples of Old Monterey architecture. Just half a block beyond is the house built in 1835 by Doctor James Stokes, a two-story, whitewashed adobe with balcony built on slender wooden posts and still surrounded by a trim garden. There were many other houses built at about the same time, but the style continued to be popular throughout the next decade, when the Pacific Building was built in 1847 for use as a hotel. A long, two-story structure with over-hanging balconies, it has served in its time as a tavern, as a minister's residence, and as a Salvation Army headquarters. One of the most picturesque of the Monterey adobes is the Old Whaling Station built in 1855 as a boardinghouse for Portuguese whaↄers and now privately owned.

The Monterey style was not confined to Monterey, even in the early days. It was copied up and down the coast, from San Diego to Sonoma. The latter town has some fine examples facing its huge plaza and one of the finest of all examples is the home of General José Castro facing the sleepy plaza at San Juan Bautista.

Spanish rule in New Mexico continued as a long succession of mili-tary governors, not too pleasantly enlivened part of the time by quarrels with the custodians of the missions. Santa Fe remained the capital around which the political and social life centered, joined sometimes by visitors from Santa Cruz to the north and Albuquerque to the south. Larger than any of these, however, was El Paso del Norte, nearer to Chihuahua and on the trail to the north.

Before the middle of the eighteenth century French-Canadian fur traders had reached Santa Fe by way of the Missouri and Platte Rivers and, after Louisiana became Spanish territory, communica-tion was opened with St. Louis. After the Louisiana Purchase in 1803 American traders and explorers began to move west, but with no welcome by the Spaniards. In 1806 Lieutenant Zebulon M. Pike, on an exploring expedition, was captured by Spaniards and brought to Santa Fe, which he described as looking "like a fleet of flat-boats which are seen in the spring and fall seasons descending the Ohio."

As soon as Mexico had achieved independence from Spain in 1821 the "no-trespassing" policy was changed and relations with the out-side world were welcomed. William Becknell, an American trader from Missouri, was the first to take advantage of the change. The following year he arrived at the plaza in Santa Fe with the first wagons loaded with goods from the East; and the famous Santa Fe Trail was opened.

Ever since the expedition of Zebulon Pike there were Americans looking with longing eyes to Texas, much nearer home than New Mexico and reported to be a land rich and desirable. One such was Doctor James Long who led a band of adventurers from Natchez, Mississippi, captured the frontier town of Nacogdoches, and set up a republic. While the leader was absent negotiating for help in the person of Jean Lafitte, the pirate, the Spaniards fell on the infant republic and drove the survivors back across the border.

Despite this very obvious lack of hospitality, to say the least, the Spanish government did permit the settlement the following year of three hundred families under the leadership of Moses Austin, a St. Louis banker. The leader died shortly afterward but the colonization was carried on by his son Stephen, who within ten years had brought in more than five thousand Anglo-Americans. Life was rigorous; the settlers lived in simple, bare log cabins, often without windows. One housewife is said to have declared: "Texas is a heaven for men and dogs but hell for women and oxen."

Colonization from the East increased, and with it troubles with the dictatorial Mexican government which had won independence from Spain shortly after the first colonists arrived. Proposals for a state government separate from Coahuila were prepared, but when Austin went to Mexico to present them he was thrown into prison. In the meantime new arrivals in Texas included Sam Houston, a veteran of Indian wars and former governor of Tennessee; Captain William Barret Travis, a popular and dashing young army officer from South Carolina; and James Bowie, brother of the inventor of the knife of that name and a great fighter and hunter in his own right. Men such as these were holding meetings to plan resistance to Antonio López de Santa Anna, by then Mexican dictator, who swore swift subjection of the Texas rebels. Stephen F. Austin, released from prison, returned in time to be made commander in chief of the Texas army.

Marching against San Antonio the Texans defeated a force of Mexicans four times their number at the old Mission Concepción. A month later, December 9, 1835, under the leadership of the great frontiersman "old Ben Milam" (aged forty-four), the little army took the city; but the leader was killed. When Santa Anna arrived with three thousand men the small band of fewer than two hundred Texans, under the command of Travis, was forced to shut itself inside the walls of the old Mission San Antonio de Valero for a last defense of the city. Among the defenders was David Crockett, frontiersman and statesman from Tennessee. A red flag, the flag of "no quarter," was hoisted by Santa Anna and his demand for unconditional surrender was answered by a cannon shot.

The details of what happened on the morning of March 6, 1836, when the Mexican hordes swarmed over the walls of the roofless little stone church of the Alamo come only from Mexican officers; for not a Texan remained alive. Outnumbered sixteen to one, the outcome was inevitable. It was one of the most heroic stands in history. Those who were not killed in the hand-to-hand fighting were shot and their bodies were burned. Among the immortals were Travis, Bowie, and Crockett.

The massacre at the Alamo was followed by another at Goliad, where the presidio chapel now looks so peacefully out over the countryside. Overtaken by the Mexicans, Colonel James W. Fannin, Jr., and his command, on their way to Victoria, were forced to surrender, whereupon they were taken to the presidio at Goliad and executed.

General Houston, replacing Austin as commander, retreated to the east in order to assemble the scattered Texas forces, and when they had reached the bayou country near the present city of Houston, with Santa Anna in pursuit, the place for battle was decided upon. With the cry "Remember the Alamo!" to which was added "Remember Goliad!" they marched to meet the Mexican army. The battle of San Jacinto is listed among the decisive battles of the world.

For ten years Texas was a republic. When, on February 16, 1846, it became one of the United States its annexation had to be made convincing to Mexico. It was, within a short time; and when the treaty of Guadalupe Hidalgo was signed on February 2, 1848, the Southwest was officially a part of the United States.

The Mexican War, as far as New Mexico was concerned, did not amount to much. General Stephen W. Kearny, commanding the Army of the West, occupied Santa Fe on August 18, 1846, without a shot being fired, and a month later set out for California.

When, in 1843, Thomas Larkin was appointed United States consul at Monterey—the only man ever to hold that job—his home became the political and social center of the capital of California. Throughout all of the minor revolutions of the Mexican period in

57. (*Top*) THE ESTUDILLO HOUSE, San Diego. (*Middle*) PATIO, Estudillo House. (*Bottom*) KITCHEN, Estudillo House

58. (*Top*) THOMAS O. LARKIN HOUSE, Monterey. (*Middle*) WHALING STATION, Monterey. (*Bottom*) DR. JAMES STOKES HOUSE, Monterey

59. (*Top*) CASA AMESTI, Monterey. (*Middle*) COLTON HALL, Monterey. (*Bottom*) PACIFIC BUILDING, Monterey

60.   VALLEJO HOUSE, Sonoma, California

61. (*Top and Middle*) MOTOR COURTS in San Diego. (*Bottom*) GUEST RANCH in New Mexico

62. (*Top*) MISSION SAN FRANCISCO DE ASÍS, the Old and the New.
(*Bottom*) CHURCH OF EL CRISTO DEL REY, Santa Fe

63. CALIFORNIA BUILDING, San Diego Exposition

64. (*Top*) COURTHOUSE, Santa Barbara. (*Bottom*) CITY HALL, Santa Cruz, California

the province it became increasingly apparent that destiny intended California for the United States, and during that period this level-headed businessman was one of the real American leaders. His letters were eagerly sought by American newspapers and his reports were responsible for much of the immigration which by that time was taking place overland. Weary of Mexican rule, many other settlers were willing to join in his plan, begun at the request of President Polk, to renounce allegiance to Mexico and seek annexation to the United States.

Two events interfered with this peaceful plan. Early in 1846 Captain John Charles Frémont, on a surveying expedition, arrived at Monterey to consult with Larkin. Here he met General Castro, who regarded him with suspicion but permitted him to purchase supplies when assured that the American officer's men, whom he had left on the interior, were not armed. The fiery Mexican general retired to his beautiful, balconied adobe home in San Juan Bautista in comparative peace.

But events moved rapidly. At dawn on June 14, 1846, in the otherwise quiet village of Sonoma, a band of Yankees seized the commandant of the presidio, General Mariano Vallejo, and raised a flag fashioned of homespun and decorated with the figure of a grizzly bear and the words "California Republic." Neither side knew that the United States was at war with Mexico.

The astonishing and equally-astonished new republic lasted three weeks. On July 7 Commodore John D. Sloat, with two hundred and fifty marines, landed at Monterey and raised the flag of the United States. That same year the American citizens built an addition to the customhouse. That same year too the Reverend Mr. Walter Colton, chaplain of the U.S. Frigate *Congress,* came to Monterey and was appointed the first American alcalde (mayor). The position was soon confirmed by popular vote, which must have satisfied the democratic conscience of this stern New Englander who never did approve of the California gaiety, drinking, gambling, and laziness. With income from the taxes levied on gambling and liquor the stanch Puritan began construction the following year of what he considered an appropriate municipal building. It still serves as such. With a two-story portico of plain cylindrical columns and simple pediment, it appears prim and precise beside the native adobes. A one-story jail was built next door. The larger building was originally built to serve also as a school, which, according to tradition, was dismissed when there was a prisoner to execute because the portico of Colton Hall made such a handy scaffold.

One morning in January of 1848 James Wilson Marshall, a young New Jersey wagon builder who had arrived with one of the overland caravans three years earlier, was busily building a sawmill on the American River near the site of Coloma. Stopping to inspect the tail-race, he picked out of the water a piece of shiny metal half the size of a pea. Pounding it between stones and finding it soft, he knew that what he held between his fingers was gold. Alone in the woods he "sat down and began to think right hard," as he wrote in his diary.

Within six months Monterey was deserted. Ships in the harbor rode at anchor without crews, shopkeepers locked their doors, soldiers at the presidio deserted their posts and others sent to bring them back disappeared. The alcalde wrote: "The blacksmith dropped his hammer, the carpenter his plane, the mason his trowel, the farmer his sickle, the baker his loaf, and the tapster his bottle. All were off for the mines, some on horses, some on carts, and some on crutches, and one went in a litter." The Reverend Mr. Walter Colton stood between the tall, skinny columns of Colton Hall and watched them go.

29

Potpourri

AFTER THE colonists in east Texas had graduated from the simplest type of log cabin, the so-called "dog-run" house, making its way westward from the Atlantic Coast, was quite commonly built. It consisted of two rooms with an open space between, where the dogs slept—as did any overflow of guests. The porch thus formed served also as a storage place for such furniture and equipment as rocking chairs, cradles, and bird cages, and for washbasins, guns, and dressed skins. When not at work the family sat there, and on rainy days the washing was hung there. A single, gabled roof covered the dwelling and batten doors and shutters, the openings.

By the time Texas became a state of the Union the Greek Revival was in full sway in the East, all the way to the Mississippi, in fact, through the northern states of Ohio, Indiana, and Illinois and through the southern states of Tennessee, Mississippi, and Louisiana. The fad spread even farther west (Colton Hall in Monterey is a crude example, brought around the Horn by a navy chaplain) and in Texas those who could afford it built in the style of the pretentious temples being erected in the Old South. But there they soon bucked up against the influence of Mexican culture where, around San Antonio, the low ranch houses, only one story in height and usually of stone, often stuccoed or whitewashed, continued to be built. The effect of Spanish occupation could not be blotted out.

In south-central Texas an entirely different influence, from central Europe, came to be felt. During the eighteen-forties many immigrants were attracted to Texas, largely Germans, Alsatians, and Poles. At first building the log cabin of the Americans, they soon reverted to native types, of which the house of half timber and half stone was the favorite. When they learned that the stone they were using was self-supporting the timber was abandoned, but the work of the wood carver continued in doorways and trim. Fine examples of these German houses are to be seen in and around Fredericksburg, seventy miles north of San Antonio, and in New Braunfels, just off the highway between San Antonio and Austin; while twenty-five miles straight west of San Antonio Castroville, with its old church and stuccoed, stone houses lining the street, is a bit of old Alsace-Lorraine transplanted in Texas.

Throughout the Spanish period New Mexico continued very happily, architecturally, with its suitable "fleet of flat-boats," and even throughout the Mexican regime California remained content with its new Monterey-style houses in the north and its low, one-story rectangular or L-shaped adobes in the south. But after the close of the Civil War came the railroad, hardly an unmixed blessing. The East began to pour west, and what it had to pour architecturally would have been better poured into the ocean.

It was a period of industrial expansion and with that came increasing wealth. It might have been all right if things had stopped there, but with increasing wealth came a desire for culture. That resulted in the importation of an artistic plague from Europe which spread like the epidemic of cholera in Mexico a few years earlier. It was reflected throughout the country. The Southwest did not escape.

There were two sources of what the rich travelers of that day thought of as inspiration. The fountains were Paris and London; the basins held the French Mansard of the Second Empire and the Victorian Gothic; and the overflow spilled clear across the Atlantic Ocean, over the Appalachians, across the Mississippi, over the Great Plains, and all the way to the Pacific. Everybody who could afford it must have a "modern" house, and the wealthier the man the more horrible the mansion.

The overpowering Mansard roof, adorned with cupolas and cast-iron railings, and the writhing Victorian oriels, bays, and porte-cocheres swept through Texas—especially Galveston—like a devastating cyclone and moved on.

Even New Mexico, with its Spanish-Pueblo heritage and its comparative remoteness, was not spared. The new fad had spent a bit of its energy in crossing the mountains but still the Santa Fe Trail had paved the way.

With the opening of the Santa Fe Trail, and more especially with the raising of the American flag in 1846, venerable Santa Fe and other cities of New Mexico—though still clinging to adobe—began to undergo changes. Brick and millwork—double-hung, glazed sash often supplemented by slatted shutters—were imported from St. Louis and Kansas City and the small grilled windows without glass began to give way to the type generally used in the Middle West and the East. Even the Indian pueblos felt the influence. Slender, square columns began to replace the hand-hewn ones and parapets with wooden balustrades decorated the tops of the adobe buildings to cover the Spanish-Pueblo architecture with a cloak called Territorial.

An interesting example of the period is the old Sena home built about 1840, in plan still Spanish, built around a patio but with slender posts supporting the roof over the arcade and with a coping of brick crowning the walls. Recently restored, it is now in use as a store and office building. At one time the Plaza was surrounded by such buildings, some of them of two stories with a porch the full height. Ox-drawn covered wagons arriving at the Plaza in the eighteen-sixties passed by lines of slender wooden columns supporting roofs to shade the passageways.

Along with the coming of the railroad came new materials and new ideas, all of them bad. Even the Governor's Palace did not escape. It was "modernized" with wooden posts to support the roof over the *portales* and crowned with a wooden balustrade of turned balusters, interrupted by paneled posts supporting Victorian urns. Even the first capitol was built in the Victorian Gothic style, only to burn down in 1892 and be replaced a few years later by an equally-nonindigenous domed structure in the style of the neo-English Renaissance. Santa Fe had come to resemble the Middle West and the East of the period.

Only Archbishop Lamy contributed something different in the way of a foreign style in the brown sandstone Romanesque Cathedral of Saint Francis begun in 1869. It was built around the walls of the Parroquía, which dated from 1713 and continued in use while the new cathedral was under construction. Had it been built to one side we might now have had them both.

In California the architecture resulting from the Gold Rush anticipated the arrival of its bastard brothers on their way west. Streets of mining towns were lined with frame false fronts behind which were general stores, hotels and roominghouses, banks and saloons. Rickety plank floors in front of them were covered with sagging, wood-shingle roofs. These hurried structures were in fact typical of mining towns. In Arizona such fronts of shiplap hid the structural adobe behind. Some of these frontier buildings still stand and are in use; others, in ghost towns, are becoming more and more dilapidated and serve only as reminders of a wild, tasteless but picturesque era.

With the slackening of the Great Bonanza and the coming of the railroad, and the consequent lumber mill in every town, the Mansard malady and the Victorian virus arrived in full force. I have before me a picture of a house built in Eureka by a lumber magnate. It fell a victim to both fads at the same time; but its Mansard porch roof, supported by wildly carved posts and supporting iron crestings and big billiard balls at intervals, is eclipsed by the many bracketed and jigsawed gables and turrets terminating in a top-heavy tower rising to a full five stories of torture. It is such an extreme case as to be weirdly fascinating. One can only look at it and say "there ain't no such animal." Yet in San Francisco thousands of such architectural abominations were destroyed in the earthquake of 1906, though many of them remain. At that time nine tenths of the city's buildings were of frame construction, a higher percentage of wooden buildings than any other city in the United States.

Not all of the Victorian Gothic houses are horrors. When Mariano Vallejo, the picturesque Mexican general, turned eminent American citizen he forsook his house in Sonoma, which town he had laid out around the largest plaza in California, and built himself a house a short distance away in the country. It is now a state monument. In the American Gothic style, with white wooden icicles dripping from its gables, it has a great deal of old-fashioned charm. But if one doesn't like it, there is a slightly earlier, half-timbered Swiss chalet next door, constructed of materials said to have been brought around the Horn in sailing ships as ballast. In the chalet, now a museum, one can see, if interested, the general's Spanish-embroidered christening robe and his silk top hat. And in Coronado, reached by a ferry from San Diego, there is a large, rambling hotel typical of the great wooden resort hotels of the eighteen-seventies and -eighties.

30

Renaissance

IN 1915 San Diego had an exposition and for this exposition Bertram Grosvenor Goodhue, who had already designed the finest modern Gothic churches in the United States, designed the California Building in a Churrigueresque style better than anything in Mexico or Spain. It would have made even old José himself sit up and take notice. A dozen years earlier Goodhue had designed a villa at Santa Barbara which did to other architects just what the California Building would have done to José Churriguera. Recognizing the possibilities of intelligent use of the Spanish tradition, a group of the leading architects began to design buildings, particularly houses, which soon took the lead in residential architecture away from the East and transferred it to the Pacific Coast.

When the Victorian and Mansard styles began to be looked upon with humor, if not horror, a wide diversity of styles began to appear. The beginning of architectural education in the leading universities, and its rapid spread, had much to do with this eclecticism. Buildings were designed in whatever style the architect chose (except when another was dictated by the client—that was all right, he could do that too) and they included nearly everything that had been done in Europe and at an earlier period in the United States. They were Colonial, "English," Italian Renaissance, French Provincial, or what have you?

Two forces had made themselves felt in the meantime: one an individual, the other a World's Fair. The Romanesque Revival of H. H. Richardson resulted in some masterpieces in the hands of the master and spread gloom along the city streets in the hands of his followers. The World's Columbian Exposition in Chicago, introducing its own Classic Revival, thrilled its visitors and did incalculable damage for more than a generation thereafter, coming as it did along with the birth of steel skeleton construction.

This eclecticism, following the spread of architectural education, still did not preclude fads in architecture; but they were better carried out. For a time, in residential work at least (the Classic still had public buildings and skyscraper office buildings in its grip), English was the vogue, with the Colonial plodding steadily along and the Italian and the French bringing up the rear. When the Spanish Renaissance in California took the palm away from the East, there was bound to be a Spanish craze throughout the country. One could hardly call it a Renaissance in most of the country.

It arrived. Nineteen twenty-five was the big "Spanish" year. Architects, with new commissions, said: "Let's make it Spanish," and went out and bought a batch of books. Short-lived, the Spanish bubble burst. The gay and colorful houses, lacking patios, fountains, and bougainvillaea, looked pathetic among bare trees covered with snow; the stucco walls cracked and the low-pitched tile roofs leaked. Although the palm was left in California, many California architects today have completely discarded every vestige of the heritage which won it for them; but they are still doing very well indeed.

I have been told recently in southern California that a Spanish house cannot be sold today. That is probably not so much because it is Spanish as it is because it is not *good* Spanish. So many of them belong to that era when certain details were appropriated while the spirit was overlooked. They are Spanish in certain extreme characteristics only. Much of the best of the old Spanish—the rambling house one room deep built partially around a patio—has recently been seized, presented with only slightly different details, filled with modern equipment, and called "ranch." The style has invaded the Middle West and the East where, with low-pitched or flat roofs, it is considered the very latest thing. The ostentatious "California" Spanish, which spread over the country twenty-five years ago and then shrank back—with narrow windows high up on the façade, tile roofs, twisted columns, and Italian fireplaces—has given way to the simpler low structures which should have been the inspiration in the first place. Incidentally Mr. Larkin's Monterey style is still doing very well in many places.

Outstanding among California cities as one above all others which has respected and retained its Spanish character is Santa Barbara. It had a good start in several old Spanish buildings in the center of what has become the city, and it has exerted every effort to keep that character. El Paseo de la Guerra, a group of courtyards and passageways containing distinctive shops, built in the heart of the old city, is a delightful spot; and the rambling white-stucco Courthouse, with its towers, loggias, balconies, and gardens, is a Spanish palace of most unusual distinction. Both the small houses of the city and the country homes are distinctive. In national Better Homes competitions Santa Barbara has repeatedly walked off with the honors. Its site, its climate, and its wealth have been of no little aid in making the clean, white city what it is today; but the co-operation of its citizens has gone farther to make its name throughout the country a synonym for beauty. The Mission Santa Barbara had set a good example.

Texas has had such a variety of backgrounds, from so many different directions, that there is really nothing of which it could have a very exclusive Renaissance. The dog-run house has been adapted to modern suburban houses in many parts of the country, the dog run, or breeze way, serving to connect house with garage. The Monterey house has been successfully adopted in Texas and, in exchange, the popular ranch house of today has its antecedent in the vicinity of San Antonio, where many of the Mexican houses, rectangular in shape and one story in height, were just one room deep and two or three rooms long, with a low-pitched roof extending over a porch or porches.

The restoration of the Governor's Palace in San Antonio has set an inspiring example, and even the spirit of the old missions has been captured in modern work without being too completely archaeological studies; but when twin mission bell towers are used on the façade of a railway station the adaptation has gone too far.

Quite the opposite has obtained in Arizona (unless one wants to copy one of its two missions, for no very good reason) for, in spite of the fact that Fray Marcos and Coronado visited there first of all, American Arizona, the "baby state," really is a baby. It is old enough to have suffered the throes of both Victorianism and eclecticism as well as the bugaboo of the bungalow, but the recent rapid growth and popularity of Phoenix and Tucson have caused the importation of some of the finest work of the modern school, especially in resort hotels and country homes, to a degree that has almost drowned out the Southwest and made Arizona simply American and International. Nevertheless there are some fine examples of Spanish Renaissance in' those cities. The Phoenix Post Office, of the early Renaissance, straight out of Spain without pausing in Mexico, is one; Trinity Episcopal Cathedral in Phoenix is another; and both the Brophy College Chapel in Phoenix and the Veterans' Hospital in Tucson go back to Mexico and Spain for their inspiration.

In the Renaissance of earlier work New Mexico shines. It should; it had the combined results of two races to fall back on. As a matter of fact it never entirely gave them up. The Santa Fe Trail, the railroad, and the resulting Territorial Style did some damage which was not repaired, and then only in part, until 1909; but since that time New Mexico has come down to earth. The one-story adobe, with or without projecting vigas, is the "modern" of Santa Fe and Albuquerque. Both cities are full of midwestern frame houses and California bungalows (Albuquerque even has a German castle and Santa Fe a red Moorish temple), but they are being supplanted now not by the modern architecture of the rest of the country but by the Spanish-Pueblo of the Spaniards and the Indians. Which is very sensible. For simple beauty, economy, and insulation a better solution has not been found. That may take a little time. But then no other state has had a successful architectural style that has lasted a thousand years.

The Renaissance began with the Governor's Palace in Santa Fe. In 1909 it was stripped of its delicate and ill-fitting Victorian excrescences and given a rebirth in its original character. It was soon followed by the Art Museum, across the street, built in 1917 as a composite of several early Franciscan missions adapted to its use. Ácoma, San Felipe, Cochití, Laguna, Santa Ana, and Pecos can all be found on its various façades. Diagonally across the Plaza, La Fonda —one of the finest hotels in the country—erected on the site of the old hotel which marked the end of the Santa Fe Trail, has been built in the Indian pueblo style, in several stories with setbacks. The Post Office near by is a good example of Spanish-Pueblo applied to a modern building; a little away from the city, the Laboratory of Anthropology and the National Park Service Headquarters have adopted the style; and many recent houses have followed suit.

The style is not exclusively Santa Fe's. In Albuquerque the University of New Mexico, originally begun in the Victorian Gothic style, officially adopted a modified type of Pueblo architecture in 1905 even before the restoration of the Governor's Palace in Santa Fe, by remodeling a brick building into a copy of an Indian pueblo; and, with that as a modest beginning, its newer buildings now give the university an architectural character that is unique among educational institutions. Especially distinctive are the Administration Building and the University Library.

Adobe houses in the Spanish-Pueblo style and mock-adobe houses also in the same style are being built to the right and to the left, not only in Albuquerque and in Santa Fe but in Taos and in many other places throughout New Mexico, and spreading over into Arizona and even to the seashore of California! The combined work of the Spaniards and the Indians has come into its own.

Fitting as it is, there is danger in this wholehearted acceptance of a return to this truly indigenous architecture, as witnessed by the influence of the Art Museum in Santa Fe. In itself it is an interesting and probably justifiable archaeological expression. But, unfortunately, after it was completed little Ácomas and little San Felipes began to rise here and there promiscuously, one of them just across the street from the Art Museum, crowning a business building. In fact, littler and littler Ácomas were in danger of making the city absurd until the day was saved by a local architect who caricatured the design by applying the littlest Ácomas of them all to doghouses and privies.

There has been considerable agitation to rebuild the agglomeration of assorted façades of the buildings now facing the Plaza on the south, east, and west to bring them "into harmony" with the Palace,

Art Museum, and La Fonda. There is no doubt that intelligent and imaginative alterations would enhance the beauty of the old Plaza; but let us hope that the change will not result in an archaeological line-up of little Ácomas.

EPILOGUE: Cities of Today – and Tomorrow

THE GREATER Southwest with its much debated outlines, in spite of the aura of Indian customs clinging to part of it and in spite of the Spanish influence which, though overrunning it only faintly, still clings—and we hope will always do so—has changed much in its populated centers and is still changing. The wonders of irrigation and of water power have been in large part responsible for their growth, but the spread of commerce and industry and the rapid development of transportation and communication have tended to mold the cities more and more into a pattern which is rather universally American or even international. The effect is seen everywhere on the city streets, in the housing developments, and in the tall buildings. The skyscraper, originating in Chicago, lovingly embraced by New York and spreading throughout the country's urban centers, has not spared the Southwest. Every city of size has its tall business buildings.

But topography, geology, and climate man has not been able to overcome entirely. What makes Phoenix and San Diego the cleanest cities in the country, as John Gunther avers and I agree, will not solve the problems of Indianapolis or Pittsburgh. Scarcity of rain and snow, irrigation, water power, sunshine, and mountains have served to make the cities of the Southwest distinctive in spite of the pattern. And cultural background has helped. Yet variations in the effect of these forces having been sufficient to preclude monotony, a few brief comments on each of the major cities of the Southwest seems called for.

The problem is where to begin. New Orleans, often spoken of as the gateway to the Southwest, is decidedly an outer gateway. Despite its erstwhile Spanish occupation, which left a faint touch of Iberia on that very Gallic quarter which one so often hears nice old ladies speak of as the Vough Care, the charming "crescent city" is pure South. So we have to look west to Texas to find where the Southwest begins. There is plenty of space in which to look. Sprawling so widely that a road atlas has to break it up into three parts to get it all on two pages, Texas reaches into almost all parts of the country except the effete East and the frozen North.

Climatically, Texas all belongs to the southern belt. But except for the badly-abused subject of its climate, that great and still remarkably independent southern empire has no unity except the loyalty of its sons. Still carrying on its books the privilege of being broken up into five states, it has never exercised it in spite of intermittent howls from Amarillo that the politicians "down in the skillet" do not know what is going on in the Panhandle or even where it is, and in spite of the remoteness of El Paso which does business with both New and Old Mexico and formerly belonged to them before there ever was a Texas.

Nacogdoches, the oldest Spanish town east of El Paso and its Indian suburbs, is now pure South; busy Houston, the state's largest city and growing by leaps and bounds, is principally southern, if it can be localized at all; and Galveston, with its docks covered with bales of cotton, looks out over the Gulf to the east and farther south. Busy and cultured Dallas and its bitter rival, the cattle center of Fort Worth, only thirty-three miles apart and alternately looking toward the west and east at the same time, cannot make up their minds whether they belong to the Middle West or the West—if one of them could the other would jump the other way—and the beautiful capital and university center of Austin tries to belong to all.

Texas presents, then, for its principal candidates for the Southwest San Antonio and El Paso, and the greater of these lies just on the imaginary border. It is where the Southwest begins.

Of the three most alluring cities in the United States two are in the Southwest. One, lying outside the gate, we have just had to pass up, so we shall begin with the second and end with the third.

Perhaps the most charming thing about that pleasant yet very metropolitan city where the Southwest begins is the San Antonio River and what has been done with it. The banks of its many irregular bends could not have been greener and more peaceful when Governor Alarcón and Father Olivares chose the spot more than two centuries ago. Skyscrapers now rise high up above and close to it; the streets which they face are busy ones, with as steady a stream of traffic as in any larger city; but the river meanders peacefully along through the heart of the city, under more than forty artistically-designed bridges, with carefully-kept lawns and walks on its banks shaded by peppers, palms, weeping willows, and oaks. No other city has such a continuous strip of beautiful and restful park so quickly reached from "the office." San Antonio has done well by its river.

The city is steeped in history. The Alamo, the cradle of its liberty, is its greatest pride, as it is to all Texas (another reason, it is said, for not dividing up into smaller states—who would get the Alamo?) Add to that its four other old missions and the Governor's Palace and San Antonio need envy no city. Spanish names are still retained on many of its radiating streets and Spain and Old Mexico still live in its center.

But San Antonio, though respectfully and even pridefully preserving the past, does not dwell too much on it. Always a military center, it is even more so now; and so appealing are its young ladies to the men stationed there that it has been called the "mother-in-law of the army." The city goes about its business with an energy unsurpassed in the North; yet it still has time to entertain its visitors with sophisticated social grace. It boasts one of the very finest hotels in the country and another old and famous hostelry, adjacent to the Alamo, is now building a large addition to shelter its guests.

The city is justly proud of its huge Municipal Auditorium, built as a war memorial and winner of a medal for design in competition with many others; and of Brackenridge Park, with its many acres of facilities for entertainment and recreation, for with all its history, and its serious business, San Antonio likes best to play. But so do people from all over the country; and they go to San Antonio to do it.

Far away to the west El Paso seems still to belong to New Mexico. That is, it does geographically, since it is reached from the east only over hundreds of miles of semidesert plateau. Physically it appears to belong to the industrial East. Culturally it is a border town—the largest in the United States—a crossroads.

As a city El Paso is comparatively young. Though the site is old the city is new. Cabeza de Vaca must have passed through on his way west; Fray Agustín Rodríguez arrived some forty years later, followed by Espejo; and in 1598 came Juan de Oñate. But it was not until after the middle of the nineteenth century that a town began to grow up on the American side of the Rio Grande. With the coming of the railroads its future was assured. Today copper, cotton, cattle, and climate are all big business.

Although it has more Mexicans than Americans and although a steady stream of children crosses the bridge from Juarez to go to school in the United States, modern El Paso is a thoroughly American city and a very busy one. Skyscrapers rise out of its midst and the chimneys of factories and foundries, mills and railroad shops pour smoke into the air to mingle with the yellow-gray fumes of the smelters. But with all the effects of its industry, El Paso's warm, dry air and bright sunshine make it a health center.

The parking space at the International Bridge is big business too, for every year a million visitors cross over into Juarez for a quick glimpse of Old Mexico. Most of them, not knowing what they are missing, do not go farther.

One really should approach Albuquerque from the west, and at night. From the south one just sneaks up on its western edge; from the north one just gradually enters, through outlying districts, without any drama; and from the east it has spread out so far up the sloping mesa that on emerging from among the Sandía Mountains one just eases slowly down into the city.

But from the west—that's different! At night, after miles of silent desert and a black sky full of stars, the lights of the city suddenly appear like a twinkling nocturnal mirage, spreading away to the left and the right along the Rio Grande, while straight ahead a multi-colored rainbow leads directly up to the sky. Albuquerque's Central Avenue has a longer stretch of brilliantly-colored neon signs than any city I know. One cannot see Broadway that way, and I doubt that it has as much color.

Or even in daylight the city spreads out, looking like an oasis. Which it is, with green cottonwoods—showing splotches of gold in the autumn—along the river forming a base on which the white city can stretch.

Albuquerque too is a crossroads. The commercial capital of New Mexico, it is the meeting place of the principal East-West and North-South highways. It serves a wide trade area and its transcontinental traffic is heavy. It is also an air center. Its airport has been designed in the accepted Spanish-Pueblo style, the renaissance of which was begun by the University of New Mexico.

The city lies low. As a health resort as well as the business and educational center of the state, its recent growth has been almost phenomenal; but its tall buildings are fewer than in most cities; most of the buildings are still of one story—the sky is the thing. Originally a one-story town, it now looks with blushes on the hodgepodge resulting from its growing pains and is trying to correct the mistakes.

Since it is a natural stopover from any direction, few people pass through the city without spending at least a night. It has therefore, in addition to good hotels, probably more and better motor courts than any city of its size in the country, if not of any size. Modern motor travel has brought about a resurrection of the old post-road inn in a new form. The Southwest leads the country in such accommodations and Albuquerque leads the Southwest. There are excellent ones at both the east and the west ends of the city.

Santa Fe grows on one. At first its narrow, crowded, traffic-filled, one-way streets and its motley array of architecture and no architecture at all facing the plaza may be disappointing. It seems just a typical small American city.

But after dinner—a Mexican one, perhaps, with a bottle of good wine—a walk in the evening along some of the narrow streets past dimly-lit doorways from which come Spanish voices and the fragrance of piñon smoke, then a seat in front of the huge fireplace in the large adobe inn at the end of the Santa Fe Trail—that's all right, everybody does it anyway—and one is ready to face the morrow with a new enthusiasm.

Then the next day another walk, perhaps over the same route, through the crooked streets shaded with huge cottonwoods, past small adobe houses and gates opening onto patios filled with hollyhocks, then a lazy seat in the plaza watching the life roundabout, and one is captured.

One begins to feel the history and is ready to see the sights in more detail. They are not all within the city limits. As a center for fascinating trips in any direction, Santa Fe is incomparable. The oldest city in the Southwest, and a drawing card because of its historical associations and the beauty of its setting, Santa Fe has of recent years been subjected to all sorts of "movements"; but it has weathered them all. Away from a railroad, away from a waterway, away from everything except beauty and history, Santa Fe never had a boom. It just goes right on being Santa Fe.

Phoenix grew out of the irrigation begun by the Hohokam Indians a thousand years ago. Once referred to by Californians as "back in the desert," the region has now become California. It feels like it and it looks like it. The wide valley in which the city is located, with mountains on the horizon, is a blooming orange grove. There are also miles of other citrus fruits, dates, figs, apricots, and gardens of nearly all kinds of vegetables.

Quite in contrast to Santa Fe, a small old city in high mesa country, Phoenix is a large young city in a desert garden. The first American to pitch a tent there did so less than a hundred years ago. Now many tall buildings rise out of its center and palatial homes and gardens line streets shaded by palms, eucalyptus, tamarisk, and olive trees and brightened by oleander hedges.

The onetime desert has become a nation's winter playground. Motor courts compete with those in Albuquerque and in the country roundabout are many resorts, from genuine cow outfits to luxury desert palaces. In the most luxurious of the latter Frank Lloyd Wright found a fertile field for his most fanciful magic.

Phoenix was well named. It has risen in youthful freshness to adult beauty—and luxury—not from its own ashes but from the sand.

Of greater historical background than Phoenix but now outstripped in size by its young rival, Tucson deals in the same commodities. Dry desert air and bright winter sunshine attract visitors from afar. Motor courts do a thriving business nine months of the year, with swimming pools as added attractions, and dude ranches near by have their devotees who come year after year and swear by the climate. Like Phoenix, Tucson has graduated from false wooden fronts to tall office buildings and fine homes (it also has the University of Arizona, in compensation for the loss of the capital); but, unlike Phoenix, the city is not surrounded by gardens and groves. Around Tucson the desert still rules, rimmed by jagged mountains; but even the desert has its attractions: the Mission San Xavier del Bac in one direction and forests of saguaro in another.

Tucson was Padre Kino's "farthest north"; San Xavier Mission was the headquarters of Father Garcés during his extensive travels; and from Tubac, to the south, Juan Bautista de Anza started on his journeys to San Francisco before he became governor of Nuevo México. Little is left in the city of that Spanish occupation. When the Spaniards were driven out of Mexico the little frontier town deteriorated.

A few years after the Gadsden Purchase a stage service was initiated from San Antonio to San Diego which included a stop at Tucson. Accommodations there, it is said, consisted of the famous "Tucson bed," made by the traveler by lying on his stomach and covering himself with his back. By 1870 the town had a hotel, four restaurants, thirteen stores, a brewery, enough saloons and gambling houses to suit everybody, and a bathtub available to anyone able to pay the fee to the Negro barber. I find no statistics on the number today, but unquestionably Tucson is as well bathed as any city in the country, in tubs, showers, pools—and in sunshine.

California is the motorist's paradise. And if he is not alert he may see the real paradise. The Golden State has more good roads than any other state in the country—and more motorists. Texas, the only larger state, is a close second in its paved highways; but it has more room. In California *everybody* is out driving.

El Camino Real, which the padres trudged, has become the basis of a network of paved highways which cover the state. Now following the sea, now dipping inland to traverse an infinite variety of landscape, the Royal Road begins at San Diego, where the missions had their beginning. Fray Junípero would not recognize the spot where he struggled against great odds to initiate his dream; and Cabrillo would be thrilled at the present aspect of his "port, closed and very good." For San Diego has become the home of the navy. One is more conscious of the navy here than of the army in San Antonio. From Point Loma, extending south like a bulwark against the open sea, one can see the whole, wide stretch of the city's water front—rows upon rows of destroyers tied up in the Bay; other ships at anchor, and shore boats running between them and the piers; planes hovering over the Naval Air Station; and retired naval officers strolling the streets, for after sailing the world they have come to San Diego to live. The balmy climate has attracted them, as it has thousands of others, with its attending easy pace of life; but, what is just as important, they are "at home." With all its other attractions San Diego, like Venice, belongs to the sea.

The Civic Center lies close to the water, the Union Station is near by, and from the highway which parallels the Bay the streets rise steeply to the business center, small for a city the size of San Diego. One is not conscious of the city's industry. As a naval base and as an aircraft-manufacturing center, San Diego has grown tremendously since World War I and even more so since the beginning of World War II. But smokestacks and smoke are little in evidence; the city is white and clean and sparkling.

In its center is the luxuriant green square of Balboa Park, the cultural and recreational center of San Diego, with the permanent Spanish palaces of two expositions. The present city stretches far to the east covering a large territory, and along the ocean to the north and La Jolla, thus surrounding "Old Town" and quietly leaving alone the restored old mission on its hillside overlooking the valley of the San Diego River to the north.

The growth and development of Los Angeles is the most fabulous phenomenon in cities today. I have in my lap a little book published only thirty years ago which speaks of the expansion of the hub of southern California "from a sleepy little half-Spanish pueblo of a few thousand to a metropolis of half a million, with a taste for the latest in everything and the money to indulge it." The city's population is a risky statistic to state. As I write, it has passed Detroit—the recent growth of which is no mean matter itself—and in the population race its warm breath is now felt on the neck of the City of Brotherly Love. Doubtless when this is read it will have become the third city in the country and destined to stay not very long at the heels of Chicago.

In area it is the largest city on earth, one fourth larger than New York, more than twice the size of Chicago, and more than three times that of Philadelphia. It has sprawled in all directions, including the south and west. Even the ocean cannot stop it; it plunges right into the Pacific to dig for oil, one of its major sources of wealth. The city is no longer in need of a harbor. An unkind visitor from the East, attending a Chamber of Commerce luncheon, is reputed to have suggested that Los Angeles lay a tube from the heart of the city to the ocean and that if she could then suck as hard as she could blow she would soon have an adequate harbor. The method used was slightly different, but in essence the city did just that. Reaching a long arm out to the ocean, Los Angeles grabbed it in, and now has one of the leading deep-water ports of the country. With the other she reaches past the Santa Monica to the San Gabriel Mountains. But water (fresh) is its life, climate is its fetish, and automobiles its first love. Although a city of homes, the automobile comes first—and last, and all the time.

There are more automobiles per capita than in any other city in the world; automobile assembly is a major industry; automobile use is a major occupation and a major hazard. But predominant as they are, automobiles are not everything. The city's airplane factories turned out more planes during the last war than all the rest of the country combined; Los Angeles is running a close race with Akron in the manufacture of tires and rubber goods; the city has outstripped Grand Rapids in the production of furniture; and, in addition to being the motion-picture capital of the world, it makes the sport clothes of the nation. One hears most about climate; the city is a mecca for sun worshipers. Working there for a short time some thirty years ago, I was told in perfect seriousness, as an explanation for my rather skimpy "salary," that the climate was considered part of one's pay. One hears less about its even more vital commodity, but without many miles of waterpipes leading from the mountains the city would dry up and disappear.

The climate has had a marked effect on the method of life and on the architecture. Closely-packed apartment buildings are taboo. There are apartments, of course, though they must bring in the outdoors. But the city, with its surrounding (and sometimes surrounded) suburbs, is essentially a community of individually-owned houses each with its lawn—constantly sprinkled, of course—and garden. This has meant spreading out, to more than four hundred and fifty square miles not including the suburbs. It has also meant, in addition to the once-ubiquitous bungalow and the "Spanish" houses of varying merit and demerit, the production of some of the weirdest architecture in the country but also of some of the best. Los Angeles and vicinity has probably gone in more than any other place in the United States for all phases of modern architecture, plain modern, supermodern, and old-fashioned modern. As might be expected, some of it is very bad, some is merely bad; but some of it is excellent. Varieties in types of sites have, together with the benefit of climate, provided fertile fields for imagination, something with which southern California is bountifully blest. Much of it has been put to good use.

Commercial buildings, particularly stores, have embraced the contemporary mode, some of them to an extreme; but public buildings have reflected more conservatively the cultural growth of the city. Thirty years ago I could find no one who could tell me where or whether Los Angeles had a public library. Now it has one of the largest and best in the country, housed in one of the most beautiful of buildings devoted to that end. The Huntington Library and Art Gallery in San Marino are world renowned, almost as much for the grounds and gardens as for the collections, and the University of Southern California, the University of California at Los Angeles, and the California Institute of Technology at Pasadena rank among the country's leading educational institutions, with campus groups in keeping with their standing.

Though built wide, Los Angeles does not rise high in comparison with other large cities. Private buildings are limited to thirteen stories and a hundred and fifty feet in height. This restriction has been enforced, with but few exceptions, to such a degree that the thirty-two-story City Hall seems a skyscraper indeed.

Los Angeles has now so far outdistanced in population its former rival at the Golden Gate that it is no longer a competition. Yet comparison is still inevitable and the rivalry continues. At least it does as far as Los Angeles is concerned. Suave, sophisticated San Francisco pays no attention. San Francisco has one of the finest natural harbors in the world. Los Angeles had to make hers. The city by the Golden Gate has its fog, which it comes by naturally. The City of the Angels, not to be outdone, now has its equivalent, which the inhabitants call smog and which hangs like a pall over the city much of the time. The increase of industry presents its problems.

San Francisco has a fine civic center atop one of her hills and Los Angeles, with greater space available but without the hills, is in the process of creating a "bigger and better" one. Its expansion poses a delicate problem. The only visible evidence of early history the City of the Angels can boast lies directly in the path of civic progress. The so-called "plaza church" stands pathetically isolated behind a maze of streetcar wires and a rush of traffic. It really does not face the old plaza at all; it is separated by a century of "progress" in the form of an uninterrupted stream of streetcars and automobiles. On an adjacent side of the plaza venerable Olvera Street extends for the distance of a block between old buildings crowded out of sight by displays of cheap Mexican merchandise and drowned almost out of existence by the antics of candid-camera fans and the cries of peanut vendors. As a rarely-picturesque spot its proposed sacrifice has caused howls of protest. The howls really should have come long ago, before streetcar tracks were laid between the plaza and the plaza church and before the automobile became an instrument of ancient-civic destruction. Even a city like Chicago argues for generations about pushing through a proposed Congress Street artery; but Los Angeles grabs a steam shovel, knocks over old buildings, and has a three-level boulevard in operation before the old-timers know what it is all about. Olvera Street appears to be doomed.

San Francisco is the biggest city in the country west of New York. The census taker will not agree with that statement, but the census taker is prone to depend on figures and in making the statement I rise above statistics. So does San Francisco. It is built almost as high as Los Angeles is wide. Its inhabitants have a right to say of Los Angeles (perhaps they do), as New Mexicans do of Texas, that it really is not any larger, it is just spread out thinner; that if San Francisco were laid out flat it could cover all of Los Angeles County and extend to Santa Barbara to boot. Even in the unimportant matter of population, if San Francisco were to include Oakland across the Bay, Berkeley with the largest university in the country, and other towns around the Bay, half of the four largest cities in the country would be on the Pacific Coast and in California. But San Francisco doesn't care. The city rises above statistics mentally too.

Therein lies the greatest difference, perhaps, between the two largest cities in the greater Southwest; the one a very metropolitan center, exuding charm but indifferent to its effect; the other a tremendously overgrown cluster of villages with the population race won by at least two laps, but still jealous.

Hemmed in by a narrow peninsula, San Francisco has had to build high; it has to cross the Bay to sprawl. It has a good foundation for its height, for the city is built on many more hills than Rome, and higher. In driving in the city a map does little good; there is no way to tell whether a street is horizontal or more or less vertical. For the latter there is still the cable car, a well-beloved institution. If the automobile, next to climate, is a fetish in a big way in Los Angeles, the cable car is a fetish in a small but devoted way in San Francisco. It is not only visitors who use them: the little cars are always packed with San Franciscans who help to swing them around on their wooden turntables, and one grip man told me that he takes his wife for a cable-car ride on his day off. With all its use and its convenience, it is San Francisco's most enjoyable outdoor sport.

That *joie de vivre* is the key to San Francisco's charm. It accounts for flowers on the street corners downtown, for some of the smartest shops in the country and for some of the most luxurious hotels and some of the best restaurants in the world. It stems from constant contact with the world. Ever since Captain Richardson, in 1835, built the first house in Yerba Buena, as it was then called, and Jacob Leese opened the first store the following year, but especially since the Gold Rush a few years later when sea captains and gold-seekers crammed the harbor, San Francisco has attracted immigrants from all directions from Boston to China. Its more than three miles of piers along its water front, crowded with ships flying the flags of all nations, has made a cosmopolitan city where one can almost smell the spices of the Orient. For if San Diego belongs to the sea and Los Angeles belongs to Iowa, Detroit, Hollywood, and increasingly much of the rest of the country, San Francisco belongs to all the world.

From the Skyline Boulevard along the ocean one can see, through rifts in the fog, rows and rows, blocks and blocks, of Lilliputian houses climbing the hills and shining white in the bright sunlight; and, when the sun strikes beyond, clusters of skyscrapers can be seen rising above the Bay. From the Embarcadero and the Ferry Building, whose clock tower is a landmark of the shore, wide Market Street leaves the rows of piers jutting out into the Bay, leaves the water front and the aroma of the Orient, the bustle and chugging of ships unloading and the raucous laughter of seamen's cafes and climbs to department stores, banks—for San Francisco is the banking capital of the West—and high office buildings. To climb Nob Hill it is necessary to take the cable car—a joy, not a hardship—to reach the tall apartment buildings, old mansions, and smart hotels.

From the Top of the Mark is a good place to see the city. It is in fact a good place for many things: a good place to have a drink and rest from strenuous sightseeing, a good place to sit by the window and try to absorb the incomparable views, or, being sated with that if such were possible, a good place to reminisce.

Alta California has come a long way since the time of Serra. So has the whole Southwest. From the early adobe missions in New Mexico, the stockaded outposts among the Comanches and Apaches, the primitive ranches in Arizona, and even the stone-vaulted church at San Juan Capistrano, it is a far cry to the busy cities of Texas, the orange groves of California, the skyscrapers of San Francisco, and the powerhouse at Hoover Dam, the noblest interior since the Cathedral of Seville. Yet the children of the builders of the latter showed us the way.

But to get back to earth, or rather to the sky, for the lights have come on while we were reminiscing and the myriad twinklings we see are below and all around us rather than above. The slowly-crawling lines of lights to our right represent traffic on the many and varied spans of the two-level Bay Bridge. More closely below is Chinatown, unique in this country; and beyond is Telegraph Hill, where artists and writers live at the top and Italians, Portuguese, Spanish, and French live at the base. Just a little farther beyond and to the left, where the black water begins, is Fisherman's Wharf, than which there is no more delightful spot anywhere—unless it be the smaller and more intimate edition at Monterey—to sniff the salt of the ocean and partake of its products. Still farther to the left begins the bridge over the Golden Gate, a worthy complement to Hoover Dam, with a clear span almost a mile long rising two hundred and twenty feet above the entrance to the harbor which Saint Francis first showed to the modern world and which Serra, as his representative on the Pacific Coast, confidently expected him to do.

Beyond is Land's End, where Fray Junípero stood as he watched the waters flowing out to the setting sun and joyfully exclaimed that Saint Francis had reached the last limit of the California continent. Like Serra, speaking for his father Saint Francis, one can stand at that spot and gaze out onto the water, out onto the surf breaking on the high cliffs to the north, and onto the limitless sea beyond, knowing that here he has come to the end of the Southwest. To go farther he must have a boat.

APPENDIX

Chronological Summary

THE INDIAN PERIOD 100 B.C.—A.D. 1540

100 B.C.—A.D. 500 Pit houses in "four corners" region. Corn cultivated. Floodwater irrigation in Arizona. Baskets. No bows and arrows.

500—900 Developed pit houses. Pottery. Bow and arrow. Ball courts in Arizona.

900—1050 Pit houses developed into kivas in New Mexico. Dwellings above ground.

1050—1300 The Classic Period. Cliff villages and community apartment villages in "four corners" region; well-developed masonry construction. Adobe compounds in Arizona; irrigation canals.

1300—1540 People from "four corners" region move closer to the Rio Grande and to the Hopi country; continue to build multistoried pueblos. People in southern Arizona revert to primitive types of shelters, or move eastward and southward.

1540 to date. People in New Mexico continue to build and live in pueblos, but under European domination. Multistoried house groups gradually give way to single-storied units.

THE SPANISH PERIOD 1540—1821

1519 Alonso Alvarez de Pineda explores the coast of Texas.

1528 Álvar Nuñez Cabeza de Vaca and others of the Narváez expedition are shipwrecked on the Texas coast.

1536 Cabeza de Vaca, passing through Texas, arrives at Culiacán, Mexico. En route he hears tales of northern pueblos.

1539 Fray Marcos de Niza enters Arizona and New Mexico; marches as far as Zuñi, then returns to New Spain.
Francisco de Ulloa explores Gulf of California. The name "California" is first applied to the peninsula.

1540 Francisco Vásquez de Coronado explores the Southwest and extends boundaries of New Spain.
Hernando de Alarcón sails up the Colorado River.

1541 Coronado marches across Texas and as far northeast as Kansas.

1542 Coronado and army return to New Spain.

1542 (*cont.*) Juan Rodríguez Cabrillo discovers San Diego Bay; explores California coast.

1543—1544 Juan de Padilla, Luís de Escalona, and Juan de la Cruz remain in New Mexico as missionaries; all martyred.

1579 Francis Drake lands on California coast; holds first Christian services there.

1581 Missionary expedition of Fray Agustín Rodríguez and two other Franciscans enters northern New Mexico; all killed by Indians.

1582 Relief expedition under Antonio Espejo learns fate of Franciscans; continues explorations.

1590 Unauthorized attempt is made by Gaspar Castaño de Sosa to colonize New Mexico. The leader is returned in chains.

1598 Don Juan de Oñate takes formal possession of New Mexico; establishes first Spanish settlement at San Juan pueblo. Franciscans are assigned to pueblos to establish missions.

1599 Indians of Ácoma revolt; subdued.

1602 Sebastián Vizcaíno explores California coast; discovers Bay of Monterey.

1605 Oñate, returning from exploring expedition to Gulf of California, carves name on Inscription Rock (El Morro) in New Mexico.

1609—1610 Santa Fe is founded by Don Pedro de Peralta as capital of New Mexico. First church and Palace of the Governor are built.

1617 Eleven churches have been built in New Mexico. Churches at Pecos and Jemez are begun.

1629 Mission churches at Ácoma, Abó, Quarai, and "Gran Quivira" are begun (the last three abandoned by 1680 because of Apache raids).

1630 Fifty Franciscan friars are at work in twenty-five New Mexico missions, with sixty thousand converts.

1659 Mission Nuestra Señora de Guadalupe is founded at El Paso del Norte (on present site of Juarez, Mexico).

1680 Pueblo Indians revolt, led by Popé; kill friars and destroy New Mexico missions. Spaniards abandon Santa Fe; flee to El Paso del Norte.

1680—1682 Refugees from Pueblo Revolt establish settlements and missions on Rio Grande near El Paso.

1685 Fort Saint Louis is established on coast of Texas by Robert Cavalieur, Sieur de la Salle.

1690 Mission San Francisco de los Tejas, the first in east Texas, is founded, near the Neches River, to offset advances of French.

1691—1692 Father Eusebio Francisco Kino explores southern Arizona.

1692 Reconquest of New Mexico is undertaken by Don Diego de Vargas; Santa Fe is taken without a blow.

1693—1695 New Mexico is recolonized and missions are re-established.

1697 Jesuits, under Juan María Salvatierra, establish first mission in Baja California.

1699 Pueblo of Laguna, New Mexico, is established by order of Governor Pedro Rodríguez Cubero; mission church is built there.

1700 Mission San Xavier del Bac is founded near Tucson, Arizona; foundations of church are begun.

1706 Albuquerque is founded by Don Francisco Cuervo y Valdés.

1716 East Texas is colonized and missions are established.

1718 Mission San Antonio de Valero is founded by Fray Antonio de San Buenaventura Olivares; Villa de Bejar established by Governor Martín de Alarcón.

1720 Mission San José is begun near San Antonio.

1731 Canary Islanders are established in settlement of San Fernando, adjacent to presidio of Bejar (San Antonio).
Missions Concepción, San Juan Capistrano, and San Francisco de la Espada are moved from east Texas and re-established near San Antonio.

1749 Presidio and mission are established at Goliad, Texas.

1751 Pima and Papago Indians in southern Arizona revolt.

1752 Presidio is established at Tubac in southern Arizona.

1767 Jesuits are expelled from all Spanish colonies by decree of Charles III.

1768 Jesuit missions in southern Arizona (then part of Sonora) and Baja California are turned over to Franciscans (in Baja California later to Dominicans). Francisco Tomás Garcés takes charge in Arizona; Junípero Serra in Baja California. José de Gálvez makes plans with Serra for occupation of Alta California.

1769 Mission San Diego de Alcalá, first Alta California mission, is founded by Serra. Governor Gaspar de Portolá reaches Monterey Bay but does not recognize it; continues to Golden Gate before returning to San Diego.

1770 Mission and presidio are founded at Monterey.

1771 Monterey mission is moved to Carmel. Missions San Antonio de Padua and San Gabriel are founded.

1772 Mission San Luís Obispo is founded.

1774 Juan Bautista de Anza reaches San Gabriel Mission overland from Sonora.

1775 Monterey is made capital of California.

1776 Presidio at Tubac, Arizona, is transferred to Tucson.
Father Garcés visits Oraibi in Hopi country; asked to leave.
De Anza reaches San Francisco with colonists; presidio established.
Missions San Francisco de Asís and San Juan Capistrano are founded.

1777 Mission Santa Clara de Asís is founded.
San José de Guadalupe, first pueblo in California, is founded.

1780 Two missions are founded on the Yuma River by Garcés.

1781 Garcés and Spanish soldiers are massacred by Yuma Indians.

1782 Mission San Buenaventura is founded.

1784 Padre Serra dies and is buried at Mission San Carlos Borromeo.

1786 Mission Santa Barbara is founded by Lasuén, who succeeds Serra.

1787 Mission La Purísima Concepción is founded.

1791 Mission church of San Xavier del Bac, near Tucson, Arizona, is completed by Franciscans.

Missions Santa Cruz and La Soledad are founded.

John Groem (Graham?), first American in California, arrives in Monterey; ill, he dies same day.

1793 Pueblo of Branciforte is founded, near Santa Cruz Mission.

1797—1798 Five California missions are founded by Fermín Lasuén: San José, San Juan Bautista, San Miguel Arcángel, San Fernando Rey, and San Luís Rey.

1803 Father Lasuén dies at Mission San Carlos Borromeo.

Louisiana is purchased by the United States.

1804 Mission Santa Inés is founded by Estévan Tapis.

1807 Lt. Zebulon Pike, on exploring expedition, is arrested and taken to Santa Fe; on his release, first information on Spanish Southwest is given to the United States.

1812 Russians build Fort Ross, on coast north of San Francisco.

Severe earthquakes in California; missions badly damaged.

1816 Thomas Doak, first American settler, lands in California.

1817 Mission San Rafael Arcángel is founded.

1818 Hippolyte Bouchard terrorizes California coast. Joseph Chapman, second American settler in California, is landed from Bouchard's ship; helps build missions, and builds first successful gristmill in California.

1819 Dr. James Long attempts settlement in east Texas; unsuccessful.

1820 Moses Austin establishes colony in east Texas.

1821 On death of Austin, colonization is carried on by his son, Stephen F. Austin.

Mexico wins independence from Spain.

THE MEXICAN PERIOD 1821—1846

1822 William Becknell opens Santa Fe Trail.

1823 Mission San Francisco de Solano, the twenty-first and last of the California missions, is founded.

1832 Thomas Oliver Larkin arrives in Monterey from Boston.

1833 Secularization of California missions is decreed by Mexico.

1834 Stephen F. Austin is imprisoned in Mexico.

1835 Pueblo of Sonoma, California, is founded by General Vallejo.

Captain William A. Richardson builds first house in Yerba Buena (San Francisco).

Thomas O. Larkin builds house which establishes "Monterey" style; residential building boom in Monterey.

Texas War of Independence; Texans win Battle of Concepción; San Antonio is captured by Texans.

1836   Siege of the Alamo, San Antonio; massacre at Goliad; General Houston wins Battle of San Jacinto; Texas is a republic.

1837   Independence of Texas is recognized by the United States.

1838   Pueblo of Pecos is abandoned; inhabitants move to Jemez.

1843   Thomas O. Larkin is appointed first and only U.S. consul to California.

1845   California mission lands are sold by Pío Pico, Mexican governor.

1846   Texas is admitted to the Union.

War between the United States and Mexico.

General Kearny occupies Santa Fe; continues to California.

The Bear Flag of the "California Republic" is raised at Sonoma.

The American flag is raised at Monterey three weeks later.

THE AMERICAN PERIOD 1846—

1848   Treaty of Guadalupe Hidalgo; Rio Grande made Texas boundary; Gila River southern boundary of New Mexico.
James Wilson Marshall discovers gold in California.

1849   Gold rush depopulates Monterey and many other cities. San Francisco becomes important port; building boom.

1850   California is admitted as a state into the Union.

1851   Bishop John B. Lamy arrives in Santa Fe to head newly-established Roman Catholic Diocese; initiates reforms.

1853   Gadsden Purchase of a strip of Sonora south of Gila River places Missions San Xavier del Bac and Tumacácori in U.S. territory.

1861—1865   Civil War.

1863   Separate territory of Arizona is created.

1867   Tucson is made territorial capital of Arizona.

1868   A settlement is established at Phoenix.

1869   First transcontinental railroad is completed.

1875   Rt. Rev. John B. Lamy is made archbishop of Santa Fe.

1881   Southern Pacific Railroad reaches El Paso.

1889   Phoenix is made capital of territory of Arizona.

1905   University of New Mexico officially adopts Spanish-Pueblo style of architecture.

1906   Earthquake and fire in San Francisco; many buildings destroyed.

1907—1909   Palace of the Governor at Santa Fe is restored and becomes Museum of New Mexico.

1912 New Mexico and Arizona are admitted as states.

1914 Panama Canal is opened.

1915 Expositions are held at San Diego and San Francisco; they have a marked effect on architectural taste.

1917 Santa Fe Art Museum is completed and dedicated.

1925 Earthquake damages Santa Barbara Mission; repaired.
      Craze for Spanish architecture sweeps the country.

1936 Hoover Dam, the world's highest and most spectacular dam, is completed; effects flood control, irrigation, water supply, and water power in the Southwest.
      San Francisco–Oakland Bay Bridge is opened.

1937 Golden Gate Bridge is opened.

1939 Golden Gate Exposition is held at San Francisco.

1941—1945 San Diego, Los Angeles, and San Francisco all increase greatly in size, due largely to war industries.

*In the tables on the following pages
asterisks are used as marks of commendation*

Listed Geographically, W

The following list includes only the nineteen pueb

Name	Indian Name	Location	Population January 1, 1	
			Family *Tota* *Groups*	
Zuñi*	Suny'tsi (Halona)	40 m S of Gallup (and Highway 66). Reached by fair road (NM 32); paved for 10 miles, the rest gravel.	551	2,75
Acoma***	Ako	50 m W of Albuquerque (15 m S of Highway 66). Reached by fair road (NM 23). Thence a steep climb on foot (tiring but not difficult).	301 (including near-by related villages)	1,50
Laguna**	Kawaik	45 m W of Albuquerque; adjacent to US 66, S.	593 (including near-by farming villages)	2,96
Isleta*	Shiahwibak	13 m S of Albuquerque; close to US 85, E. Easily accessible.	298	1,49

o East and South to North

which are still occupied today. (See map, page 84)

Language	Description	History	Mission–Church
Zuñi	Large village* on river—red sandstone and red adobe. Vegetable gardens across river. Trading post.	One of the "Seven Cities of Cíbola," first pueblos seen by Spaniards (1539–1540). Present village built c 1695, after Revolt, near site of former Halona. Origin not known. Ancestors may have come from Chaco Canyon.	Red sandstone and adobe mission church (1705) now in ruins. Part of walls and balcony remain.
Keres	Striking site*** on mesa top, 357 feet above valley. 2-3 story houses* in rows. $1 admission fee; $1 photography fee; motion pictures $5.	Continuously occupied since arrival of Spaniards in 1540. Origin not known. Ancestors may have come from Mesa Verde. Most of the inhabitants have now moved into the valley and to new villages.	Adobe mission church*** of San Estéban Rey (1629) the largest and finest in New Mexico; repaired and well restored in 1924.
Keres	Built on rocky hill* S of highway; interesting blend of Indian and Spanish architecture. $1 photography fee.	Established in 1699, on Spanish order, by Keresan-speaking people, probably from Ácoma, Santo Domingo, and Cochití.	Mission San José** built in 1699 (the last of the early missions); stone and adobe. Interesting, though crude, decorated interior**.
anoan (Tiwa)	Interesting; built around plaza*; other scattered one-story houses; photography by permission of the pueblo governor.	Most southerly pueblo; stands on or near site it occupied when Spaniards spent winter of 1540–1541 near by. History before that time not known. Did not take active part in Pueblo Revolt of 1680.	Adobe church (early 17th C) unwisely restored with wooden spires and peaked roof; the few remaining old details* interesting.

Name	Indian Name	Location	Population January 1, 1949	
			Family Groups	Total
Sandía	Nanfíat	12 m N of Albuquerque; 100 yds. E of US 85.	29	147
Jemez	Heminsh	28 m NW of Bernalillo; 5 m N on NM 4 from San Ysidro and US 44.	182	911
Zía*	Tsi-ya	18 m NW of Bernalillo, on N bank of Jemez River; 1 m N on side road from NM 44, across bridge.	54	271
Santa Ana	Tamaya	9 m NW of Bernalillo on N bank of Jemez River; 1 m N on sand road from NM 44; across ford, apt to be treacherous.	60	300
San Felipe**	Katishtya	12 m NE of Bernalillo; 3 m NW on side road from US 85; across river and a bit S.	163	815

iguage	Description	History	Mission–Church
ınoan (iwa)	Small village; much Mexicanized.	The only surviving village of the province of Tiguex, Coronado's headquarters, 1540–41. In 1680, after Pueblo Revolt, inhabitants moved to Hopi country and built village on Second Mesa. In 1742 they returned to the Rio Grande, founded present village.	Old church of 18th C now replaced by a modern church.
ınoan (owa)	Typical one-story adobe houses, on a beautiful valley site.	Present village c 1700; in vicinity for 300 years previously. May have come from Mesa Verde and Chaco Canyon (pottery related). Joined by remnants of people from Pecos, abandoned in 1838.	Chapel of San Diego modern (1937) near ruins of old church. (Ruins of Mission San José de Jemez** at site of ancient pueblo, is 12 m N.)
.eres	Attractive site* on a basaltic mound above river; small, not prosperous, hostile.	Claim same site as in 1540, therefore perhaps as old as Acoma. Inhabitants may have come from Mesa Verde, or from Zuñi.	Adobe church* (1692), rebuilt on ruins of earlier church; massive buttresses and pierced belfry on front; gallery over entrance.
.eres	In midst of sand dunes on river bank. Practically deserted during cropping season, except for guard.	Founded late 17th C. Formerly on a mesa a few miles east. Earlier history unknown. Possibly from Mesa Verde.	Adobe church* (late 17th or early 18th C), low, with wooden gallery; pierced belfry above, at right.
.eres	Covers a large area along river; streets composed of one-story brown adobe houses; plaza at far end.	Present village built c 1700. Claim, with Cochití, origin in Tyuonyi, Frijoles Canyon. Occupied several different sites in the meantime.	Present adobe mission church*** (early 18th C) with twin towers, open belfries, and gallery, one of best of New Mexican mission churches.

Name	Indian Name	Location	Population January 1, 1949	
			Family Groups	Total
Santo Domingo**	Kihwa	18 m NE of Bernalillo; 6 m NE of San Felipe; (or 4 m W on side road from US 85; or via Peña Blanca from Cochití).	230	1,152
Cochití	Kotyiti	25 m NE of Bernalillo; (25 m SW of Santa Fe). 15 m NW on side road from US 85, across bridge over Rio Grande (to W bank), 1 m S.	53	413
Tesuque	Tathunge	8 m N of Santa Fe; 1 m W on side road from US 64; easily accessible.	33	166
Pojoaque	Posunwage	14 m N of Santa Fe; ¼ m E on side road from US 64.	5	26
San Ildefonso**	Pohwoge	18 m NW of Santa Fe; 4 m W from US 64 on NM 4 (paved); then 1 m N on side road.	36	180

Language	Description	History	Mission–Church
Keres	Pueblo** large, prosperous, interesting, with rows of adobe houses, and kivas; hostile (no photographs).	Moved several times because of floods. Present village founded after reconquest in 1692. Ancestors may have come from Mesa Verde; also claim Frijoles Canyon ancestry.	Church* recent, in good Spanish-Pueblo style, with balcony and exterior color decorations.
Keres	Typical one-story adobe houses around plaza. 2 kivas.	Claim origin in Frijoles Canyon; occupied several sites before founding of present village c. 1500.	Church (1694) unfortunately remodeled, with arcade and tin steeple; an example of "benevolent vandalism."
Tanoan (Tewa)	Flat, gray adobe village. Most-visited pueblo, being nearest to Santa Fe.	Present village founded c 1700; former village, 3 miles east, abandoned at time of Pueblo Revolt. Origin not known.	Original mission destroyed in Pueblo Revolt. Sacristy of later church (ruined) remodeled into present small church of gray adobe.
Tanoan (Tewa)	Only a few scattered houses; of no interest.	Early history unknown. It had been dwindling in size for many years, until, a few years ago, it was virtually extinct. It has been revived, and a few emigrants have returned.	Modern brick church; of no interest.
Tanoan Tewa)	Flat; spreads over large territory, around 2 large plazas**. Interesting village, noted for pottery** Most photographed kiva** 50 cent photography fee.	Present village founded c 1700; plazas relocated twice. Older village was 7 or 8 miles west.	Present church modern and uninteresting; on site of earlier church.

Name	Indian Name	Location	Population January 1, 19	
			Family Groups	Total
Nambé		16 m N of Santa Fe; E on side road from US 64.	30	151
Santa Clara	Khapo	25 m NW of Santa Fe; 2 m S of Española on NM 5, then ¼ m E on side road.	116	584
San Juan	Ohke	30 m NW of Santa Fe (5 m N of Española); ¼ m W of US 64.	164	821
Picurís (San Lorenzo)	Pinwel-tha	50 m NE of Santa Fe; 20 m S of Taos. 17 m on side road (NM 75) from US 64. Not easily accessible.	26	133
Taos***	Toa-tha	73 m NE of Santa Fe, via US 64; (70 m to Taos; 3 m beyond to Pueblo of Taos).	187	938

guage	Description	History	Mission–Church
noan (ewa)	Scattered; largely Mexicanized.	History unknown. Pueblo being absorbed by amalgamation with Mexican village.	Recent church, built in Spanish-Pueblo style, on commanding site above valley, on the road to the scattered pueblo.
noan (ewa)	On a low hill, short distance off road to Puyé; not distinctive.	Present village established c 1700, after Pueblo Revolt. Had previously occupied several sites. Claim to have come from Puyé.	Church, built in the 18th C, now in ruins. The small modern church, in Spanish-Pueblo style, was built in 1918.
noan (ewa)	Present village not distinctive; its proximity to the highway caused it to lose its Indian character.	Present village established in 1598; had previously occupied other sites near by. First Spanish capital established near by in 1598 by Oñate; abandoned a decade later for Santa Fe.	Present church is modern (since 1900). Small modern chapel across the street.
noan (iwa)	Small scattered village in a picturesque, high mountain valley.	Once one of the strongest pueblos, and active in Pueblo Revolt. Present village founded c 1692 near earlier village. Now the smallest pueblo except Pojoaque.	Old church of San Lorenzo (c 1692) has been unfortunately remodeled, with pitched roof and wooden cupola.
noan (iwa)	Best extant example of terraced Pueblo architecture; house groups 4–5 stories high*** Now many small houses too. Village in two parts separated by stream*. 25 cent parking fee; $1 photography fee.	Present village founded c 1700, after earlier pueblo had been sacked and destroyed by the Spaniards. Inhabitants may have come from Chaco Canyon; pottery related.	Church of 1704 now in ruins (used as a cemetery). Small 19th C church is picturesque (visitors not invited inside).

Listed Geographica

The following list includes only th

today. Sites of missions no longer existi

Name	Location	Founded
Nuestra Señora de Guadalupe de El Paso*	In Juarez, Mexico, across Rio Grande from El Paso; corner Calle 16 Septiembre and Calle Nicolas Bravo.	1659; church co pleted in 1668.
Corpus Christi de la Isleta del Sur	In town of Ysleta, 12 m SE of El Paso on US 80.	1681, by refugees fr Pueblo Revolt in N Mexico.
La Purísima Concepción del Socorro	3 m S of Ysleta, on a side road (paved). (15 m SE of El Paso).	c 1683, followi Pueblo Revolt.
(Capilla de la Elizario)	On paved side road 3 m W of Clint, which is 21 m SE of El Paso	Following Pueblo R volt of 1680.

F TEXAS

om West to East

issions of which something may be seen
e not listed. (*See maps, page 150*)

Description	History	Present Condition
•unded on 3 sides by a ;h wall, with ancient metery in front. Flat of; single bell tower. uick walls of adobe icks plastered; beamed iling* carved brackets*	Founded for the conversion of the Manso Indians, it became the nucleus for settlements at "The Pass." A new, larger church has been built next to it, opening into old church.	Little changed, except modern roof replaces thick roof of earth, and pews replace use of serapes and small stools. Still in use.
riginally on an island in e Rio Grande; since the ver changed its course has been on the Texas le. Curved gable; tower ith overpowering dome.	Built by Tiwa Indians from New Mexico, under the protection of Spanish soldiers. In one of a group of 14 pueblos.	Old mission destroyed by fire in 1907. Present building (locally called Carmel) is a modern reproduction. Active.
a quaint, scattered village, church is wide and w, with a high, square, erced belfry.	The original mission was abandoned because of trouble with Indians; the second building was destroyed by a flood; the third has now been replaced by a recent structure.	Present building built on ruins of one erected in the early 19th C. In use.
he simple presidio apel (not a mission) ces the old plaza. With hite walls and curved, erced belfry, it resembles California missions.	Originally founded on the Mexican side of the Rio Grande, the present site is the third.	The present structure was built in 1877, the fourth to be erected. In use, and well kept.

Name	Location	Founded
San Antonio de Valero*** (The Alamo)	In San Antonio, on the E side of Alamo Plaza, between E. Houston and E. Crockett Sts.	May 1, 1718, by Fr Antonio de San Bu naventura Olivares.
Nuestra Señora de la Purísima Concepción de Acuna**	San Antonio, 3 m S of Alamo Plaza. Roosevelt Ave. to Mitchell St.; W to Mission Road; turn S.	In 1716, in east Tex Re-established on present site March 1731.
San José y San Miguel de Aguayo***	San Antonio, 2 m S of Mission Concepción. (5 m S of Alamo Plaza.)	Feb. 23, 1720, by Fr Antonio Margil Jesús. Present chur begun May 19, 1768
San Juan Capistrano	San Antonio, 7 m S of Alamo Plaza; follow Mission Rd., or S on 181 to Bergs Mill, turn W.	In 1716 in east Tex near Nacogdoches. Re-established on present site in 1731.
San Francisco de la Espada*	San Antonio, 1 m S of San Juan Capistrano, on Espada Road.	In 1690 in east Tex near the Neches River. Re-establish on present site in 173
Mission Nuestra Señora del Espíritu Santo de Zuñiga and Chapel of the Presidio Nuestra Señora de Loreto de la Bahia**	Goliad State Park, via Texas 29, 2 m S of Goliad, which is 90 m SE of San Antonio; 140 m SW of Houston.	In 1722, to serve th Karankawa Indians.

Description	History	Present Condition
e church*** and walls N* are all that remain original mission-fort, lt in a grove of cot-wood (alamo) trees. chased by the state in 3; area later con-ted into a park**	Present building c 1756; mission prospered; de-clined; secularized 1793. Church especially famous as place where Texans made last stand against Santa Anna in 1836. All were killed. Now a state monument and museum, it is Texas's most-vener-ated shrine.	Except for repairs, the church*** of the mid-18th C remains. New roof and arched top of present front added in 1849.
lt of adobe and tufa; n cruciform; twin vers at front** and ne and lantern over ssing. Arcaded clois-on S.	After failure of east Texas missions, threats of French in Louisiana prompted re-establish-ment of missions in San Antonio in 1731. Present building begun shortly thereafter.	Best preserved of Texas missions. Open daily and Sunday. Small adm. fee; custodian guide.
est of the Texas mis-ns. Great quadrangle* ludes church, pueblo, diers' quarters, gran-. Church has elabo-ely-carved façade*** l baptistry window*** gle tower.	Established by Fray An-tonio after he had been driven from east Texas by the French, it soon be-came the largest and most prosperous of the Texas missions.	Granary** and adjacent Old Mill** recently re-stored, as well as church*** No group of buildings in the country contains more of histor-ical and architectural in-terest.
all and simple, with ck walls, and flat seg-ntal arches; recently tored. Pierced campa-rio*	Another of the group re-established in San An-tonio in 1731. Present building (now largely re-stored) begun shortly thereafter.	Church largely rebuilt. Still in use. Appears new and largely deserted.
arming tiny church** stone, with campa-rio* rising above front ll surmounted by a ought-iron cross. oorish arched door-y**	Re-established in San An-tonio at the same time as Missions Purísima Con-cepción and San Juan Capistrano.	With much original con-struction, it retains at-mosphere of mission days. Still in use.
esidio chapel** of ne, has arched en-nce, semicircular top façade, and stubby ver with pyramidal of.	Originally founded at site of LaSalle's Fort St. Louis in 1722; moved in 1726 to the Guadalupe River near Victoria; in 1749 to the present location.	The mission is a modern restoration; the presidio chapel is original; beau-tiful site* on a hill over-looking fertile valley.

Listed Geographica

The following list includes only the
today. Sites of missions no long

Name	Location	Founded
San José de Tumacácori**	48 m S of Tucson on US 89.	By Padre Kino 1691; present build built by Francisc much later.
San Xavier del Bac***	7 m S and 2 m W of Tucson, via US 89, then W on side road; or W from Tucson, then S via Mission Road.	By Padre Kino 1700; present build built by Francisc much later.

m South to North

ssions of which something may be seen
sting are not listed.

Description	History	Present Condition
urch** built of adobe l brick, with thick ls. Baroque façade; e bell tower, on R. me. Adjacent mission ldings in ruins. Mor-ry chapel* in ceme-y at rear.	Site first visited by Kino in 1691; said Mass in a brush shelter. Small chapel built c 1701; only a *visita* in Jesuit times. Taken over by Francis-cans in 1768; present building begun shortly before 1800; dedicated 1822; secularized 1827.	Building fell into decay and was plundered. Made a national monument in 1908. Though a partial ruin, much of interest re-mains. Interesting mu-seum* and patio*
utiful setting*** in ert near Tucson. urch has carved Chur-ueresque façade** ssive towers** only e with dome. Dome er crossing. Lavishly-orated interior***	Kino first visited site in 1692. Mission established to Christianize Indians, and as headquarters for ranch; abandoned in 1751 because of Pima Revolt. Again active 1754–67 un-til Jesuits were expelled. Present building begun c 1772 by Franciscans; ded-icated 1797; secularized in Mexican times. Reoc-cupied 1859. Restoration begun 1906. Again in use by Franciscans.	Well restored; now kept in good condition by Franciscan missionaries who act as guides.

THE MISSION

Listed Geographic

The following list is complete, of the twenty-e
includes also the three related chapels or churc

Name	Jurisdiction	Location	Date Foun
San Diego de Alcalá*	San Diego	7.5 m NW of San Diego Civic Center (6 m NW of Balboa Park; 6 m W of Old Town). On hill, looking down Mission Valley.	July 16, 1
San Luís, Rey de Francia***	San Diego	4.7 m E of Oceanside, which is 35 m N of San Diego on US 101. On slight eminence overlooking valley.	June 13, 1
(Asistencia of San Antonio de Pala)*	San Diego	20 m E and a little N of San Luís Rey. In village of Pala, via drive among hills on winding, paved road.	1
San Juan Capistrano***	San Diego	30 m N of Oceanside on US 101, in village of same name. 60 m S of Los Angeles.	Nov. 1, 1

F CALIFORNIA

m South to North

ssions, regardless of existing condition, and
ich are still standing. (*See map, page 182*)

By Whom	*Order of Founding*	*History*	*Present Condition*
ιípero Serra	1	The first Alta California mission founded; named for Saint James of Alcalá, Spain. First occupied site in "Old Town." Moved in 1774 to present location. Attacked by Indians in 1775; Father Luís Jayme killed. Present church built 1808–13.	After gradually crumbling to ruins, church restored in 1931. Church is all that remains. Most interesting feature is façade with curved pediment* and (restored) belfry.
mín Lasuén, sted by An- ιo Peyri, who ιained in rge for al- st 34 years.	18	Named for Saint Louis (Louis IX) of France. Largely the work of Peyri, prosperous from the start. Present church built 1811–15; dome completed 1829. Cruciform in plan; only one tower completed. Restored by Fathers O'Keefe and Wallischeck. Again in use.	Largest and one of finest of missions. Fine façade with curved pediment* and tower*** Interesting mortuary chapel**
ιre Peyri, as a ιch of San s Rey Mis- ι.		Founded to serve Indians living inland from San Luís Rey; dedicated to St. Anthony of Padua. It suffered after secularization, but has been repaired, and again serves its original purpose.	Church restored. Primitive interior* interesting. Campanario*** fell in 1916, but has been rebuilt.
ιípero Serra, sted by Pad- Pablo Mu- ιegui and ιgório Amúr- ι	7	Named for St. John of Capistrano, Italian theologian. Prosperous from beginning. Great stone church built 1797–1806; destroyed by earthquake 1812. "Serra's" original church restored 1910–33 by Father John O'Sullivan.	Sanctuary*** only of stone church remains, but the whole site** including belfry* cloisters** and Serra's church** makes a beautiful and popular pilgrimage.

Name	Jurisdiction	Location	Date Foun
San Gabriel, Arcángel**	San Diego	314 Mission Drive, San Gabriel. 9 m W of Los Angeles downtown; 4 m S of Pasadena.	Sept. 8, 1
(Nuestra Señora, Reina de Los Angeles)	San Diego	100 Sunset Blvd., Los Angeles; facing the Plaza; near Union Depot and Civic Center.	1
San Fernando, Rey de España*	Santa Barbara	In San Fernando (a separate town, surrounded by Los Angeles); 22 m NW of downtown Los Angeles.	Sept. 8, 1
San Buenaventura	Santa Barbara	In modern small city of Ventura, 70 m NW of Los Angeles; (28 m SE of Santa Barbara). Identified by two tall pine trees.	March 31, 1
Santa Barbara***	Santa Barbara	Los Olivos Street, between Garden and Laguna Sts., Santa Barbara. (2 miles above harbor.)	Dec. 4, 1

By Whom	Order of Founding	History	Present Condition
ring presi-cy of Serra, Padres Cam-, and Somera.	4	Named for the archangel; San Gabriel, after difficulties at start, became one of the most prosperous of missions. Present stone church built 1794–1806.	Church and part of patio remain. Façade is simple, without tower. Buttressed side* and campanario*** most interesting. Ornate retablo.
lres from San briel Mission. he pueblo was nded by Gov-or Neve.)		Known as the Plaza Church; established for colonists of the pueblo of Los Angeles. Present church, financed by sale of brandy from San Gabriel Mission, built 1818–22, with help of a Yankee, Joseph Chapman.	Still standing, is the oldest church in the city. Belfry a modern restoration. Of greater historical interest than architectural merit.
mín Lasuén, sted by Pad-Dumetz and la.	17	The last of four missions established by Lasuén in the summer of 1797; named for St. Ferdinand III of Spain. Adobe church completed 1806, damaged in earthquake of 1812 and rebuilt; then fell into decay.	Adobe church now restored, and in use; other buildings being restored. Most interesting part is original monastery** or "long building," facing street.
ípero Serra e last mis-n founded by 1), assisted by lre Cambón.	9	Founding delayed; first buildings destroyed by fire. Present stone church completed 1809, damaged by quake in 1812; repaired. Retained as parish church; other mission buildings destroyed.	Only the church remains; curious façade; tower; buttresses. Interesting side doorway*. Interior badly renovated.
mín Lasuén e first mis-n founded by 1), assisted Padres Pa-na and Orá-s.	10	First church (1787) replaced by larger adobe structure (1792), destroyed by earthquake in 1812. Present stone church built by Padre Ripoll, 1814–1820; damaged by earthquake 1925; repaired. Now the mother house of the Franciscan province.	On commanding site*** best preserved and one of finest of missions. Church has unique Classic façade*** twin towers*** Well-preserved interior*. Fine fountain** in front. Beautiful cemetery* at side.

Name	Jurisdiction	Location	Date Foun
Santa Inés*	Santa Barbara	At edge of Danish village of Solvang, 3 m W of Santa Ynez; 3 m SE of Buellton. (35 m NW of Santa Barbara.)	Sept. 17, 1
La Purísima Concepción	Santa Barbara	20 m NW of Santa Inés Mission; near Lompoc, in a valley in the country.	Dec. 8, 1
San Luís, Obispo de Tolosa	Monterey	Chorro and Montgomery Streets, San Luis Obispo. (110 m NW of Santa Barbara.)	Sept. 1, 1
San Miguel, Arcángel**	Monterey	9 m N of Paso Robles, which is 30 m N of San Luis Obispo. On US 101.	July 25, 1
San Antonio de Padua*	Monterey	40 m NW of San Miguel, (13 m on US 101, W 27 m on side road— now paved—through Jolon). Or from King City on paved side road.	July 14, 1

By Whom	Order of Founding	History	Present Condition
évan Tapis e only mis- a founded by a), aided by res Calzada, tiérrez, and rés.	19	The last mission founded south of the Golden Gate. First church destroyed by quake in 1812. Present adobe church built 1815-17. Campanario collapsed in 1910; replaced by one of concrete.	Church and monastery remain, in use. (Second story of latter a recent addition.) Simple gabled church. Restored concrete belfry. Interior* retains old decorations.
mín Lasuén	11	Mission had a turbulent history; first buildings replaced in 1800, to be in turn destroyed by the earthquake of 1812. New group of buildings, on new site, in almost complete ruins when reconstruction was begun in 1934 by CCC and National Park Service.	In a lovely valley site* behind beautiful gardens* the present group is almost entirely a modern reconstruction.
ipero Serra, sted by Padre é Cavaller.	5	After first thatched buildings were burned, tile was employed for roofs, the first in California. Present adobe church built c. 1793.	After having been badly renovated, covered with siding, and crowned with a wooden steeple, the church has again been restored to its original appearance.
mín Lasuén, sted by lre Buenaven- a Sitjar.	16	One of the four missions founded by Lasuén in the summer of 1797, it was prosperous from the start. Present church built 1816-18; decorated 1821 by Estéban Munras from Monterey.	Directly on highway, garden* and arched corridor* attractive. Original church has simple gabled façade. Interior** has exposed beams and mural decorations.
ipero Serra, sted by Pad- Pieras and ar.	3	Founded soon after the Mission San Carlos in an oak glen to SE. First church completed in 1773, replaced 1780 by another, and 1810-13 by the present church of brick and adobe. Monastery fell into ruins, but has been restored (1949-50) for use as a Franciscan school for lay brothers.	Now repaired and monastery restored. Beautiful setting** Fine façade** with curved gable and low bell towers.

Name	Jurisdiction	Location	Date Foun
Nuestra Señora de la Soledad	Monterey	40 m N of San Antonio de Padua; near side road W of US 101; (reached via King City and Greenfield).	Oct. 9, 1
San Carlos de Borromeo***	Monterey	At the ᴄdge of the village of Carmel, 4 m S of Monterey.	June 3, 1
(Capilla Real de Monterey)	Monterey	Church St., between Camino El Estero and Figueroa St., Monterey.	1
San Juan Bautista**	Monterey	30 m NW of Monterey. On side road (State 156), 3 m from US 101.	June 24, 1
Santa Cruz	San Francisco	Facing the Upper Plaza, Santa Cruz; on N shore of Bay of Monterey. State Highway 1, 85 m S of San Francisco.	Sept. 25, 1

By Whom	Order of Founding	History	Present Condition
rmín Lasuén	13	A dreary history in a dreary location. Never successful. Buildings, simple adobe structures, soon fell into ruins.	Now only a few heaps of crumbling adobe marked by a wooden cross, 100 yds. from the road, in the midst of truck farms.
nípero Serra, Monterey. oved a year er to Carmel.	2	The second mission, founded within a year after San Diego. Serra's headquarters, and place of burial. Stone church built 1793–97 by Lasuén; fell into decay; repaired at various times.	Now completely restored. Beautiful setting**. Fine façade* towers*** and exterior stairway**. Curious parabolic-arched interior*. Gothic vaulted baptistry***
nípero Serra, a mission. hen mission as moved, it as retained as esidio chapel.		Served as chapel of the presidio, and also as the "Royal Chapel," the place of worship of the royal governors. Present stone church completed 1795, then enlarged; in continuous use since. The only surviving presidio chapel in California.	Still intact. Elaborately carved Neo-Classic façade. Pyramidal roof on tower added in 1893.
rmín Lasuén, sisted by Pads Catala and artiarena.	15	At first troubled by hostile Indians and by earthquakes. Present church, of adobe and brick, built 1803–12. It is cruciform as a result of blocking up of side aisles, leaving open two transeptal chapels. Reredos decorated by Thomas Doak, first American in California.	Facing the plaza** and old houses** in the sleepy village, the large church** with aisles blocked up, is still well preserved. Long monastery arcade*; peaceful garden.
rmín Lasuén	12	Adobe church built 1793–94. Mission never successful. Destroyed by earthquakes of 1840 and 1857.	Nothing remains of original buildings. A half-size model (built 1931) faces the plaza near the site and contains a few old relics.

Name	Jurisdiction	Location	Date Found
Santa Clara de Asís	San Francisco	On present campus of University of Santa Clara (45 m SE of San Francisco).	Jan. 12, 17
San José de Guadalupe	San Francisco	15 m N of city of San Jose; opposite southern extremity of San Francisco Bay.	June 11, 17
San Francisco de Asís*	San Francisco	Dolores St., between 16th and 17th Sts., San Francisco. .4 m S of Market St. (1 m SW of Civic Center.)	Oct. 9, 17
San Rafael, Arcángel	San Francisco	16 m N of San Francisco; across Golden Gate Bridge; on US 101. In town of San Rafael.	Dec. 14, 18
San Francisco de Solano	San Francisco	In town of Sonoma; 43 m N of San Francisco; on State Highway 12. 21 m SE of Santa Rosa.	July 4, 18

By Whom	Order of Founding	History	Present Condition
ᴜring presi-ncy of Serra, Padre Tomás la Peña.	8	First site abandoned because of floods. Church built 1781–84, designed by Padre Murguía, who died four days before the dedication. Destroyed by earthquake of 1812; a new church was built 1817–22. Used as college chapel until destroyed by fire.	Only a remnant of adobe cloisters remains, at rear of new University Chapel, patterned after last mission church.
ᴇrmín Lasuén	14	Another of the four missions founded in the summer of 1797. A new church, completed in 1809, replaced first wooden structure; destroyed by earthquake in 1868.	Only a portion of the old monastery remains, and contains some old relics.
ᴜring presi-ᴇncy of Serra, ʏ Padre Palóu, a site selected ʏ De Anza.	6	After use of temporary buildings of wood and thatch, a church was begun in 1782. Meager early records do not make it clear whether that is the church seen today; but the present church was completed before 1795.	Facing a wide boulevard, church* only is still intact. Fine, decorated interior**. Interesting old cemetery*
ɪcente Sarría, sisted by Pad-ᴇs Gil, Abella, ᴅd Durán.	20	At first an asistencia of San Francisco de Asís, founded for the sake of the health of the Indians. Simple church and mission house built 1818; now entirely destroyed; replaced by a modern church.	Nothing remains of original buildings. A copy, near by, was under construction in 1949–50.
ᴀdre José Alta-ɪira (unsanc-ᴏned by Padre-ᴛesidente Sar-ᴀ). Later approved.	21	Founded, with the consent of the governor but not the Franciscan authorities, to offset the advances of the Russians (who sent presents to the new mission). Like San Rafael, simple adobe structures.	At corner of large plaza* faced by old houses**; restored and in use as a state museum.

INDEX

Abeyta, Bernardo, 141
Abó, 96-98, 101, 104, 122, Pl. 10
Acapulco, 67, 69, 70, 71, 155
Acevedo, Francisco de, 97, 104
Ácoma, 4, 33, 36, 101, 115-124, 130,
    133, 252, Pls. 12, 16
    battle of, 117
    Church of San Estéban Rey, 119-
    122, Pl. 11
    massacre at, 116-117
Adobe, 37, 39, 90, 100, 197, 202, 214,
    251, 258; see also Houses, adobe
    adobe bricks, introduction of, in
    California, 228; in New Mexico,
    92, 105
    arches of adobe bricks, 100
Agriculture, 16, 17, 19, 21, 23, 34, 95,
    105, 164
Aguayo, Marqués de San Miguel de,
    165, 170
Aguílar, Isidoro, 198
Alamo, the (San Antonio), 161-162,
    256, Pl. 28
    siege of, 161, 162, 241-242
Alarcón, Hernando de, 61, 62, 67
Alarcón, Martín de, 159, 255
Albuquerque, 10, 96, 125-126, 138,
    155, 240, 251, 252, 257-258
    airport, 257
    as farming and trade center, 125-
    127
    Church of San Felipe de Nerí, 126
    founding of, 125
    motor courts, 258
    Plaza, 125-126
    University of New Mexico, 252,
    257
Alburquerque, Duke of, 125
Alcaraz, Diego de, 53
Altamira, José, 225
Altars, 97, 141, 193, 206, 219, 224, Pls.
    15, 39
Alvarado, Hernando de, 62, 63, 64,
    116
Alvarado, Pedro de, 67, 69, 73
Amarillo, 10, 255

Amazons, 47, 48, 53, 66, 67, 72
Americans
    in Arizona, 247, 251, 259-260
    in California, 219, 235-240, 242-244,
    247-250, 260-266
    in New Mexico, 240, 242, 245-247,
    251-253, 257-258
    in Texas, 241-242, 244-245, 250-
    251, 254-257
Amúrrio, Gregório, 197
Anasazi, 23, 33, 37, 40
    defined, 23
Anián, Strait of, 46, 68, 69, 70, 235
Anza, Juan Bautista de, 176, 189-190,
    193, 200, 223, 259
Apache, 18, 19, 96, 101, 104, 106, 110,
    129, 138, 153, 163, 174-175, 177,
    265
Apalachen, 51
Aqueduct, 138, 159, 205
Arches, 100, 133, 152, 153, 154, 155,
    202, 204, 208, 212, 218, 219, 224,
    228, 229
Arellano, Tristan de, 63
Arizona, 1, 2, 13, 16, 17, 18, 20, 22, 34,
    56, 62, 65, 111-114, 172-180, 185,
    189, 247, 251, 252, 265
    missions, 175-180, 288-289
Arkansas River, 11, 64
Arvide, Martín de, 144
Asinai (Texas) Indians, 157
Audiencia, 50, 53
Austin, Moses, 241
Austin, Stephen F., 241
Austin, Texas, 255
Ávila, Alonzo Gil de, 104
Ávila, Pedro de, 104
Ayeta, Francisco de, 104, 107, 152
Aztec, New Mexico, 22, 32-33, Pl. 7
Aztecs, 19, 41-42, 48, 138
Aztlán, 42

Babbitt, Maj. E. B., 161
Bakavi, 113
Ball courts, 39
Bandelier, Adolf F., 35, 99

Dorantes, Andrés, 54, 55, 56, 57
Doric architecture, 211, 216-217, 218, 224
Douglass, A. E., 22
Drake, Francis, 69-70
Drought, 29, 35, 95, 105, 110
Durango, 73, 74

Earthquakes, 198, 200, 203, 205, 207, 208, 218, 222, 223, 247
East Texas, 156-158, 164, 165, 170 missions
    Nuestra Señora de Guadalupe, 158
    San Francisco de los Neches, 169
    San Francisco de los Tejas, 157, 169
    San José de los Nazones, 168
Echeandía, José María, 236
Eclecticism, 249, 251
Education, architectural, 249
El Dorado, 47, 48, 63
El Morro, 89, 118, Pl. 9
El Paso, 1, 4, 10, 11, 109, 153, 154, 155, 156, 255, 256-257
El Paso del Norte, 81, 151-155, 240
Enchanted Mesa, 115, 119
Encomienda, 73, 76
England, colonies of, 156
Enriquez, Fernández de la Cueva, 125
Escalona, Juan de, 133
Escalona, Luís de, 74
Española, 11, 34, 136
Espejo, Antonio de, 75, 76, 116, 256
Estancia Valley, 96
Estebanico, 54, 55, 56-58, 60, 116, 173
Estudillo, José Antonio, 237
Eureka, 247
Exploration, Spanish, 2, 44, 45-75, 174

Façades, 119, 165, 167, 194, 206, 212
Fages, Pedro, 187, 188, 204, 210
Fairs, 145, 155
Fannin, James W., Jr., 242
Fannin massacre, 242
Farms and farming, 23, 118, 125-128, 173, 174, 227
Ferdinand III, of Spain (Saint), 87, 201, 209
Ferrelo, Bartolomé, 69, 71
Fireplaces, 93, 98, 238

Fitch, Henry, 236-237
Flagstaff, 26
Floods, 153, 154, 197, 199, 200, 222
Floors, 93, 145, 208, 219
Florida, 2, 3, 49-52
Food storage, 20, 24, 27, 28, 77, 127, 146
Fort, 24, 90, 159, 166, 169
Fort Ross, 226-227, Pl. 55
Fort Saint Louis, 157, 159, 170
Fort Worth, 10, 255
Fountains, 201, 205, 212, 216, 229
"Four Corners," 20, 21, 23, 36, 37
France, colonies of, 156-158, 175
Francis, of Assisi (Saint), 85-87, 90, 100, 155, 185, 186, 190, 225, 266
Franciscans, 4, 73, 86-87, 95, 99, 102-103, 104, 121-122, 139, 176, 180, 185, 207, 228, 232
Fredericksburg, 245
Frémont, John Charles, 243
French influence on architecture, 246
Furniture, 127, 160, 177, 208, 228, 238
Fuster, Vicente, 198

Gables, 128, 140; *see also* Pediment curved, 153, 161, 170, 178, 194, 196, 212, 216, 218, 229
    false, 123, 146
Gadsden, James, 172
Gadsden Purchase, 172, 260
Galleries, 131, 132, 133, 141, 142, 143, Pl. 21
Gallup, 29, 59
Galveston, 52, 246, 255
Gálvez, José de, 184-186, 190
Gaona brothers, 179
Garay, Francisco, 50
Garcés, Francisco Tomás, 114, 176-177, 179, 189, 259
Gateways, 141, 144, 146, 166, 258
Gente de razon, 127
Geography of the Southwest, 9-15
German influence on architecture, 245
Gila River, 11, 12, 14, 36, 37, 39, 40, 61, 172, 174, 189
Giusewá, 100-101, 129
Gold, 46-48, 49, 51, 63, 67, 244
Gold Rush, 244, 247, 265
Golden Gate, 68, 71, 188, 225
Golden Hind, 69